Stitching the Self

Stitching the Self:
Identity and the Needle Arts

Edited by
Johanna Amos and Lisa Binkley

BLOOMSBURY VISUAL ARTS
LONDON • NEW YORK • OXFORD • NEW DELHI • SYDNEY

BLOOMSBURY VISUAL ARTS
Bloomsbury Publishing Plc
50 Bedford Square, London, WC1B 3DP, UK
1385 Broadway, New York, NY 10018, USA
29 Earlsfort Terrace, Dublin 2, Ireland

BLOOMSBURY, BLOOMSBURY VISUAL ARTS and the Diana logo are trademarks of
Bloomsbury Publishing Plc

First published in Great Britain 2020
This paperback edition published in 2021

Cover design by Adriana Brioso
Cover image: *Monster Spirit*, 2008, 35 × 58 cm, hand embroidery on cotton, silk threads.
Courtesy of the artist Anna Torma.

A catalogue record for this book is available from the British Library.

A catalog record for this book is available from the Library of Congress

ISBN: HB: 978-1-3500-7038-7
PB: 978-1-3502-4241-8
ePDF: 978-1-3500-7039-4
eBook: 978-1-3500-7040-0

Typeset by RefineCatch Limited, Bungay, Suffolk

To find out more about our authors and books visit www.bloomsbury.com
and sign up for our newsletters.

For Sandra—mentor, champion, friend

Contents

List of Plates ix

List of Figures and Table xi

Notes on Contributors xiii

Acknowledgments xvi

Introduction: Stitching the Self   *Johanna Amos and Lisa Binkley* 1

Part One   Emerging Identity: Reconsidering the Narratives of the Needle

1   The Identity of an Embroidering Woman: The Needle Arts in
Brussels, Belgium, 1850–1914   *Wendy Wiertz* 21

2   "Experiments in silk and gold work afterwards to bloom": The
Embroidering of Jane Burden Morris   *Johanna Amos* 33

3   Becoming the Boss of Your Knitting: Elizabeth Zimmermann and the
Emergence of Critical Knitting   *M. Lilly Marsh* 49

4   "Knitting is the saving of life; Adrian has taken it up too":
Needlework, Gender, and the Bloomsbury Group   *Joseph McBrinn* 67

Part Two   Elaborating Identity: Expressing Ideology, Crafting Community

5   *Whig's Defeat*: Stitching Settler Culture, Politics, and Identity
Lisa Binkley 83

6   "From Prison to Citizenship," 1910: The Making and Display of
a Suffragist Banner   *Janice Helland* 97

7   *Our Lady of the Snows*: Settlement, Empire, and "The Children
of Canada" in the Needlework of Mary Seton Watts
(1848–1938)   *Elaine Cheasley Paterson* 111

Part Three Recovering Identity: Locating the Self Through Needlework

8   "Je me declare Dieu-Mère, Femme Créateur": Johanna Wintsch's
     Needlework at the Swiss Psychiatric Asylums Burghölzli and
     Rheinau, 1922–1925   *Sabine Wieber*   125

9   Hybrid Language: The Interstitial Stitches of Anna Torma's
     Embroideries   *Anne Koval*   141

10   Suturing My Soul: In Pursuit of the *Broderie de
     Bayeux*   *Janet Catherine Berlo*   155

Notes   171
Index   221

Plates

1.1 Hélène De Rudder, née Du Ménil and Isidore De Rudder, *Autumn*, 1904. Embroidery, 200 × 260 cm. Brussels, Musée de la Ville de Bruxelles-Maison du Roi, inv. E 1904/2/3. © Brussels, Musée de la Ville de Bruxelles-Maison du Roi.

1.2 Irène D'Olszowska, Round collar of Brussels needlepoint with a pattern of peacocks and flowers, *c.* 1905. Needlepoint, 125 × 18 cm. Amsterdam, Rijksmuseum, BK-BR-364. © Amsterdam, Rijksmuseum, free of copyright.

2.1 William Morris (designer), Jane Morris (maker), May Morris (maker [?]), "Acanthus," *c.* 1878. 264 × 205 cm. Amgueddfa Genedlaethol Cymru National Museum of Wales.

2.2 May Morris (designer) and Jane Morris (maker), Bedcover (KM233), *c.* 1910. Wool and silk on linen, 261 × 212.5 cm. © Society of Antiquaries of London (Kelmscott Manor)/V&A.

4.1 Vanessa Bell, *Portrait of Virginia Woolf (née Stephen)*, 1912 [poss. March]. Oil on board, 15¾ × 13⅜″, NPG 5833. © Estate of Vanessa Bell. Courtesy National Portrait Gallery, London.

4.2 Virginia Woolf (embroiderer) and Angelica Garnett (designer), *Leda and the Swan*, chair cover. Monk's House, Rodmell, East Sussex, NT 768172.1. © The National Trust.

5.1 Jessie Campbell, *Whig's Defeat, c.* 1860. Hand-sewn, cotton, 222 × 175 cm. Photo courtesy of Agnes Etherington Art Centre, Queen's University, Kingston, ON.

6.1 Women's Social and Political Union (WSPU), Suffragette Banner, 1910. © Museum of London.

7.1 Mary Seton Watts (née Mary Seton Fraser Tytler), *Self-Portrait,* watercolor, 1882. © Watts Gallery Trust.

7.2 Mary Seton Watts, *Our Lady of the Snows*, 1906. Mother of pearl, moonstones, crystal, garnets, aquamarine. Silk and velvet painted and applied on to satin ground, embroidered with gold and silver thread. Collection of McGill University. Presented to the Royal Victoria College, McGill University, Montreal, Canada in 1907. Pictured *in situ* at the Royal Victoria College, 2016. Photograph by author.

8.1   Johanna Natalie Wintsch, *Aragon—RE/ICH*, 1924. Silk on linen, 31 × 31 cm. Sammlung Rheinau (StAZH).

8.2   Johanna Natalie Wintsch, *Albertine Schenk*, 1923. Silk on cotton, 31 × 31 cm. Sammlung Rheinau (StAZH).

9.1   Anna Torma, detail from *Monster Spirit,* 2008. Silk embroidery on cotton. Photo credit: Anna Torma.

9.2   Anna Torma, detail from *Bagatelles*, 2011. Silk thread embroidery and watercolor on silk fabric. New Brunswick Museum, Saint John, NB. Photo credit: Istvan Zsako.

10.1 Installation View of the Bayeux Embroidery. © S. Maurice—Bayeux Museum, Bayeux, France.

10.2 Louise Bourgeois, *Cell 1*, 1991. Mixed media, 83 × 96 × 108″; 210.8 × 243.8 × 274.3 cm. Photo: Peter Bellamy. © The Easton Foundation/VAGA at Artists Rights Society (ARS), NY.

Figures and Table

Figures

1.1 Duchess d'Ursel, née Antonine de Mun, "Riri à la fenêtre du salon d'Hingene s'essayant à faire de la mignardise. Juillet 1890." Pen and ink drawing, 260 × 165 mm, *Album 1888–1891*. Brussels, private collection, 35r. © Hingene, Kasteel d'Ursel, Stefan Dewickere. 22

1.2 *La classe de broderie à l'école Bischoffsheim*, c. 1903. Photo Gautier, in Anonymous, "L'École professionnelle Bischoffsheim," *Bruxelles Féminin*, 1 December 1903, 8–9. Free of copyright. 25

2.1 William Morris (designer) and Elizabeth Burden (maker, attributed), *Guenevere*, c.1861. Wool on holland ground, 115.6 cm (figure height). © The Society of Antiquaries of London (Kelmscott Manor). 34

2.2 Frederick Hollyer, Photograph of the Burne-Jones and Morris families, 1874. Albumen print. © National Portrait Gallery, London. 43

3.1 The salutation "Dear Knitter," and her manuscript signature closings "Good Knitting" and "Sincerely-Elizabeth," emphasized the personal and direct address of Zimmermann's *Newsletters*. Image of Zimmermann's closing signature to *Newsletter* 11, Fall 1963. Published in *The Opinionated Knitter*, 61. Used by permission of Schoolhouse Press. 55

3.2 Zimmermann's Percentage System provided a method whereby the individual knitter could make custom fitting adjustments reflecting personal design choices. Sketch of the Percentage System for Icelandic Yoke Sweater, *Newsletter* 14, Spring 1965. Published in *The Opinionated Knitter*, 76. Used by permission of Schoolhouse Press. 56

4.1 Vanessa Bell (designer) and Ethel Grant (embroiderer), *Chair cover*, 1932. Beech wood, paint, cane, needlework, 1070 × 515 × 530 mm. Monk's House, Rodmell, East Sussex, NT 768191.1. © Estate of Vanessa Bell. Image courtesy of Henrietta Garnett and The National Trust. 76

4.2 Duncan Grant (designer) and Ethel Grant (embroiderer), *Firescreen*, *c.* 1930. Canvas, gilt, wood, 1090 × 835 × 95 mm. Monk's House, Rodmell, East Sussex, NT 768212. © Estate of Duncan Grant. All Rights Reserved DACS, 2017. Image courtesy of The National Trust. 77

5.1 Maker unknown, *Whig's Defeat,* date unknown. Once displayed at Henry Francis du Pont's summer home. Image courtesy of Winterthur Museum, Delaware. Note: Two of the blocks feature printed fabric of George Washington and Henry Clay's images. Quilt in Private Collection. 86

5.2 *Whig's Defeat* detail, fringed edging. Author's photograph. 89

5.3 Andrew McPherson, Lorneville, ON, *c.* 1880. Photograph courtesy of Bonnie Harwood. 90

6.1 WSPU "From Prison to Citizenship" banner procession, 18 June 1910. © Museum of London. 104

7.1 Children at work in the Tinsmith's Shop of Barnardo's Stepney Home, *c.* 1910. © Barnardo's Archive [Arc2001]. 119

7.2 "Group of boys," British Home Children at receiving home in Ontario, Canada. National Library and Archives of Canada. [C-034837]. In the public domain. 121

8.1 Johanna Natalie Wintsch, *Dr. Gehry,* 1923. Silk on cotton, 31 × 31 cm. Prinzhorn Collection, Heidelberg, Inv. Nr. 6039–2. 126

9.1 Anna Torma, *Monster Spirit,* 2008. Silk thread embroidery on cotton fabric, 45.7 × 35.6 cm. Photo credit: Anna Torma. 151

9.2 Anna Torma, detail of *Vanitas I,* 2011. Silk thread embroidery and appliqué on silk fabric. Photo credit: Anna Torma. 153

10.1 Detail, Bayeux Embroidery: Mont St. Michel. © S. Maurice—Bayeux Museum, Bayeux, France. 160

10.2 Detail, Bayeux Embroidery: Normans setting a house on fire. © S. Maurice—Bayeux Museum, Bayeux, France. 164

Table

6.1 Banner signatures. 99

Notes on Contributors

Johanna Amos is adjunct assistant professor at Queen's University, Canada, in the Department of Art History & Art Conservation. Her research focuses on nineteenth-century British art and material culture, with a particular emphasis on fashion, textiles, and women artists. She has written for *RACAR* and *Victorian Review*, and has presented her research in Canada, the United States, and the United Kingdom. In 2017 she was a research fellow at Winterthur Museum, Garden & Library, and she currently contributes to a SSHRC-funded project on the role of practice in art and design education.

Janet Catherine Berlo is Professor of Art History at the University of Rochester, New York, and holds a PhD in history of art from Yale. She is co-author of *Native North American Art* (2nd edn 2015), *American Encounters* (2007), and author of many other publications on Native American and American art history and textile history. Berlo has received grants for her work from the Guggenheim and Getty Foundations.

Lisa Binkley is the W.P. Bell Postdoctoral Fellow in the Centre for Canadian Studies at Mount Allison University, Canada. Her work focuses on Indigenous and settler textiles as material culture, and the relationships between Indigenous and settler women during the long-nineteenth century. Her current research brings together archival research, oral histories, material culture, and community engagement. She has published on settler and Indigenous quiltmaking in Canada and her book, *Material Identities: Quilts in Canada and their Makers, 1800–1900*, is forthcoming from the University of British Columbia Press.

Dr. Elaine Cheasley Paterson is Associate Dean, Academic and Associate Professor of Craft Studies in the Department of Art History at the Faculty of Fine Arts of Concordia University in Montréal, Canada. Her funded research concerns women's cultural philanthropy in early-twentieth-century British, Irish, and Canadian craft guilds of the home arts movement and tracing a lineage from this historical material to the current resurgence in do-it-yourself, maker culture, and craftivist practices. Her publications include *Sloppy Craft: Postdisciplinarity and the Crafts* (2015), with Susan Surette; "Crafting Empire:

Intersections of Irish and Canadian Women's History," *Journal of Canadian Art History* (2014); and the upcoming edited volume *Craft and Heritage: Intersections in Critical Studies and Practice* (2019).

Janice Helland, PhD is Professor Emerita, Art History, Queen's University, Canada. She is the author of *British and Irish Home Arts and Industries, 1880–1914: Marketing Craft, Making Fashion* (2007), co-editor of *Craft, Community and the Material Culture of Place and Politics, 19th–20th Century* (2014), and has published articles in journals such as *Textile History, Costume, Journal of Design History, Journal of Modern Craft*, among others.

Anne Koval is an independent curator, poet, and professor of Art History, and Museum and Curatorial Studies at Mount Allison University, Canada. Recent publications include "*Evan Penny: Ask Your Body*: 2017 Venice Biennale" (2018); "Calling the Cuckoo: Linda Rae Dornan," in *More Caught in the Act: An Anthology of Performance Art by Canadian Women* (2016); and "From Poet to Painter: The Aestheticism of Swinburne and Whistler," in *Poetry in Painting: The Lyrical Voice of Pre-Raphaelite Paintings* (2017). Her poetry is published in *The Radcliffe Line and Other Geographies: Sarindar Dhaliwal* (2018) and *What We See: A Modest Atlas of Survivals* (2020). Her curated exhibitions include *Paper Doll* (2012), *MUSE* (2014), and *Fairy Tails* (2020).

Dr. M. Lilly Marsh is a professional weaver specializing in local wool fibers, currently practicing in upstate New York. She completed her PhD in American Studies at Purdue University in 2016, and is also a founding board member of the Hudson Valley Textile Project, a consortium of fiber-oriented makers, producers, and processors dedicated to a farm-to-fashion production chain of economically and environmentally sustainable cloth production and garment design in the Hudson River Valley.

Dr. Joseph McBrinn is Reader in Design History at Belfast School of Art, Ulster University in Northern Ireland. He previously taught at the National College of Art and Design in Dublin. He has written and lectured widely on Irish art, craft, and design. He has served on the editorial advisory boards of *The Journal of Modern Craft, Textile: Cloth and Culture* and *The Irish Arts Review*. His most recent publications focus on the intersection of disability and design in interwar Britain. He is currently engaged on a biography of the Irish artist Evie Hone (1894–1955).

Dr. Sabine Wieber is Lecturer in History of Art, Architecture and Design at the University of Glasgow, UK. She is a trained design historian and researches

Austrian and German domestic interiors between 1850 and 1930 with a particular focus on gender, national identity, and the Medical Humanities. She co-curated the critically acclaimed exhibition "Madness & Modernity: Kunst und Wahn in Wien um 1900" (Vienna 2010) and is currently completing a book manuscript on *Jugendstil Women and the Making of Modern Design*.

Dr. Wendy Wiertz is a postdoctoral researcher at KU Leuven (Belgium). Her current research project concentrates on war lace, lace produced in occupied Belgium under the auspices of the Commission for Relief in Belgium (C.R.B.) and sold in the United States and other Allied countries during the First World War. The basis for this research was laid in the U.S. during Wiertz's tenure as a 2018–19 Fulbright and honorary Belgian American Education Foundation scholar. Prior to this, Wiertz completed her PhD in art history with a focus on aristocratic amateur women artists in Belgium during the nineteenth and early-twentieth centuries. She has also worked as an exhibition curator, a board member of Dynastie et Patrimoine culturel, and a teaching assistant at KU Leuven.

Acknowledgments

This collection began as a conference session, *Stitching the Self: Exploring the Power of the Needle*, at the Universities Art Association of Canada (UAAC) annual conference at NSCAD University in Halifax, NS in 2015. Some of those papers grew into the chapters presented here, and we feel wonderfully fortunate to add to this initial seed the work of several incredible scholars, many of whom inspired our own research. It has been a pleasure to work with each of our contributors, and we thank them for their care and commitment to this project, and for their advice and patience as we learned our way as editors. Bloomsbury has been similarly supportive of this collection; we are grateful for their enthusiasm, and to the team we have worked with throughout: Frances Arnold, Hannah Crump, Pari Thomson, and Yvonne Thouroude. We are also indebted to the anonymous readers who provided thoughtful comments on how to improve this work. As with many academic works of this nature, little would be possible without the financial support of multiple organizations, and we particularly thank the Queen's University Fund for Scholarly Research and Creative Work and Professional Development (Adjuncts) for funding the addition of color plates to this volume, and the fellowship program at the Winterthur Museum, Garden & Library for time, space, and their excellent research library. We have both been nurtured by remarkable mentors—especially the incomparable Janice Helland—friends, and families. We thank them from our hearts—you are everything to us.

Introduction: Stitching the Self

Johanna Amos and Lisa Binkley

Since 1997, hundreds of prisoners across England and Wales have engaged in the production of embroidered cushions, quilts, and other household wares through the charity Fine Cell Work (FCW). Founded by Lady Anne Tree, the organization recalls the philanthropic and benevolent social efforts of nineteenth-century reformers, as well as the numerous instances in which stitching has been embraced for its recuperative properties, including among soldiers, in asylums, and, more recently, as part of the healing work of Canada's Residential Schools Truth and Reconciliation Commission.[1] Participants in Fine Cell Work's scheme develop skills in the fine needle arts, and earn a commission for each piece completed. The program thus offers inmates the means to succeed upon their release, both practically and financially.

But Fine Cell Work's mission is also rehabilitative in another sense; testimonials allude to the occupation of needlework as a preventative against self-harm, and to the meditative quality of stitching, how it focuses and quiets the mind.[2] The act of creation, whether according to individual inspiration or commissioned designs, further produces a tangible and valued object, a work of art. As one worker writes, "what I find most gratifying about FCW is that my efforts are not judged in light of my crimes, nor the fact that I am in prison, but rather on their own merits—the artistry, the attention to detail and the aesthetic pleasure they give to people."[3] For those who engage in Fine Cell Work's mission, the needle offers the potential for creativity and authorship, recovery and self-transformation.

The issues raised by the efforts of Fine Cell Work are those at the heart of this collection. In focusing on the needle as a tool for expression, the chapters in this volume explore the multiple ways in which stitching—whether worked by the embroiderer, knitter, quilter, or dressmaker—enabled individuals and communities to remake themselves and the world around them. For, as Heather Pristash, Inez Schaechterle, and Sue Carter Wood suggest, needlework offers a "space in which to stitch not only a seam, but also a self."[4] In doing so, this collection seeks to herald Michael Yonan's call for greater efforts to be made to bridge the fields of art history and material culture.[5] While both are ostensibly "discipline[s] of objects," material culture studies has embraced numerous forms of material expression, from tools to toys to gardens.[6] Art history, on the other hand, has tended to adhere to "The long-held belief that certain classes of objects are somehow intrinsically more worthy of close analysis" than others, demonstrating a preference for high art, and the more traditional fields of painting, sculpture, and architecture.[7] Textiles, then, present an ideal vector through which to explore potential areas of connection and overlap; as the globe's most ubiquitous form of material culture—playing a role in both mundane daily activities and significant ceremonial occasions—they confound such distinctions and hierarchies. As Julia Bryan-Wilson observes, textiles cannot be understood "as a singular artistic 'medium' but as a field of cultural production or matrix that moves nimbly between and beyond high and low."[8]

Much has changed since Rozsika Parker published her ground-breaking study of needlework and femininity, *The Subversive Stitch: Embroidery and the Making of the Feminine*, in 1984; textiles, and needlework in particular, are now more generally accepted as a form of artistic expression, and are understood to be intimately linked to social, cultural, and historical experience. However, the persistence of the art/craft divide has continued to mar our understanding of historical work, especially that produced by women. As Maureen Daly Goggin writes, "Although scholars have begun to recoup fiber arts, redefining the conditions, practices and products of needlework as *art*, there is still much work to be done to deconstruct the stubborn patriarchal art/craft binary."[9] Contemporary artists who work with fiber, including Sheila Hicks, Erin M. Riley, Ghada Amer, and Tracey Emin, have demonstrated that textile-based work has arrived in the contemporary field, even as the gallery space necessitates a disavowal of some of fiber's most evocative characteristics, and in particular its tactile quality. These works are made with museum display in mind; yet, for fiber works produced outside the modern design or feminist art movements of the mid-twentieth century, the situation is more complex. Quilts, samplers, portieres, clothing, and cushions still reside on the margins of art history. Thus the suggestion put forward by Griselda Pollock and Rozsika Parker in *Old Mistresses* in 1981 that what characterizes fine art and separates it from the decorative or craft is not the gender of the maker but rather where the work was created—in the studio or the home—and for whom—for public display or the family—has proven to be a somewhat unshakeable definition.[10]

With essays that touch on works from the nineteenth century to the present, this volume challenges the divisions that result from an uncritical acceptance of the social and historical conditions that determined realms of production and display by not only attending to objects that have fallen outside the scope of traditional art history, but by placing these works—a settler quilt, a psychiatric patient's embroideries, a suffrage banner—on the same continuum as contemporary fiber art. These works are knit together here through agency and intention, and in particular through a consideration of how makers plied the needle (or set of needles) in order to position the self differently—to fashion the self as an artist, educator, individual, activist, or work of art; to forge new social ties, whether familial, professional, or political; or to recall identities lost or left dormant through processes of dramatic personal change or displacement. In doing so, we draw upon a critical thread in material culture scholarship: that the act of making simultaneously transforms the material world as well as the maker. This notion is beautifully articulated by Alice Barnaby in her study of British women's manipulation of muslin into clothing and drapery in the early part of the nineteenth century; she writes, "The processing of raw material into a refined and ornamented material refers equally to both the woman and the muslin; both were rendered equally eloquent through the woman's handling of the muslin. As she sat in the drawing room and worked upon the muslin, it also worked upon her in a reciprocal act of improvement."[11] Barnaby contends that the gestures and behaviors associated with stitching inscribed the body with the ideal feminine characteristics of the period—delicacy, stillness, and refinement—at the same time that the products essential for articulating femininity and women's role within domestic space—graceful garments and comfortable surroundings—were created. While a number of the essays in this volume also explore this relationship between femininity and needlework, not all acts of the needle conformed to cultural expectations, and some chapters explore the ways in which practitioners employed the needle to defy class, gender, and psychological norms, or utilized the needle's feminine associations strategically to gain political, economic, or social advantage. These chapters thus suggest that the products of such investment were not simply singular artful works, but new relationships, positions, and identities.

The gendering of needlework, and textile labor more broadly, in the nineteenth century, and more particularly the cementing of its association with femininity, continues to have ramifications for those who create as well as those who study textile objects. As any contemporary image of an apparel factory will attest, the characteristics ascribed to women historically form the foundation on which their current participation in the manufacture of cloth and clothing is premised, while for those women who employ fiber as an artistic medium, there is a perception that their gender has, in part, determined this decision. At the same time, contemporary male practitioners who choose to take up the needle still face scrutiny and assumptions about their gender or sexual identity, and in particular, if they choose to pursue this area as an amateur practitioner—a maker of rugs, embroidery, or knitted sweaters—rather than as a fashion designer or studio artist. In the realm of scholarship, textile history is perhaps one of the few areas of art history in which women's contributions have been more satisfactorily investigated and revealed,[12] while men's labors in fashion and needlework remain understudied.[13] Joseph McBrinn's work in this volume and elsewhere serves as a powerful corrective to this circumstance, as it begins to unravel gendered assumptions about textiles through an exploration of work produced under an array of desires and circumstances, including financial necessity and personal expression.[14]

While a number of the chapters included here deal with women's contributions—a reflection perhaps of the fact that textiles have represented one of the most accessible forms of artistic labor for women for generations—this work as a whole does not center on the relationship between needle arts and femininity. Rather, contributors view gender as one facet of a subject's position, and explore how gender contributed to their experience. Anne Koval, for instance, notes how the perception of textile design as women's work allowed artists in socialist Hungary to create subversive works, while Johanna Amos and M. Lilly Marsh demonstrate how the needle offered women access to business enterprises from which they were otherwise largely excluded. We see this moving away from exclusively gendered considerations of labor as essential to opening up larger conversations around textiles and artistic masculinity—particularly given that textile practices outside of the West often highlighted male expertise and ingenuity, a link that was disrupted by European interference.[15]

This collection also furthers recent attempts to complicate narratives of professionalism and professionalization in the arts. While traditionally viewed as a trajectory of achievement, Kyriaki Hadjiafxendi and Patricia Zakreski have recently argued for a reframing of this model of professionalization, suggesting that the categories of amateur and professional existed in an "overlapping and dialectical relationship" in the nineteenth century,[16] while Kristina Huneault takes the position that the very notion of professionalism is fraught; as she notes, it is "a complex and historically contingent construct."[17] Stephen Knott's 2015 study of amateur craft similarly contends with the standard categorizations of amateur and professional activity, and seeks to destabilize assumptions about amateurism as trivial and insignificant work.[18] Critically, Knott situates the emergence of the contemporary, and derisive, definition of amateur practice amidst the rise of industrialization, demonstrating that the historical emphasis on "curiosity or a love of acquiring knowledge" gave way to an attitude of productive leisure, as labor became increasingly standardized and fragmented into discernible blocks of time.[19] Moreover, while amateurism and professionalism have often been constructed in opposition to one another, this is not absolutely reflected in their relationship to the market economy. Amateur activity rarely results in direct financial compensation, though it might forestall an expense, and although professional activity is often determined by remuneration, by the willingness of a purchasing public to consume an artist's work, the granting of professional status by academic and professional organizations is not necessarily a reflection of financial success. Further complicating this picture, Huneault points to the distinction between forms of professionalism in different art economies: "a commercial art professionalism, and a fine art one."[20] Those who taught classes or produced work for commercial publishers and advertisers were professional in the sense that they made their living through the arts, but this was not the measure through which many institutions accorded status.

Practitioners of the needle arts often trouble concrete notions of amateur and professional status, both directly and indirectly, and perhaps most notably by producing objects for forms of exchange other than those governed by capitalism. As several chapters in this collection demonstrate, individuals used needlework products and skills to position themselves, typically more favorably, in a variety of social and cultural networks. Lisa Binkley, for instance, notes that a demonstration of needle skills, through elaborate and ornate appliqué quilts, was essential to signifying a woman's readiness for marriage and cementing a marriage contract in settler Canada, while Sabine Wieber suggests that Johanna Wintsch may have presented gifts of needlework to the physicians charged with her care at Burghölzli and Rheinau asylums, not only as an appreciative gesture, but also as a means of ingratiating herself with her doctors, perhaps positioning herself for an earlier release. Similarly, Johanna Amos argues that Jane Morris mobilized her skill with the needle through gifts, clothing, and commercial products in order to reposition herself within a network of artists, simultaneously transforming her appearance, as well as her style of working. Wendy Wiertz examines the plethora of possibilities that needlework skills afforded middle-class Belgian women in the nineteenth century, from artistic excellency to valuable teaching posts, and M. Lilly Marsh explores Elizabeth Zimmermann's use of her knitting needles to craft a multifaceted business empire, despite the fact that she was denied membership in the professional craft organization within her home state. And, all of the chapters included here demonstrate the extraordinary skill and ability with which women and men have plied their needles historically and into the present. While many of the objects that they produced were created under what would traditionally be defined as amateur circumstances, their products defy such easy categorization, exhibiting none of the inferiority that typically accompanies the term.

It is thus one of the aims of this volume to question the "methodological privileging of professionalism," an act that we regard as overdue and essential if traditional notions of art and artistry are to be redefined.[21] For, as Huneault demonstrates, emphasis on these narratives has ramifications. In her analysis of Dorothy Farr and Natalie Luckyj's exhibition *From Women's Eyes: Women Painters in Canada*, the first national survey to deal with women's contributions in this area, Huneault suggests that the curators' "embrace of the professional model (and its concomitant devaluation of amateur practice)" allowed them to highlight the numerous instances where women established professional careers and reputations, despite the adversity with which they had to contend.[22] However, at the same time, it "led them to find women artists lacking."[23] Challenging the importance of professionalism, then, or considering it as one point in a constellation of methods for defining artistic achievement, as Hadjiafxendi and Zakreski suggest,[24] has implications for women's work, or that which does not conform to gendered expectations of production, as well as for craft, collaborative modes of creation, and for work produced outside Eurocentric definitions of art.[25]

Piecing Together

The field of textile scholarship is incredibly broad, and has become increasingly vibrant in recent years. While historically the literature tended to focus on the relationship between cloth and industrial development, trade, and labor, or upon the collection and appraisal of textiles from particular geographic regions, current analyses have grown increasingly sophisticated. Parker's *Subversive Stitch*, and Annette B. Weiner and Jane Schneider's exploration of the social significance of textiles, *Cloth and Human Experience* (1989), were key to this transition, setting a precedent for studies that demonstrate the complex relationship between the making of textiles and gender, culture, and politics, and encouraging a reconsideration of a range of textile objects and processes to which this work is indebted.[26]

One of the most prominent threads in more recent textile scholarship upon which we rely is the reconceptualization of textile work, particularly that in the needle arts, to define producers as social beings: creating, communicating, and circulating cultural values. In *The Spectacle of Women: Imagery of the Suffrage Campaign, 1907–14* (1988), for instance, Lisa Tickner illuminates the activities of the suffrage movement through an examination of hand-stitched banners made by women as a demonstration of their commitment to the cause. Through her exploration of the production and use of these banners, Tickner brings to light the emergence of a community of women with a common interest that crossed social divides.[27] In 2001, Laurel Thatcher Ulrich expanded on this idea of textiles as an expression of women's identities and experiences by addressing the addition of embroidery to wool, cotton, and linen coverlets in the early-nineteenth-century United States.[28] Regardless of whether the coverlets were acquired from a local merchant or made by a local weaver, it was common practice for young women to add decorative embroidered embellishments to the cloths as symbols of gentility and education. As Ulrich demonstrates, the popularity of embroidering coverlets in the early decades of the nineteenth century indicates the importance of home manufacturing and economic privilege, and, as trade embargoes between Britain and the United States limited textile imports from Europe at this time, illustrates the emergence of an American identity in cloth production and the needle arts.

A number of textile historians have also delved more recently into the entangled histories of textile objects, illuminating how particular materials are implicated in processes of colonization, globalization, industrialization, and exchange across cultures.[29] Beverly Lemire, for instance, has focused the study of the global consumption of textiles through the examination of a particular fiber. *Cotton* (2011) investigates how this substance, once introduced to the Northern Hemisphere, "became the driving force in global exchange," reshaping the economic direction of industrializing nations and profoundly influencing the development of the regions supplying cotton to the rest of the world.[30] Mills, factories, and slave plantations were all results of the expansion of the cotton trade. An examination of the very foundation of numerous textile objects, Lemire's analysis complements her earlier work on the exchange and transformation of a particular type of cotton—calico—which has its material and design origins in hand-painted Indian chintz, yet became an "English" fabric through dual processes of domestication: through British consumption and industrial imitation.[31] Amelia Peck similarly considers the effects of the circulation of trade textiles, not only on technology, the economy, and patterns of consumption, but on the broader material and visual culture of regions at multiple nodes within this transaction. As she notes, "Because the scope of the textile trade was so widespread by the mid-seventeenth century, the constant interchange of exotic design motifs, fibers, and dyes between these now interconnected markets brought into being, for the first time, a common visual language of design that was recognizable throughout the world."[32]

However, this volume relies more particularly on a facet of this scholarship: that which considers how makers and objects are inflected by these complex histories, and carry the weight of such interactions with them, whether the work addresses this directly or not. In this vein, Jessica Hemmings's recent collection, *Cultural Threads: Transnational Textiles Today* (2015), reveals a selection of works from contemporary textile art and design to be "material vectors," hybrid objects that reflect the notion that "we live in a world in which individual identities are now built from multiple points of reference."[33] Christine Checinska's contribution to Hemmings's volume, for example, evaluates the *Soundsuits* of African-American artist Nick Cave and the mixed-media paintings of Ivorian-French artist Ernest Dükü in order to suggest that stitching, as a form of cultural expression, might be viewed as a means of remembrance, retention, and renewal among the African diasporas.[34] Stitching is thus a vehicle for uniting the self, "a way of suturing the rupture of movement, piecing one sense of being to another."[35] Although it deals with a different context of migration—from Hungary to Canada—Anne Koval's chapter in this volume charts a similar desire to knit identities together through textile labor—labor steeped in familial and cultural history—as it resides in the work of contemporary fiber artist Anna Torma.

Central to the focus of this volume is the notion that textiles exist between and across the fields of material culture and art history. As such, it builds upon attempts to define and critique the relationship between textiles and what have traditionally been defined as the fine arts. Jonathan Holstein and Gail van der Hoof's landmark exhibition *Abstract Design in American Quilts* (1971) rekindled enthusiasm for quilts in the twentieth century. Coinciding with the renewed interest in pioneer life and colonial settlement that sparked the quilt revival of the 1970s and early 1980s, this exhibition is often seen as pivotal in textile scholarship for igniting a reconsideration of the art/craft divide following modernity.[36] Holstein and van der Hoof were largely interested in evaluating quilts for their visual properties, positing that these objects might be comparable to the finest works of twentieth-century abstract art. As Holstein states, "quilt makers did in effect paint with fabrics; the visual aspects of these quilts were in no sense foreign or strange to them, [it is] as if they were some form of avant-garde art."[37] Though controversial, this approach paved the way for further studies of the artistry and skill of quilting,[38] perhaps most interestingly among the marginalized communities of the American South, including that at Gee's Bend.[39] It further provided conceptual footing for the work of artists such as Faith Ringgold, whose *tangka* paintings and story quilts embraced quilting and other textile mediums as a means to document the African-American experience and to critique the gendered and racist practices of artistic institutions that continued to marginalize work typically characterized as "craft." As Elissa Auther has shown, textile-based practices were a foundational aspect of the feminist art movement of the 1960s and 1970s, employed in the works of Judy Chicago, Faith Ringgold, Harmony Hammond, and Miriam Schapiro, among others, as a means to highlight women's heritage and expertise and to push for a re-evaluation of the tenets upon which the art historical canon was founded.[40] This social oppositional potential of textiles has not been forgotten in the twenty-first century, and knitting and crochet have become some of the most common techniques in craftivist practice—activism which often plays upon the gendered, communal, and globalized nature of textile production in order to disrupt or critique neoliberal networks of power.[41]

This work has roughly coincided with what has often been described as the "material turn" in the humanities, a shift that has sought to emphasize the potential for objects to be used as evidence, and in particular, as a means to recoup unwritten histories. As pioneering material culture scholar and art historian Jules Prown writes, "In any age there are certain widely shared beliefs— assumptions, attitudes, values—that are so obvious that they remain unstated. As such, they are most clearly perceivable, not in what a society says it is doing in its histories, literature, or public and private documents, but rather in the way in which it does things."[42] While Prown saw the decorative arts as an ideal field in which to uncover such cultural histories, more recent analyses have looked at a broader range of material goods and practices, from scrapbooks to silver, butter sculpting to beadwork, in order to illuminate the widest possible array of human experiences, and to reveal the individual as well as the cultural motivations inherent in making. These analyses also rely upon Arjun Appadurai's now famous assertion that objects have social lives—lives that are constructed as things pass through stages of making, use, and circulation.[43] And, as Gillian Rose elaborates, these processes of circulation not only transform objects, but people and spaces, sometimes in uncertain ways: "objects and contexts not only define each other, but may change and disrupt each other."[44] Thus, a single object has the potential to generate multiple instances of meaning over the course of its existence, and the capacity to shape the world around it.

Maureen Daly Goggin and Beth Fowkes Tobin's edited volumes have effectively built upon this scholarship, focusing on women's creation and consumption of goods in order to highlight less understood spheres of knowledge, and exploring women's "gendered material practices," or manipulation of the material world, to consider objects as well as "the ways in which objects were conceptualized, produced, circulated, used, and exchanged."[45] Goggin and Tobin see women as active and creative, contributors to the social and cultural sphere, a theme that is picked up by Hadjiafxendi and Zakreski in their volume on women, craft, and professionalization.[46] Hadjiafxendi and Zakreski argue that through organization and artistry, women crafted objects as well as identities that reflected the complex engagement between the domestic and the industrial, the amateur and the professional in Britain during the nineteenth century. Janice Helland, Beverly Lemire, and Alena Buis's *Craft, Community and the Material Culture of Place and Politics, 19th–20th Century* (2014) elaborates upon this by exploring the potential of craft in establishing and reaffirming communal identities and relationships as communities encountered the forces of colonialism. Produced under periods of aggressive assimilation, the resultant objects presented new craft forms, reflecting the hybrid identities of their makers and context of creation, but also anchoring their creators to the past.[47] These studies see objects as revelatory: illuminating both their maker and the social context of their existence. The present volume, then, seeks to use the needle to unite this emphasis on determination and generation within the field of material culture with current textile scholarship, particularly those explorations that foreground the social, the cultural, and the artistic.

Such an approach is somewhat akin to that advocated for by Pristash, Schaechterle, and Wood in their essay "The Needle as the Pen: Intentionality, Needlework, and the Production of Alternate Discourses of Power," cited above, and from which the current volume derives its name. In this work, Pristash, Schaechterle, and Wood propose viewing needlework as a form of epideictic rhetoric, or rhetoric that "highlights the skill or artistry of a speaker over the development of an argument," that emphasizes and fosters communal values, and helps "its audience to imagine possibilities that need to be enacted in the world."[48] In doing so, they pull upon a familiar thread in textile scholarship: the link between writing and speaking and cloth, between text and textiles.

In English, numerous words and phrases have their roots in terminology associated with textile tools, qualities, and labor ("dyed-in-the wool," "spinning a yarn"),[49] and Victoria Mitchell notes that "in Hungarian, the word for fibres is the same as that for vocal chords."[50] Similarly, Jasleen Dhamija suggests that "being one of the oldest techniques mastered by the human race, fabric has lent its vocabulary to some of the most esoteric philosophical concepts," including *sutra*, from the Sanskrit word meaning "to string together."[51] Feminist theorists have also linked the acts of text and textile production in order to acknowledge the alternate means through which culture might be generated and individual narratives recorded, and, as Elaine Showalter has shown, how the strategy of piecing used in quilting might be comparable to the practice through which many early American women writers crafted texts.[52] Similarly, in "Beyond *Bricolage*: Women and Aesthetic Strategies in Latin American Textiles," Janet Catherine Berlo suggests that the textile works of the Maya, Kuna, and Shipibo might "share an aesthetic structure with verbal or literary modes."[53]

These comparisons between textuality and textiles have been incredibly fruitful, not least because they regard needlework as the equivalent of documentary forms of evidence—an act that has implications for women's work as well as non-Western forms of creation—however, as John Styles observes, if textiles are a "material language," and objects "a kind of text, then it is one that is (and was) exceptionally unstable, elusive, and ambiguous, easy to manipulate and almost impossible to read consistently."[54] Pristash, Schaechterle, and Wood's consideration of needlework as a form of epideictic rhetoric has thus become crucial for this study, as it emphasizes a desire to consider both process—"the sheer act of creating"—and product—"our primary information. When a rhetor is long dead"—as meaningful factors in the creative equation.[55] In this framework, the needle can be regarded as an extension of both hand and mind, enabling creation and connection, or as Pristash, Schaechterle, and Wood suggest, it becomes an implement through which to "shape identity, build community, and prompt engagement with social action."[56] Building upon this proposition, the present volume, *Stitching the Self: Identity and the Needle Arts*, centers on the needle as a vehicle through which identities, both individual and communal, were fostered and circulated in the period 1850 to the present.

In the collection cited above, Zakreski and Hadjiafxendi underline the concept of crafting, suggesting that the term implies a state of transformation which alters both the maker and the material with which they engage.[57] Needlework is similarly transformative, and it is the contention of this volume that viewing practice alongside product reveals the needle as a mechanism for exploration and identity construction. Contributors thus examine how needlework provided a space for growth, (re)definition, and salvation. In doing so they also challenge the lingering divisions in the field of art and textile scholarship—art and craft, amateur and professional, public and private, masculine and feminine—and through focused explorations of particular objects and makers, suggest that needlework allowed practitioners to travel the spectrum between these spheres.

Scope and Organization

This collection brings together the work of art and crafts historians, emerging and established scholars, and draws upon a range of methodological approaches, including object-based, geographic, feminist, political, and historical analyses. Binding the care of the connoisseur with the scope of the social historian, contributors consider objects closely, in many cases engaging with makers and works previously overlooked. A selection of the chapters presented here deal with a singular work in great detail, and, as such, offer a possible model for reading unique objects in meaningful ways. Such analyses are essential for the field of textiles, where it is often difficult to unite a body of work around a particular maker.

While studies of needlework traditionally focus on embroidery, this volume casts a wider net, and includes essays on quilting, knitting, dressmaking, as well as embroidery, recognizing that the needle itself represents a powerful vehicle for articulating identity. However, although broad in this sense, this collection is limited in others. Each author engages with the issue of artistry, a focus which complements the temporal and geographic range of the volume. Contributors highlight needlework processes and products in the West in the period 1850 to the present, finding narratives of creative intention within a culture and at a time when forms of labor were increasingly gendered, and in which the arts, and eventually, the crafts were progressively subjected to calls for professionalization, processes which largely excluded needlework and needleworkers from the realm of artistic production. Although such a focus would perhaps imply an emphasis on women's work, this collection does not demand this, and select chapters deal with male production or collaboration between men and women, illustrating that the gendered division of labor had ramifications for practitioners of both sexes. And while the case studies presented here do focus on Western works, they do so with an awareness of the wider cultural context in which these objects were formed. Lisa Binkley's chapter, for instance, situates a woman's use of quilting cotton against the background of immigrant experiences and abolitionist politics, while Elaine Cheasley Paterson's analysis of Mary Seton Watts's embroidery demonstrates that Watts is inseparable from her experiences as an imperial citizen; this worldview informed her approach to arts education.

Emerging Identities

Stitching the Self is divided into three thematic sections, which, though not chronological, reveal instances of artistry, activism, and self-determination. The first, Emerging Identity: Reconsidering the Narratives of the Needle, considers whether new narratives of creativity might lay dormant in the needlework of established figures.

Wendy Wiertz begins with an abstract approach to this idea, challenging the literary and visual trope of the silent, stitching woman of the middle and upper classes with an examination of the work and career of Belgian artist Hélène De Rudder. Like many of her peers, De Rudder received training in the needle arts as part of a genteel education. However, she did not rely on the needle for domestic comfort alone, but rather sought public recognition for her work through the Belgian Salon des Beaux-Arts, establishing herself as a talented artist and craftsperson. Johanna Amos also considers how an examination of needlework can disrupt well-established narratives by looking in particular at the work of Jane Burden Morris. Famed for her relationship to two famous men—her husband, William Morris, and the painter Dante Gabriel Rossetti—Morris is often identified as the "muse" of the Pre-Raphaelite movement. Amos moves to complicate this narrative by looking at Morris's contributions in the field of needlework—her preparation of items for both her husband and Rossetti, as well as the creation of dress for her own wardrobe—in order to argue that Morris used the needle to reinvent herself as a contributor to an artistic community in both practice and visual presentation.

M. Lilly Marsh explores the pioneering work of renowned knitter Elizabeth Zimmermann, emphasizing how needlework practice could be utilized to disrupt ideas of the amateur maker during the mid-century American economic boom. Through a series of successful patterns, publications, and television programs, Zimmermann inspired knitters to engage with their craft in a creative and critical manner, and unlike Mary Walker Phillips, whose creation of experimental wall hangings in traditional and novel materials allied her with the modern design movement, dawned a generation of practitioners capable of applying the design skill more typically associated with the professional to the home economy, destabilizing the traditional relationship between domestic and creative work.[58] Finally, Joseph McBrinn revisits the textile projects of the celebrated Bloomsbury group, considering how both the women and the men of Bloomsbury found solace in the therapeutic properties of stitching, including embroidery, knitting, and crochet, yet also utilized the practice to play with and disrupt needlework's gendered associations. McBrinn further demonstrates that although lauded for their progressive, modernist approach to sexuality and gender identity, it was Bloomsbury's engagement with Victorian forms of needlework that made their critique of Victorian heteropatriarchy all the more astute.

Considered together, these narratives address needlework practices and practitioners who mobilized education and social connections to produce objects that accommodated the traditional associations of needlework with gentility, resourcefulness, and training, and at the same time challenged existing social, cultural, and economic norms and expectations. For Hélène De Rudder, Jane Burden Morris, Elizabeth Zimmermann, and members of the Bloomsbury group, the needle offered a powerful vehicle through which they could construct alternate identities, and explore the liminal space between the public and the private, the amateur and the professional.

Elaborating Identities

Building upon the illuminating narratives of the first section, and in particular upon the consideration of the ways textile objects might disrupt social norms and expectations, the chapters that form part two, Elaborating Identity: Expressing Ideology, Crafting Community, investigate "alternative discourses" and the political dimension of needlework objects, as well as the activist associations of needlework practice.[59]

Lisa Binkley considers how the *Whig's Defeat* quilt, although likely produced as an example of Canadian maker Jessie Campbell's expertise in fine needlework and her readiness for marriage, also served to situate Campbell within her community as well as larger local and global political spheres. The daughter of Scottish Highland immigrants, Campbell appropriated an American design, made in celebration of the defeat of the Whig party in the United States (1844), in order to reference the dissolution of the British Whigs and their role in the forced migration of Highlanders. In doing so, Campbell asserted the significance of her Highland heritage, even as her connections to settler Canada deepened through marriage. Her coverlet thus alludes to the hybrid identities assumed by many nineteenth-century immigrants. Janice Helland considers a more overtly political textile object, a suffrage banner made collaboratively and under the guidance of Ann MacBeth at the Glasgow School of Art (GSA). The central panel in the "From Prison to Citizenship" banner is comprised of a series of embroidered signatures, signatures which document numerous women's participation in hunger strikes undertaken while serving prison sentences for their political activism. As such, it memorializes the work of less familiar figures in the suffrage movement, and demonstrates the use of the needle to advocate for social change. However, in utilizing the emerging modern design language of the GSA, and in acknowledging the acts of civilian women, this banner also disrupts the particular material and visual qualities typically associated with suffrage banners. Rather than asserting a femininity that "came close to repressing their politics and inhibiting their effect," the "From Prison to Citizenship" banner more closely echoes the militant actions of the Women's Social and Political Union.[60] Elaine Cheasley Paterson similarly explores the circulation of social values in her analysis of Mary Seton Watts's banner *Our Lady of the Snows*. In this chapter, Paterson illuminates the banner's roots in the philanthropic and social activism of Watts's earlier career, which saw craft as an elevating or civilizing influence, and the promotion of this ideology in an imperial context through the banner's presentation to Canada and residence at Royal Victoria College. Paterson demonstrates how the gifting of this banner coincided with the physical removal of children from center to periphery through the "child-savers" movement, and similarly forms part of the dialogue which formulated "Greater Britain" at the turn of the century.

In the chapters by Binkley, Helland, and Paterson, the authors emphasize both process and final product as significant to the social and political activities in which the makers were active. Through stitching, women became empowered practitioners and forged relationships to broader communities and social movements. For example, by making and using a quilt with nuanced political connotations, Campbell reinforced the depth to which her Scottish Highland community and its subsequent diaspora in Canada responded and adapted to their political environment and surroundings. Helland similarly highlights the shared experiences of hunger strikers and how the use of the suffrage banner in the "From Prison to Citizenship" procession made a community of voices visible on a national stage. This notion of advocacy is picked up and inflected by Paterson in her consideration of the *Our Lady of the Snows* banner, which to this day hangs at McGill University in Montreal, as representative of Watts's initiatives in educating the poor in the values of craftsmanship, viewing this as a means through which they might transform their lives.

Recovering Identities

The final section of this collection, turns from the public to the intimate, emphasizing the personal dimension of the needle arts. The chapters in Recovering Identity: Locating the Self Through Needlework consider how the act of stitching fosters self-realization and strength in periods of transition, and how the resultant objects record these moments of memory and transformation.

Sabine Wieber opens this section with an examination of the needlework of Johanna Wintsch, produced during her institutionalization at Burghölzli and Rheinau asylums. While stitching often figured in psychiatric treatment due to its calming and meditative, not to mention productive, qualities, Wieber argues that Wintsch's needlework may have also provided Wintsch with a space in which to carve out a personal identity, apart from that dictated by the institution. She further suggests that this articulation allowed her to resist aspects of her confinement. Anne Koval picks up on the soothing and restorative potential of needlework in her analysis of contemporary needle artist Anna Torma. Part of the Hungarian diaspora, Torma utilizes embroidery and quilting, skills learned from her female relatives, to document and reclaim aspects of her family history. Torma also visually ties the mundane and the familiar, borrowing images from her children's drawings, with long-standing artistic traditions, using the needle to imitate the illuminations of medieval bestiaries or the drawings of anatomical texts. Janet Catherine Berlo's "Suturing My Soul" concludes this section, yet also serves as a powerful coda to the volume as a whole. Binding a career of academic and personal experiences in the textile arts to an analysis of the Bayeux "Tapestry," Berlo attempts to chart the meaning of the needle for women across time and geography, to realize a "poetics of embroidery." She thus illuminates the power of the needle for all who endeavor to employ it, and the scholarly potential in investigating the echoes of needlework practice. As the other essays in this volume illustrate, Berlo insists that needlework provides an intimate record of creativity; in tracing its stitches, we connect with the minds and hands of those removed from us by time or distance.

In closing this volume, Wieber, Koval, and Berlo build on the earlier chapters by emphasizing how the lives and experiences of each of the needle artists in this collection are embedded in the threads of their textile creations. With each stitch, fiber, and image, makers expressed their ideas, trials, joys, and sorrows. Like all of the authors here, they suggest that it is impossible to look at needlework without considering the narrative behind the object. Whether rarified or quotidian, these works are a valuable register of personal experience, marking the ways through which the needle facilitated transition: emergence, elaboration, and recovery.

Stitching the Self

Numerous scholars have pointed to the potency of textiles, "the most intimate of thing-types," as Judy Attfield describes.[61] As materials that clothe the body and the home, and which, like the body, are ephemeral, wearing and fading out of existence, they have strong associations with individual and collective identity. Identities, as Cheryl Buckley and Hilary Fawcett suggest, are never "fixed but always in the process of making."[62] Similarly, stitches can be worked or laid, yet they can also be dropped or undone, seams can be sewn together or ripped apart, fragments can be pieced and made anew. It is in this context that the needle becomes a numinous tool. Through it, individuals not only articulate facets of themselves, but alter their physical being, increasing skill and dexterity; they remake the self, as they allow the self to become manifest in the world.

Part One

Emerging Identity: Reconsidering the Narratives of the Needle

The Identity of an Embroidering Woman: The Needle Arts in Brussels, Belgium, 1850–1914

Wendy Wiertz

Introduction

A drawing dated 1889 depicts a girl quietly sitting in front of a window (Figure 1.1). Her head bent, her eyes fixed on her hands, she is fully concentrated on crocheting a fine ribbon. Likely, she does not even notice her mother sketching her rapt form. This girl is Riri d'Ursel, the later Countess de Boissieu (1875–1934), and the daughter of the high-ranking Duchess d'Ursel, née de Mun (1849–1931).[1] This private moment of a hand-working daughter captured by her mother is but one of the many nineteenth-century visual examples of girls and women embroidering, knitting, crocheting, tailoring, and dressmaking.[2] According to these images, the hands of girls and women never stopped for a moment's rest. As Rozsika Parker has demonstrated, such images contributed to the stereotype of femininity: silent and still, confined to the home, and committed to a family.[3] Is this the only narrative? In this chapter, I question this visual stereotype by investigating if and how needlework fostered new identities among girls and women, focusing on those of the upper and middle classes in Brussels during the period 1850–1914.

The first part of this chapter focuses on Belgian women's education in the needle arts during the second half of the nineteenth and the beginning of the twentieth century. Drawing upon educational manuals, magazines, books, and visual culture, which offered a prescription of the curriculum for home and institutional education, I demonstrate how home tutoring and schools employed the needle arts towards different goals, both domestic and professional. In the second part, I examine the career of one of Belgium's most well-known needlewomen, Hélène De Rudder, born Du Ménil (1869–1962). She is a clear example of an embroideress who transformed from a craftswoman to an artist.

Figure 1.1 Duchess d'Ursel, née Antonine de Mun, "Riri à la fenêtre du salon d'Hingene s'essayant à faire de la mignardise. Juillet 1890." Pen and ink drawing, 260 × 165 mm, *Album 1888–1891*. Brussels, private collection, 35r. © Hingene, Kasteel d'Ursel, Stefan Dewickere.

In the third and last part of this chapter, I concentrate on how the needle arts were employed by other women, the status of needlework, and how these skills could lead to new identities as (semi-)professional craftswomen and teachers, thus showing how women stretched the prescribed boundaries of femininity. This chapter is set within the context of Art Nouveau's celebration of the decorative arts, as well as a shift in education policy.

The Place of the Needle Arts in Young Women's Education

"Faut-il conclure de là que l'industrie féminine (je parle évidemment ici des femmes privilégiées que la nécessité de gagner leur vie n'oblige pas au travail) est dans le marasme? Certes non [...]."[4]

Alma, author for the women's journal *Bruxelles Féminin*, was delighted to observe that Belgian girls and women still practiced aspects of "feminine industry," including the needle arts, in 1904. These "modern Penelopes," as she called them, were women whose privilege freed them from work, and who chose to use their time wisely, not wasting their efforts on grand art. As she stated, "Le nombre de jeunes femmes et de jeunes filles qui chez nous, occupent leurs loisirs à exécuter des ouvrages délicats, artistiques et pratiques, croît chaque jour. Ce sont là passe-temps très intelligents et beaucoup plus intéressants [...] que les essais infructueux de grand art auxquels se complaisant encore quelques snobinettes."[5]

Many women, however, not only chose needlework, the so-called feminine industry, but combined different techniques. The aristocratic sisters Marie (1848–1925), Jeanne (1850–1926), and Henriette (1855–1940) Countesses de Villermont, who were tutored at home in Brussels and at the Belgian countryside, were three such women. Drawing, painting, and playing music, as well as sewing and embroidering, were all part of their education. They also received a lesson in making bobbin lace.[6] The sisters learned these skills from their mother and governess. The eldest, Marie, later recalled in her memoirs, "Ma mère dont les doigts de fée étaient infatigables n'aimait rien tant que de passer de longues heures de la journée sur la terrasse du château à broder, faire de la tapisserie, ou coudre pour les pauvres."[7]

In addition to the instructions received from their mother and governess, the sisters de Villermont could consult printed examples in magazines or pattern books. These pattern books existed from the early-sixteenth century. Drawing and painting manuals only appeared from the end of the eighteenth century onwards, demonstrating that the needle arts were an important pastime centuries before drawing and painting, and remained so during the nineteenth century.[8] Almost all girls and women from the upper and middle classes learned embroidering, knitting, crocheting, tailoring, and dressmaking. They learned the skills at home from female relatives, governesses, or received lessons from private teachers and at school.

The schooling system in Belgium during the second half of the nineteenth century was characterized by the *Schoolstrijd* (School War), an ideological, pedagogical, and financial conflict between Catholics and liberals. This conflict changed the schooling landscape. During the first half of the century, girl's education had been mainly entrusted to congregational schools and private pensions; however, after 1850 non-confessional schools were founded. All institutes included needlework in their curriculums, and whatever the school's ideology, the vision of women's social role remained the same: "as domestic helpmates, women played a critical role in the family, showcasing their husbands' success and ensuring the family's biological and ideological continuity."[9] *Écoles ménagères* (schools specializing in domestic science) were particularly focused on teaching young women how to run a household. These schools targeted two groups of women: those who would go into service, and, preferably, those who would marry, settle, and become devoted wives and mothers. However, this bourgeois ideal of the angel in the house, promoted by books, education manuals, magazines, and visual culture was not possible for everyone: some women had to gain a livelihood because they remained unmarried or because their fortune declined.[10]

Different educational systems could prepare women for a profession, but none explicitly advertised this goal. This changed with the creation of the *école professionelle*. In Brussels, the first professional school for girls was founded in 1865 and was later called *école* Bischoffsheim after its most important initiator, the banker, liberal politician, and philanthropist Jonathan-Rafaël Bischoffsheim (1808–1883). The institute was modelled after the French Élisa Lemonniers' professional schools for poor girls and proclaimed a number of revolutionary objectives for the period.[11] Aside from the secular nature of its teachings, it declared the importance of a general theoretical level of instruction for future women artisans, organized apprenticeship training outside of the workshop, and legitimated the principle of paid work for women. These objectives constituted a total break from the dominant ideal of the angel of the house.[12]

Stressing the legitimation of the principle of paid work for women was new and contributed to their emancipation. The Brussels professional school offered a mixture of theoretical and professional lessons permitting their students to choose from technical drawing; embroidering; manufacturing clothing and lingerie; painting on porcelain, glass, and fabric; fabricating artificial flowers; and accounting (Figure 1.2). Unlike its French counterpart, the *école Bischoffsheim* predominantly recruited lower middle-class students. To be recruited, the students had to fulfil a number of conditions: the girls had to be twelve years old, finished primary school, and they needed to pay a small enrolment fee. Later, efforts were made to include girls from the lower classes. The school proved to be a success, and by 1900 around forty-eight such professional schools existed in Belgium, though of varying quality.[13]

In the same decade that the first professional school for girls opened its doors, the Brussels Academy of Fine Arts considered the integration of the applied arts. Auguste Orts (1814–1880), a lawyer, liberal politician, and the chairman of

LA CLASSE DE BRODERIE.   Photo Gautier.

Figure 1.2 *La classe de broderie à l'école Bischoffsheim, c.* 1903. Photo Gautier, in Anonymous, "L'École professionnelle Bischoffsheim," *Bruxelles Féminin*, 1 December 1903, 8–9. Free of copyright.

public works for the Brussels City Council,[14] raised the issue of admitting women in this field. He argued that women could earn a living through the applied arts, including the needle arts, before they married. If there should be financial difficulties after marriage, they could continue working without having to leave their home. In this way, they could fulfil their roles as wives and mothers.

One supporter of Orts's idea was the painter Louis De Taeye (1822–1891). He drew attention to the fact that the expense of educating women in the applied arts was less than when men attended the program. According to De Taeye, this was due to the choice of materials: women frequently pursued painting on porcelain, fans, fabrics, or glass; the design and creation of clothing; or the manufacture of artificial flowers, whereas men specialized in wood- and metalworking. Although Orts and De Taeye did not argue that women were better suited to practices in the decorative arts than the fine arts, this belief was widespread and had been reinforced by numerous empirical studies conducted by doctors and scientists.[15] However, the efforts of Orts and De Taeye to admit women into the decorative arts section were in vain; when the Academy of Fine Arts opened an applied arts section in 1886, women were barred despite the many advantages proposed. Women would have to wait three more years before they could enter the prestigious institute, though they were welcomed in both the applied and fine arts.[16]

Education manuals, magazines, books, and visual culture advised that needle arts were an integral part of girls' education. Educational systems ranging from home tutoring to confessional and non-confessional schools did include these arts in their curriculums. No educational system explicitly legitimated the principle of paid work for women through these skills, except the professional *école* Bischofssheim. This was quite revolutionary from an emancipatory viewpoint. In the same period, the discussion of admitting women in the applied arts section of the Academy of Fine Arts was raised; however, it was only in 1889 that women were admitted to the Academy. This opened the way to a career in the applied and fine arts, and potentially to new identities.

Case Study: Hélène De Rudder, née Du Ménil (1869–1962)

An obvious example of a needle worker whose identity was transformed from craftswoman to artist is Hélène De Rudder. She was and is Belgium's most well-known and appreciated embroideress of the late-nineteenth and early-twentieth centuries.[17] Born Du Ménil, she moved in 1886 with her parents to Uccle, close to Brussels. Belonging to the lower middle class, she needed to learn a profession. She enrolled at the Brussels *école professionnelle* Funck, an institution modelled after the *école* Bischoffsheim. She learned how to sew and manufacture clothing before taking up embroidery. In addition to the classes at the *école* Funck, she took private drawing lessons from Maria De Rudder, sister of the established sculptor Isidore De Rudder (1855–1943).

Isidore De Rudder descended from an artists' family and followed in their footsteps. In 1869, he registered at the Brussels Royal Academy of Fine Arts and trained to be a sculptor. After his studies, he embarked on a successful career as a sculptor, but he was also interested in the applied arts, gained merit as a designer, and was embedded in the Brussels art scene. From 1890, he started to design and execute smaller objects in bronze and ceramic for companies including the bronze company Luppens and porcelain manufactures Vermeren-Coché and Boch. He also collaborated with the silversmith company Maison Wolfers.[18]

Hélène Du Ménil married De Rudder in 1890 and started to collaborate with her spouse. Although most contemporary authors were convinced Hélène De Rudder, née Du Ménil was only the executor of her husband's designs, this impression was corrected by Isidore De Rudder in his unpublished memoirs. He replaced author Sander Pierron's sentence, "N'est-ce pas lui qui a dessiné tous les projets de ses cartons?" with "C'est lui qui dessinait tous les cartons des projets conçus par la brodeuse et l'aidait à réaliser ses rêves d'artiste."[19] This correction explains why most embroideries are signed only by Hélène De Rudder. She took credit as the designer and executor. A minority are left unsigned, bear the name of both spouses, and a few feature only the name of Isidore De Rudder.[20]

Hélène De Rudder, née Du Ménil first exhibited her embroidery at the 1895 exhibition of the Brussels *Cercle Pour l'Art*.[21] Immediately, her work was lauded and numerous exhibitions both within and outside Belgium followed over the next twenty years. Through the intermediation of her husband, De Rudder received large commissions from local authorities and from museums. The most prestigious ones are those she executed for the Wedding Rooms of the Brussels and Saint-Gilles City Halls, the Ghent provincial government building, and the hall of honor of the Tervuren Colonial Palace. This official recognition was extraordinary for a woman. Besides these orders, she also embroidered at the request of private individuals. De Rudder, née Du Ménil executed her works with the help of embroiderers who worked under her supervision.[22]

Many commissions were exhibited before they were hung at their final destination. Each time, the press lauded the size, the iconography, the style, and the technique of the works. The press and public were astonished with the monumental size of the embroideries measuring over two meters. Iconographically, De Rudder, née Du Ménil was inspired by flora and fauna, allegorical animals, and scenes from legends, fables, and mythology. Stylistically, the works belong to Art Nouveau, yet they are also reminiscent of the work of Renaissance artist Sandro Botticelli (1445–1510), the Pre-Raphaelite Brotherhood, as well as Japanese prints. Technically, De Rudder, née Du Ménil mainly employed patchwork application. Different pieces of tissue—sometimes used—were glued to the fabric and finished off with embroidery.[23] Unfortunately, the monumental embroidered panels made in this technique deteriorated much faster than those of all-over stitchery, as used in the *Seasons*, including *Autumn* (Plate 1.1). The anonymous critic of the women's magazine *Bruxelles Féminin* lauded these large panels seen at the 1903 Brussels *Salon des Beaux-Arts* and even hoped De Rudder would realize a renaissance of the needle arts.[24]

De Rudder, née Du Ménil and her team started working on *The Four Seasons* in 1900, finishing them a few years later. Each panel, embroidered in silks, measures 191 centimeters in height and 225 centimeters in width and shows the succeeding seasons combined with the different life stages of a woman as a girl, young bride, mother, and grandmother. *Autumn* is the third panel in the series and depicts a young mother breastfeeding her second child outside on a porch. Her firstborn, a little girl sits at her left, eating grapes. Above the little girl, a peacock with its magnificent tail sits on the porch fence, looking at the young mother. On the right side, the rich harvest of autumn is shown on a table covered with red linen. The fruits of the land are displayed with the game shot during the hunt: rabbit, duck, pheasant, and wild boar. In the background, branches and leaves from different trees such as the oak tree shield the intimate scene from the landscape. The borders around the scene are filled with seasonal leaves, flowers, and animals. While the border at the top shows Libra, Scorpio, and Sagittarius, the three signs of the zodiac linked to the Autumn, the border underneath depicts four geese flying away from a lake. Iconographically, the message of the series is conservative, as women are given the role of dutiful wives and mothers, but the Art Nouveau style and the high quality of the execution definitely set De Rudder's accomplishments as an expert in the needle arts, and she was often considered more than a craftswoman.

Hélène De Rudder, née Du Ménil was lauded as an artist.[25] Her reputation was rooted in a number of factors. She married and collaborated with an established artist. He drew the cartoons after her ideas, provided her with a network, and acted as her intermediary for commissions. She was also fortunate that during the second half of the nineteenth century, the needle arts, and the applied arts in general, regained appreciation. At world exhibitions, the ideal was to combine artistic beauty with mass production. The arts and crafts movement also gave embroidery a new incentive by inventing new designs and opposing the mere imitation of paintings. Finally, Art Nouveau, the style prominent when De Rudder's monumental embroidered panels were celebrated, tempered the hegemony of painting and sculpture to the benefit of the applied arts.[26] After 1914, Art Nouveau and large embroidered panels were no longer in vogue. Nevertheless, during and shortly after the Great War, Hélène De Rudder, née Du Ménil made smaller pieces in lace and continued to participate in exhibitions until she closed her studio in 1925.[27]

A New Identity Through the Needle Arts? Female Needleworkers Gain Recognition

While the name of Hélène De Rudder, née Du Ménil seems to have eclipsed the reputation of many other needlewomen, she was not the only one stretching the prescribed boundaries of women's femininity. Certainly, many women from the upper and middle class were busy embroidering, knitting, crocheting, tailoring, and dressmaking at home, but it was during the second half of the nineteenth and the early part of the twentieth century that female needleworkers found a stage at the numerous organized exhibitions in- and outside Belgium.

Aristocratic and bourgeois women belonging to the upper classes chose charity bazaars and fancy fairs as their venue. The press often devoted one or more articles to the events due to the charitable character and the illustrious participants and visitors, including female members of Belgium's royal family. In Brussels, the yearly *Fancy fair* drew many exhibitors, visitors, and press attention. The elite magazine *L'Éventail* wrote on 28 February 1892 that Queen Marie-Henriette (1836–1902) received an embroidered cushion from Baroness de Gericke. The most remarkable object, however, was a "joli chapeau de dame, œuvre de Mlle Devleeschoudere, la modiste attirée des actrices du Théâtre du Parc."[28] Unfortunately, this platform and the attention did not include a change of identity for the participants. Although the aristocratic and bourgeois women found a stage, received attention from co-exhibitors, visitors, and the press, and developed new skills through the sale of their work, communication, and even organization of the event, these aspects were considered traditional characteristics for these ladies. Creating needlework for the poor was one aspect of charity, the latter belonging to the aristocratic and bourgeois duties summarized in *Noblesse oblige*.[29]

Middle-class women practicing the needle arts chose to display their objects at other locations such as the world exhibitions and the Brussels *Salons triennaux des Beaux-Arts*. Since the first world exhibition was mounted in 1851, different countries had followed the successful formula. Between 1885 and 1914, no less than seven international exhibitions were staged in Belgium.[30] Each time, a separate section displayed a wide diversity of works made by women, including needlework. Although, the far-reaching abilities of women in distinct scientific and artistic fields were shown, the overall message was very conservative: a woman's goal in life was foremost to be a devoted wife and mother. For this reason, *écoles ménagères* received more attention than *écoles professionnelles*. The choice of women for applied arts, including needlework, was reassuring: they lived at least partly up to the stereotype in following feminine pursuits. Even though, the needle arts were revalued during the second half of the nineteenth century and Hélène De Rudder, née Du Ménil was considered an artist, most women and their works were seen as craftswomen and craft. A last disadvantage was that the works of women were first judged according to the gender of the maker instead of the object's qualities. In this way, women never formed any competition for the arts and crafts made by men.[31] Nonetheless, they were mentioned in the press and received positive reviews which enhanced their visibility, self-confidence, and emancipated them. For example, one critic wrote after seeing the Liège *Palais des femmes* in 1905, "[N]ombre de femmes ont exposé de superbes cuirs repoussés, des broderies décoratives, des ornements d'église, des drapeaux, des tapisseries, des meubles artistiques. Le grand prix a été décerné à Mlle Suzanne Weiller pour son superbe paravent, œuvre tout à fait hors pair."[32]

Women found a stage at world exhibitions, but these were not the only venues where needlework was shown. In 1903, the Brussels *Salon triennal des Beaux-Arts* organized for the first time a section for the applied arts which was warmly welcomed in the press. "Enfin voici le clou du Salon actuel, ce qui en constitue vraiment cette année l'attrait et la nouveauté: le compartiment de l'art appliqué."[33] The huge success of the initiative was repeated during the following events of 1907, 1910 and 1914.[34] However, other cities where *Salons des Beaux-Arts* were mounted did not follow the Brussels example. The Brussels context was unique as the Art Nouveau style, with its attention to the applied arts, was much more present in Belgium's capital than elsewhere in the country. This was possibly due to Brussels's status as the capital, its flourishing economy, its rising middle classes, its openness to new ideas regarding society, philosophy, economy, arts and culture such as the English arts and crafts movement, and the presence of Art Nouveau architects and artists such as Victor Horta (1861–1947).

At the 1903 exhibition, seventy-seven male and female professionals and amateurs displayed objects made in wood, glass, ceramics, enamel, metals, leather, embroidery, and tapestry in the applied arts section. The needle arts were well represented: fifteen of the thirty-two women and three of the thirty-five participating men showed at least one object made in the needle arts.[35] During the next exhibition in 1907, thirty-nine of the fifty-nine female exhibitors displayed one or more needle works.[36] Six of them had already participated in the 1903 exhibition: Henriette Bosché (active during the first half of the twentieth century),[37] Hélène De Rudder, Alice Deschreyver, Irène D'Olszowska (born c. 1880),[38] Julie Foerster,[39] Hermina Nilles, and Clara Voortman (1853–1926).[40] Little is known about Alice Deschreyver and Hermina Nilles. Julie Foerster was educated at the *école professionnelle* Fernand Cocq in Ixelles, near Brussels at the end of the nineteenth century. Her specialization was designing and manufacturing clothes. Henriette Bosché was a teacher at the same institute between c. 1910 and 1920. Clara Voortman became a professor at the Ghent Academy for Fine Arts where she had trained under painter Jean Delvin (1853–1922) and introduced applied arts to the program. The women often combined teaching positions with different art disciplines: Bosché, D'Olszowska, and Voortman all drew, painted, and practiced the needle arts (Plate 1.2). As artists and craftswomen, they continued to exhibit. As the popularity of the *Salons triennaux des Beaux-Arts* started to decline towards the start of the First World War, they also displayed their works at smaller exhibitions of artist's societies and in galleries and received attention from the press.[41] However, most of the time they sent paintings and drawings as the vogue for the Art Nouveau slowly disappeared and a stricter separation between high and low arts was again introduced.

Conclusion

The stereotype of a needleworking woman who is still, confined to the home, and committed to the family was spread throughout the nineteenth century. This was no different for girls and young women of the upper and middle classes in Brussels during the second half of the nineteenth and the beginning of the twentieth century. The majority of girls and young women learned the skills for maintaining a household, but some of them used these talents to stitch a new identity. They grew to be teachers, (semi-)professional needleworkers, and artists. This was possible due to the foundation of professional schools which stressed the legitimation of the principle of paid work for women, women's emancipation at the turn of the twentieth century, the revaluation of the applied and needle arts under the influence of Art Nouveau, and the attention from the public and the press during world and national exhibitions and fancy fairs.

This overview of the status of needlework and needleworkers in Belgium at a time of social upheaval and shifting stylistic preferences shows the multiple challenges and opportunities with which women in this field were presented. The case study of de Rudder helps to clarify how some of the broader trends played out for individual practitioners—and at the same time emphasizes the extraordinary circumstances of her situation.

"Experiments in silk and gold work afterwards to bloom": The Embroidering of Jane Burden Morris[1]

Johanna Amos

In the early 1860s, Jane Burden Morris (1839–1914), wife of the arts and crafts designer William Morris and model to the Pre-Raphaelite painter Dante Gabriel Rossetti, began work on a series of embroidered wall hangings, which included a depiction of the medieval queen Guenevere (Figure 2.1).[2] Based upon a portrait study of Morris herself in medieval attire, the panel was one of several featuring legendary female figures designed by William Morris and intended for display within Red House, the Morrises' first family home. Like many of the objects produced for Red House, *Guenevere* was part of a series of experiments in the decorative arts that secured the establishment of Morris, Marshall, Faulkner & Co. (later Morris & Co.) in 1861. However, a reworking of her own image in medieval guise, *Guenevere* also heralds a shift in the trajectory of Jane Morris's own life, from working-class daughter to middle-class wife and member of an influential artistic circle—a shift in which the needle played a transformative role.

Framing the needle as an active force in Morris's life, this chapter explores three avenues through which Morris used needlework to redefine her identity— to stitch an alternate self—and examines her contributions as art embroiderer and artistic collaborator, the remaking of her appearance through the production of dress and fashion, and her use of handcrafted gifts and shared labor to establish and cement personal relationships. In doing so, it suggests that Jane Morris, though long overshadowed by her more famous male colleagues, not only contributed to the success of the arts and crafts movement, but that her self-definition through needlework can itself be viewed as an artistic act.

Figure 2.1 William Morris (designer) and Elizabeth Burden (maker, attributed), *Guenevere, c.* 1861. Wool on holland ground, 115.6 cm (figure height). © The Society of Antiquaries of London (Kelmscott Manor).

Prick and Pounce: Laying the Ground

Jane Morris's interactions with the needle almost certainly began at an early age. Raised in Oxford, the daughter of a stablehand and a washerwoman, Jane (née Burden), like her family, numbered among the working poor. However, this background did not prevent the Burden children from receiving some education, and the 1851 census lists both Jane and her sister Elizabeth as "scholars."[3] Given Jane's abilities in later life, it is likely that she mastered her letters at school, as well as basic sewing and embroidery skills. Embroidery in particular would have been crucial for, as Leena Rana points out, needlework formed an important part of girls' education in the mid-nineteenth century, "particularly [for] those from impoverished conditions."[4] Despite this, the first projects by Jane's hand known to survive are those worked for Red House, the home in Bexleyheath commissioned by William and Jane Morris shortly after their marriage in 1859, and to which they relocated in 1860.

Designed by Philip Webb, the home became the site of an experiment for working out William Morris's developing ideas on interior design, a space in which the world was made anew. As his biographer explains:

> Only in a few isolated cases [...] was there anything then to be bought ready-made that Morris could be content with in his own house. Not a chair, or table, or bed; not a cloth or paper hanging for the walls; nor tiles to line fireplaces or passages; nor a curtain or a candlestick; nor a jug to hold wine or a glass to drink out of, but had to be reinvented.[5]

In this endeavor the Morrises were joined by their closest friends: Webb; the painter Edward Burne-Jones and his wife, Georgiana; Rossetti, and his artist wife Elizabeth Siddall; and the painter Ford Madox Brown. Together the friends created a program that is often described as medieval in character, and which featured stained glass windows, wooden furniture with crenelated ornaments and Gothic arches, embroidered tapestries, and murals and painted furniture with scenes from the *Canterbury Tales* and medieval legends. Jane Morris was thoroughly involved in the decoration of the home—she pricked and painted ceilings and posed for several of the painted figures—however, her greatest contribution to the scheme lies in the embroidered hangings that decorated the Morrises' bedroom, and the set of figure embroideries intended for display within the dining room.

The first of these, known as "Daisy" (Society of Antiquaries, Kelmscott Manor) after the scattering of flowers across the work's surface, is unusual for the period in both its design and execution. William Morris was responsible for the pattern, which departs from the rigid schemes of the popular Berlin woolwork to offer a slightly wild collection of bouquets.[6] Though avant-garde in one sense, the design is also far from novel, and was itself borrowed from the pages of a fifteenth-century manuscript copy of *Froissart's Chronicles* then held by the British Museum.[7] Jane Morris worked the pattern in red, pink, green, and yellow wools on a navy serge ground, a material that represents an unexpected choice, and one for which she was responsible. In a set of notes written decades later, Morris recalls her selection of this "rough and inexpensive fabric,"[8] chosen at a time when "hunting up" materials for this type of work proved difficult, again pointing to the unusual quality of both design and stitch.[9] While the blue serge would, as Wendy Parkins indicates, have been familiar to Morris, coming from a working-class background, her selection of it here "suggests a capacity to recognise objects in a new context," and to discern value in the otherwise overlooked, a process with which Morris herself might have identified.[10]

Morris may also have determined the type of stitches employed in the piece. As Linda Parry writes of the understated outline and couching stitches, "It is likely that this simple yet effective stitching was actually suggested by Jane Morris, a skilful practitioner," who would have had to divide her time between decoration and the management of a growing household.[11] However, Jane herself noted that the stitches utilized in the Morrises' early embroidery endeavors were partially learned from studying medieval and antique examples:

> It is not easy to imagine the great difficulty we had [. . .]. There were no lessons to
> be had, everything had to be laboured at for a time often successful, often not but
> the failures were amusing too. [. . .] We studied old pieces and by unpicking &:
> we learnt much but it was uphill work fascinating but only carried through by
> his enormous energy and perseverance.[12]

While Jane credits her husband as the driving force behind the project, William Morris had only begun to experiment with embroidery around 1855, and Jane had entered their marriage a skilled practitioner.[13] In learning a set of historic stitches, then, Morris was adding techniques to an already established repertoire, and would have understood better the effects and potential of the stitches, even of those that were new to her. "Daisy" is thus a product of shared knowledge and creativity; it records how the Morrises utilized research and skill to revive old techniques, judgement to determine which were best suited to contemporary work, and represents their first steps in creating a language that evoked, rather than imitated, the medieval.

These techniques were furthered in a series of embroideries of notable female figures, intended for display in the Red House dining room. Though frequently linked to Chaucer's fourteenth-century poetic work *Legend of Goode Wimmen*, few of the figures depicted are actually the same.[14] Designed by William Morris, the figures might also have been inspired by a sixteenth-century set of hangings depicting legendary women displayed at Hardwick Hall, and which he was likely to have seen on his visit to the house in 1855.[15] According to Jane, twelve figures were planned for Red House, though only seven were fully or partially completed, including Helen of Troy, Lucretia, Penelope, Aphrodite, St Catherine, Hippolyte, and Guenevere.[16] Worked in crewel wools on holland ground by Jane and her sister, Elizabeth, the figures, once completed, were to be cut from the linen and appliquéd to an elegantly embroidered serge background, though this was only done in three cases.[17]

Although unfinished, the Guenevere embroidery is unique among the sequence in that it is the only figure that appears to be closely modelled on one of Red House's occupants; the image is almost identical to that of the heroine in William Morris's painting *La Belle Iseult* (1858; Tate), for which Jane posed. In this sense, *Guenevere* was appropriate for Red House, a home in which the occupants and visitors were regularly depicted as medieval characters in murals and painted furniture—Burne-Jones's sequence of murals in the drawing room, for instance, features William and Jane as a fifteenth-century king and queen— yet also unusual, as Jane herself was closely involved in the object's execution.

Accounts of the activities of Red House suggest an atmosphere of joy and playful experimentation, and the images of the Morrises and their friends in medieval garb must be seen as contributing to and a consequence of this atmosphere. However, Wendy Parkins argues that the images of Jane in regal attire take on further significance when considered in relation to her working-class origins; these images may "have served a didactic purpose—reassuring Morris and others that his wife was qualified to reside in his 'palace of art.'"[18] Yet Jane's proximity to the execution of this particular object suggests something more—it is an attempt to figure herself not only into a middle-class life, but an artistic one. As one of Jane Morris's first forays into artistry, the series to which *Guenevere* belongs is emblematic of the expanding opportunities presented by the needle: the stitches and techniques employed here, and in Red House more broadly, were the first in the art embroidery movement, and a founding block in the Morris design firm; *Guenevere* heralds a manipulation of appearances that would shortly become crucial in Jane's own self-presentation; and as part of the shared activity of Red House, the series demonstrates the joys and advantages of collaboration in fostering creativity and sustaining friendships.

Threading the Needle: Artistry and Embroidery

Several of the surfaces and objects that adorned Red House were never fully realized; their fragmentary character serves as a reminder of the enthusiasm with which the members and guests of the home embarked on new projects, discarding the personal for more ambitious aims, including the production of wares for Morris, Marshall, Faulkner & Co., or the Firm, established in 1861. Like the ornamentation of Red House, the Firm was a collaborative effort, and W. Morris, Rossetti, Brown, Burne-Jones, Webb, and Peter Paul Marshall were all engaged in the creation of designs and cartoons for commercial goods for domestic and church interiors. While the work of several of these contributors has been celebrated in the various accounts of the enterprise,[19] the contribution of women to the establishment of the Firm, and more particularly that of Jane and her sister, has received less attention[20]—this despite Violet Hunt's assertion that "Mrs Morris was famous for her embroidery, and sitting 'lily-like, arow,' with Red Lion Mary [W. Morris's housekeeper] and Mrs W[ardle] ... laid, with her needle, the foundations of the firm."[21]

This neglect has its roots in the labor practices of the period, and in the distinction between amateur and professional. Indeed, despite arts and crafts practitioners' objections to the fragmentation of labor under industrialization, many, including William Morris, often subdivided production into two stages, design and manufacture. Gender further complicated this division, as Anthea Callen has demonstrated, and in the area of embroidery production more specifically, men typically contributed the designs, while women stitched.[22] For women like Jane Morris and Elizabeth Burden, this marginal position was compounded by their proximity to William Morris himself. Both lived with the Firm's managing partner, and, as neither of their names appear in the early accounts or meeting minutes of Morris, Marshall, Faulkner & Co., it is likely that information was communicated and embroidery work completed domestically, and possibly without compensation beyond the general success of the family enterprise.[23] However, the effective execution of the Firm's products, particularly in the early days of incorporation, must have been crucial, and reviews of the Firm's initial work suggest that the tasteful execution of embroideries formed part of Morris, Marshall, Faulkner & Co.'s emerging reputation.

The International Exhibition of 1862 offered the first major venue for showcasing the Firm's wares, and a range of furniture, glassware, and embroidered hangings were displayed in the Medieval Court. No complete record of the tapestries assembled survives, but given the date, the early works from Red House were almost certainly among the hangings exhibited.[24] Although reactions to the display were mixed, with many reviewers pointing to the disjuncture between the Firm's medieval-inspired wares and the modern Victorian interior, the tapestries were honored with "an award for faithfulness to medieval tradition," and garnered some praise in the press.[25] *The Building News*, for example, claimed that in the hangings "the harmony of colour is exquisite; there is scarcely a false tone among them. The design of the ornament is also in keeping with the workmanship and the material. And all are thoroughly medieval."[26] In this account, appreciation for the work seems to hinge on design and execution working in harmony to create an overall pleasing object, not in the form of the ornament alone. Thus, while William Morris's enthusiasm for ancient styles and techniques may have initiated the experiments from which these tapestries resulted, it was the skill and handiwork of Jane Morris and others that demonstrated that such objects could be artfully executed, and, despite the misgivings of some reviewers, popularly accepted.

As the Firm grew, embroideries remained a solid segment of the business. The Firm maintained a small staff of experienced needlewomen, all trained in the particular art embroidery techniques for which Morris work was known, and who produced ecclesiastical embroideries, as well as domestic screens and hangings, and other soft furnishings. Under this expansion, it has been suggested that Jane Morris took on a leadership role in the management of the embroidery division,[27] and a few letters confirm that she was responsible for at least some coordination of workers and materials until May Morris took over in 1885.[28] She also continued to complete work for the Firm, though it is difficult to trace to what extent, as many of the items that can be definitively tied to Morris's hand remained in the family collection, and were thus not produced with distinctly commercial aims. Nevertheless, a few of Jane Morris's extant embroideries seem to have been executed as stock or as commissions for some of the Firm's most prestigious clients. These include the "Acanthus" embroidery, alternately described as a coverlet or a curtain, currently housed at National Museum of Wales.[29]

"Acanthus" (Plate 2.1) was designed by William Morris and executed in 1878 for Theodosia Middlemore, who displayed it at her summer home, Melsetter House in Orkney. Here it seems to have been used as a hanging, as May Morris described it on a visit to the home as a curtain, "looking delightfully delicate and suitable."[30] In 1913, Middlemore lent the embroidery to the British Arts and Crafts Exhibition in Ghent, where it was displayed as a bed cover, and it was further shown at a similar exhibition in Paris the following year.[31] Given that these exhibitions were intended to showcase the best of British design abroad, it is significant that this piece was selected. Dramatically different from the embroideries exhibited in 1862, "Acanthus" still demonstrates a splendid harmony of design and artful execution.

At least two other embroideries of this design exist, one worked by May Morris, the other by one of the Firm's embroiderers, suggesting that this was a popular pattern; however, the contrast between these works also provides some insight into each embroiderer's interpretation of the design. May's version (V&A T.66-1939), produced *c.* 1900–10, is worked in blues, pinks, and reds, while Jane's features more organic tones: golds, pinks, and greens. The dimensions are also different: Jane's is the largest at roughly 2.5 x 2 meters, while the Morris & Co. example (V&A T.153-1979), worked *c.* 1880, possibly as a sample for the Firm's shop, is less than half this, and features only a fragment of the overall design.[32] This manipulation of design to suit the occasion, as well as the tastes of the embroiderer, is in line with art embroidery theories of the period. While Mary Smith Lockwood and Elizabeth Glaister argued in their treatise on the needle arts that "The first condition of an ideal work of art is that it should be conceived and carried out by one person," they also suggested that in circumstances where this was not possible, and embroiderers were confined to working to a prepared pattern, there was still "so much left to the judgment and taste of the worker as to justify her in calling the result of her labours an Art."[33]

Although there is little evidence to indicate that Jane Morris occupied the same professional status as the Firm's other embroiderers, or even that of her daughter May, who, in addition to assuming management of the Firm's embroidery division, became a successful designer in her own right, Jane Morris's status cannot satisfactorily be described as amateur. Morris's contributions enhanced the development of the Morris design enterprise, and while her works satisfy both commercial and domestic aims, as the embroideries for Red House indicate, work produced for the Morris home was often called upon to represent the business in professional settings, whether through display at international exhibitions, or within the interior spaces in which William Morris entertained his most prominent clients. Jane Morris, then, occupies a similar position to the multitude of "industrious women" who "existed between binaries of public and private," amateur and professional in the nineteenth century.[34]

This overlap between domestic creativity and more formal realms of production is also evident in Morris's creation of items of dress and drapery to be used as props in the paintings of Dante Gabriel Rossetti.[35] As with Morris's work for the Firm, the pieces created for Rossetti's images emerged collaboratively, with Rossetti contributing to the consideration of form and material, and Morris to style and ornamentation. In their exchange over the gown that forms the focal point of Rossetti's portrait of Morris, *The Blue Silk Dress* (1868),[36] for instance, Rossetti demonstrates a somewhat developed sense of women's clothing and an interest in its material properties, writing, "the sleeves should be as full at the top as is consistent with simplicity of outline, and perhaps would gain by being lined with some soft material."[37] His remarks, however, also convey the confidence he had in Morris's judgment and ability; when considering the design of the embroidered ornament for the neck and cuffs of the gown, he deferred to her sensibilities, stating, "of this you will be the best judge."[38]

Evidence that Morris regularly worked with Rossetti to provide his canvases with a particular look and styling also lies in an exchange of letters between the painter and his studio assistant, Henry Treffry Dunn. In the early 1870s, Rossetti was frequently resident at Kelmscott Manor, a country home in Oxfordshire which he leased with the Morris family. Away from his London studio, he wrote to Dunn on multiple occasions to request the delivery of furniture, jewelry, and drapery, either sourced from his personal collection or London's network of bric-a-brac shops, to be used as visual and material aids in the execution of his art. Following one such plea, Rossetti wrote again to Dunn indicating that one of the objects previously requested, a headdress likely intended for the work *Marigolds* (1873), was no longer needed, as "Janey made up something."[39] Although lacking in detail, the letter hints at the dialogue that existed between Rossetti and Morris, and at the potential for creativity and improvisation on Morris's part as the need arose.

Similar to her early work for Morris & Co., Jane Morris's skill with a needle added essential qualities to Rossetti's art; she provided texture and color, and enabled the convincing execution of an artistic product. Rossetti himself intimated the critical role Morris's dresses and drapery played in his practice; when pieces of one of Morris's costumes went missing in transit, Rossetti bemoaned the fact, writing to the critic Theodore Watts-Dunton, "I don't know how to get on with the picture without them."[40] Indeed, the work for which these items were intended, *Madonna Pietra*, was never completed.

Embroidering: Fashioning the Self

While several of the items Morris made for Rossetti were used strictly as modelling costume, there are indications that some of the dresses in the painter's store were originally garments in Morris's personal wardrobe. Rossetti wrote to Morris early in 1880, noting the "extreme usefulness of the dresses of yours which I have," and inquiring as to whether she had any more "'Old Clo' of an artistic cut and material," which she might be willing to contribute to his work.[41]

Though seemingly designed for use in Rossetti's portrait of her, Morris's blue silk gown also travelled between studio and closet,[42] and the two pictures for which this dress was used, *Mrs. William Morris* and *Mariana*—one a portrait, the other a literary subject—suggest the dual character of the gown, and point to similarities between Morris's self-presentation in daily life, and the styling of her figure in Rossetti's art. This relationship was noted by many of Morris's contemporaries; the American author Emma Lazarus, for instance, described Morris as "very beautiful and exactly like all the Rossetti pictures," dressed in "an esthetic [sic] dress of dark dull red, with a garnet necklace and cross."[43]

Written accounts suggest that for much of her adult life, Jane Morris engaged in a particular form of artistic self-fashioning, wearing an unconventional style of clothing best described as artistic dress.[44] Less restrictive than the corseted and bustled fashions typical for the middle classes in Victorian Britain, artistic dress became a favorite among women engaged in artistic pursuits; handmade or hand decorated, the style was also a visual and material indication of one's allegiance to the arts and crafts and aesthetic movements. Although never broadly accepted, the style was notable enough to merit mention in the ladies' periodical *Queen*, and one article describes the qualities most sought by the style's adherents:

> They loved the soft, heavy folds of India cashmere, wrought in delicate borders by the embroiderer's hand; the richness of velvet and plush and the dim delicacy of muslin unspoilt by starch; their eyes were open to the mellow colour of long strings of amber beads, rich oriental necklets of quaint device . . . They recognised the value and beauty of all such things, and shrank from the gaudy extravagant ugliness and the *bizarrerie* without grace of the fashions of the Second Empire.[45]

Although none of Morris's garments are known to survive, both visual and written descriptions of her dress relate qualities similar to those articulated above. Observed entertaining at home or at studio gatherings, Morris is described as wearing gowns of "cream crêpe, sparingly trimmed with old gold satin, and made high to the throat,"[46] and "crinkled white garb with a gold string around her waist or absence of a waist"; highlighting her acceptance of the unboned silhouette as well as soft fabrics delicately ornamented.[47] A further, and particularly evocative description appears in the recollections of May Morris; she recounts "a delicious, simple gown of shot blue and brown that was a great favourite with the little girls. It had some fragile ornament of gold thread at the throat and the wrists, and was of a delicate, faintly-rustling texture, that we never tired of stroking."[48] These textual references are further in keeping with the dress

Morris wears in a photograph of the Morris and Burne-Jones families taken in 1874 (Figure 2.2); it drapes from the shoulder, is lightly belted at the waist, and has voluminous sleeves. The gown is also sparingly trimmed, save for a faint ruffle at the throat and simple ruching employed at the cuffs, and appears to be made of supple fabric. Such photographic and textual accounts of Morris's artistic clothing appear until late in her life, suggesting a long-term identification with this form of self-presentation. However, Morris's motives for adopting the style are not recorded and must be inferred.

Figure 2.2 Frederick Hollyer, Photograph of the Burne-Jones and Morris families, 1874. Albumen print. © National Portrait Gallery, London.

In marrying William Morris, Jane affirmed her connection to the Pre-Raphaelite circle; she also entered middle-class society. Such a transition would have entailed learning the techniques of middle-class femininity, including its codes of dress—techniques with which Morris was likely only superficially familiar. One of the women credited with assisting Morris in navigating this transformation was Sara Prinsep (née Pattle), mother of the artist Valentine Prinsep, and doyenne of the artistic community at Little Holland House, a venue frequented by the Pre-Raphaelites and their associates. The daughter of a British civil servant, Prinsep and her sisters spent time in India during their youth, and cultivated an unusual style of dress more in keeping with the hot and humid climate of the subcontinent than the drawing rooms of London.[49] Accounts and images of the Pattle sisters emphasize "gracefully flowing robes ... made of rare Indian stuffs," ornamented with delicate jewelry.[50] G. F. Watts's painting of Prinsep's sister, Sophia Dalrymple (1851–53; Watts Gallery), for example, features a gown of softly draped white silk or muslin, loosely belted at the waist, with little ornamentation.[51] This illustration of the sisters' unconventional style anticipates the "crinkled white garb with a gold string around her waist or absence of a waist" Morris was recorded wearing in 1881.[52]

In assisting Morris in her transition to middle-class artistic wife, Prinsep may have encouraged or inspired an alternative approach to fashion, and one already somewhat popular with the artistic set. Certainly, the unconventional style would have been appealing to someone uncertain about the set of new, and rigid, social behaviors and expectations she was tasked with mastering, and who, as Rossetti's portrait in the blue silk dress articulates, likely cultivated an artistic persona. Such an adoption further makes sense within the context of Red House itself—not only because Morris participated in the artistic development of the home, and a loose style of clothing would have allowed her to do this more freely, but also because it conforms to the scheme of activity within the house more broadly. As Mackail indicates, at Red House, William Morris's mission was to remake the world, an endeavor that seems to have extended to the bodies of the home's key participants.[53]

Jane Morris's embrace of artistic dress, in addition to her contributions to Red House and the initial products of the Morris firm, suggests that she utilized her needle to engage with and eventually master her new surroundings. Her continued use and development of what might be viewed as an artistic performance, especially in tandem with Rossetti's visual representations of her, legitimized Morris's place within the artistic circle, and made plain her commitment to a set of artistic practices with the potential to permeate all the material facets of a home.

Finishing: Ties that Bind

There is no question that Morris was highly skilled and took deep pride in her abilities with a needle; however, as the interactions outlined above indicate, there are few projects—aside from the clothing made for personal use and enjoyment— in which Morris was the sole author. Rather, needlework intersected with the growth of personal and professional relationships, involving the exchange of knowledge, materials, designs, and techniques, as well as shared labor and invention. In particular, it was a critical aspect of family life. In her husband's memorials, Georgiana Burne-Jones suggests that stitching was part of the daily experience at Red House in the early years of the Morris marriage: "Oh, how happy we were, Janey and I, busy in the morning with needlework or wood-engraving."[54] Certainly it formed part of the strength of the partnership between husband and wife, and as Jane taught her daughters, she perpetuated the techniques developed by her, her sister, and William Morris in the early days of the Firm.[55] Jane further participated in the execution of designs crafted by May's hand, extending Morris work to another generation.

However, Morris also utilized needlework to cement and tend to personal relationships outside the family sphere. Her surviving correspondence mentions a handful of handcrafted gifts, sometimes bestowed in times of emotional strain. In the fall of 1887, for instance, Morris wrote to Theodore Watts-Dunton: "I am sending you a bit of embroidery I finished for you long ago, it is not by any means one of my best things but you chose it from several and I have nothing better at hand. I send it just as it is but if you would like it made into a cushion I will do it for you."[56] While the physical appearance of the embroidery, outside the rough indication of size, remains unclear, Morris's letter demonstrates that she did not rank it among her finest work, and although she seems to face some anxiety over parting with such a piece, her care for her friend outweighs these concerns. At the time, Watts-Dunton, an aging bachelor, was contending with a bout of neuralgia, and was still caring for A. C. Swinburne, whom he rescued from alcoholism in 1879.[57] No stranger to illness herself—Morris both suffered from an undiagnosed medical condition and faced the challenges of caring for an epileptic child—she may have empathized with Watts-Dunton, sending the embroidery as a reminder of her friendship at a trying time.[58] As a handcrafted object, the embroidery signifies care and attention, and represents an attempt to bring warmth and color to Watts-Dunton's life at a time when few outside pleasures could be enjoyed.

Philip Webb similarly benefitted from Morris's attentiveness and skill in the needle arts. In a thank-you note written to Morris in 1869, Webb teases, "I take it as very kind of you, that the nice comforter you have sent me, is not knitted in the form of a rope. This piece of soft work done by your hands shall be to me as a promise that you are not going to withdraw from me, what had hitherto been unfailing kindness on your part."[59] The letter jokingly hints at a lapse, possibly in communication or wellbeing, on Webb's part, but also emphasizes his appreciation of the knitted scarf, and recognition of the significance of its handcrafted nature.

That Webb celebrated Morris's engagement with the needle, and saw this as a shared interest, is further evident in a letter from 1871. Here, Morris writes to Webb, thanking him for an embroidery design: "I shall never dare ask you for any design again, I had not expected anything half so elaborate or beautiful, thank you very much for it, I shall work it carefully in fine wool on blue serge I think, taking care to get different shades of blue for the flowers."[60] This exchange again demonstrates the latitude offered by embroidery design—Morris interprets the pattern, and determines the materials most suitable for a particular effect—and captures the esteem within which Webb held Morris's abilities; although the design is lost, Jane's assessment of it suggests something stunning and complex, a tribute to her skill and sense of taste. However, it further indicates the place of collaborative labor in Morris and Webb's friendship, that a shared interest in design and creativity were cherished elements of their connection.

Conclusion

Following William Morris's death in 1896, Jane Morris continued to collaborate with her daughter on embroidery projects, investing more thoroughly in the personal dimension of artistic production rather than the professional commissions of the Firm. One of the most stunning works from this period is a hanging or coverlet now frequently displayed on her late husband's bed at Kelmscott Manor, designed by May and worked by Jane (Plate 2.2).[61] Executed primarily in stem stitch on natural linen, the coverlet features bouquets of flowers separated by winding knots, and is bordered by a sequence of insect and animal motifs, representing the flora and fauna that surrounded Kelmscott Manor. The coverlet is deeply personal; it is also a monumental work, impressively executed.

Like the embroideries completed alongside her husband early in her career, the bed coverlet demonstrates the shared enthusiasms of the Morris family. It is a celebration of natural materials, nature as subject, organic pattern and winding forms, and, like the products of Jane's needle in design as well as fashion, suggests a concern with how we might live. However, while the early embroideries utilized ancient techniques in order to telescope the talents and values of the past, here those techniques are refined to create a modern work that does not pretend to be medieval. It is the culmination of a life's experimentation with stiches, and, at the same time, an embrace of the interests and values that circulated within the Morris home throughout Jane's life. Indeed, the depiction of Kelmscott Manor, the only home Jane herself would ever own outright, in the lower margin of the coverlet, is a salient reminder of the domestic, and the forces that existed with the Morrises' walls: creativity and collaboration, and the space in which to stitch a self.

Becoming the Boss of Your Knitting: Elizabeth Zimmermann and the Emergence of Critical Knitting

M. Lilly Marsh

At mid-twentieth century, hand knitting in the United States was practiced as a minor and fading chore of the household economy. Pattern publication in national women's magazines was decreasing and the premier specialty publication, *Vogue Knitting Book,* had closed by the late 1960s. By 1990 the practice had rebounded with major new publications in periodicals and books, innovative and revived artisanship practices, and major international conferences and gatherings. A driving figure in this resurgence was the knitter, writer, teacher, designer, and publisher Elizabeth Zimmermann. From the publication of her initial article in 1955 to her retirement in 1989, Zimmermann emphasized knitters as independent craftspeople responsible for their own material and design choices, in opposition to the popular knitting industry's identification of knitters as uncritical pattern-followers. Her philosophy of critical practice was communicated to knitters through her independently-published semi-annual newsletter (1958 to the present), two cable television series (broadcast across the US and Canada), four books, as well as numerous articles and North American teaching engagements. This approach intersected with increasing feminine autonomy and an increasing interest in the fiber arts in the post-World War II period, and helped to shape a new identity of "the knitter" as an original and self-determining craftsperson.

Zimmermann's view of knitting as a fine studio craft also diverged from that of the contemporary fine craft world, which increasingly emphasized professionalization. Nonetheless, she pursued the recognition of her professional peers and was accepted into the Wisconsin Designer Craftsman organization in 1958. Her practice, publications, and philosophy were founded upon a productively porous boundary between functional domesticity and professional craft practice, rather than the segregation of the two typically found in contemporary craft theory. In prioritizing innovative technique, functionality, and high-quality materials, and segueing easily between domesticity and professionalism, Zimmermann effectively generated an alternative identity to both the Wisconsin Designer Craftsman's non-domestic, professional ideals, and the yarn manufacturers' passively domestic consumers.

Building on recent work in craft and cultural history, this chapter traces a feminist cultural history of domesticity and professionalism in the evolution of craft process as identity formation by analyzing the dialogic relationship between Elizabeth Zimmermann and North American knitters.[1] In resistance to both the contemporary knitting industry and the professional craft organizations, Zimmermann insisted on a self-representative and domestic practice of critical knitting. In modeling this identity, and by giving her knitters the appropriate tools, I argue that Zimmermann was able to facilitate an alternative and durable identity for the North American knitter that valued intellectual engagement, domestic production, and originality at any skill level. Zimmermann's conceptualization of the knitter was one who was self-expressive in design, critically knowledgeable in technique and materials, independent of pattern following, yet engaged thoroughly with other knitters in seeking new techniques and inspiration. While this newly flexible identity was experienced by many as deeply liberating, it was not without negative effects. It exacerbated the problematic area of intellectual ownership in craft. Without the boundaries offered by clear accreditation (cultural or professional), the intellectual ownership of knitting designs and techniques became subject to great confusion even among the most knowledgeable public practitioners of the craft.

State of Mid-century Play in Professional Knitting and Knitting Craftsmanship

American knitting at mid-century was dominated by the commercial authorities of the yarn manufacturers and the periodical publishers, who shaped their market through their specialty pattern book publications and in national women's magazines. Knitting patterns were ubiquitous in women's magazines but an analysis of three specific publications, Conde Nast's *Vogue Knitting Book*, *Women's Day*, and the mid-west regional magazine *The Workbasket*, offers a broad demographic view of the knitting public.[2] *Vogue Knitting Book* was exclusively an upper-, or aspirational, class publication which featured exotic locations and high-fashion sensibilities towards hand knitting. *Women's Day* magazine and its various specialty publications were reliably middle or lower-middle class, and had a firm grasp on domestic economics and functional fashionability. *The Workbasket* was distinctly working class, with a strong interest in the production of income by the housewife. While each of these publications kept pace with the larger cultural and economic shifts of the period, they exhibit a surprising uniformity regarding knitting, despite their disparate audiences and purposes, with a strong, culturally conservative class and gender orientation around knitting representations.[3] Their collective emphasis on the finished object—whether for fashion, function, or profit—coupled with a highly detailed and specific project-based form of instruction, generated a strict focus on the product, rather than the process, of knitting. Each magazine presented projects with minutely detailed directions with little or no overall guidance in general knitting practice. Instruction was strictly limited to the most basic, with no alternative or advanced techniques offered. Strong partnerships between manufacturers and editorial staff emphasized brand name yarns as the source for successful projects rather than good design or knowledge of knitting technique on the part of the knitter. Designs were uncredited. The techniques and principles of knit garment construction were ignored in favor of standard dress-making principles in generating flat, shaped elements to be sewn into whole standard-sized garments. Furthermore, the lack of wider information regarding knitting techniques left the individual knitter dependent upon the minutely detailed project instructions with limited options for modification to size or fit, or application to subsequent projects. The knitter could either follow the pattern as written or not knit at all. This was acceptable if the knitter inhabited the ideal commercially-sized and shaped body, but was much less useful in fitting the actual knitter's body or those of their friends and families. Reproducing a commercial product to commercial standards, the knitter was rendered invisible, as both maker and inhabitant, in favor of standardization.

American knitters fared no better in the realm of book publication, as few new books were introduced, and older texts were often simply reprinted without updates. A typical introductory knitting book of the period, *Betty Cornell's Teen-Age Knitting Book*, was far more interested in inculcating gender-appropriate behavior in young middle-class women than in teaching actual knitting.[4] These appropriately feminine behaviors tallied nicely with ideas about knitting that were based on absolute obedience to pattern following and creating the final object of the practice, that is, the production of an object, and a woman, designed to attract young men.

If Betty Cornell was descriptive of the industry's conceptualization of the American knitter as an ideal pattern-following woman, Ida Riley Duncan's work was illustrative of how industry viewed its relationship with American knitters across very firm boundaries. Author of two texts, Duncan addressed an audience of shopkeeper-experts aiming to attract the knitting consumer. Her *Knit to Fit* (1963, 1966, and 1970) was a formal curriculum for credentialing industry professionals in both teaching and design, complete with homework and an appendix of correct responses. Her students were advised to be discreet with professional knowledge around "laymen,"[5] and careful of their "prestige."[6] Duncan, carefully credentialed on the title page as "former Assistant Professor of Home Economics at Wayne State University," was an authoritative gatekeeper of valuable specialist information. Her goal was the preparation of industry professionals, not the general advancement of the domestic knitting consumer, and her text clarified and hardened that boundary.

Elizabeth Zimmermann intersected with this state of American knitting in 1949, when her family moved west from the New York City area to Shorewood, Wisconsin. An unpublished 1971 Zimmermann manuscript offers a reflection on her background in English and German knitting experiences as well as her early days among American knitters. In her childhood in England, knitting was universally practiced amidst family and friends and the knitter looked to this local intimate community for advice and directions. In her youth, Zimmermann, fully confident in her skills, considered herself "absolutely the boss" of her knitting, resolving any problems herself, or in consultation with her equals.[7] According to Zimmermann, in Germany, authority resided in the shopkeeper and her assistance was exclusive to her customers and highly authoritative. German shopkeepers, as per Duncan's model, provided minutely detailed, custom-fitting instructions with complete authority over the individual knitter. In Germany, Zimmermann related having "received the most expert instructions," and noted, "They would actually take a large sheet of brown paper, draw the sweater-pieces on it with masterly sweeps of the hand, and make every single decrease or increase. It was inspiring and my independence of knitting instructions melted like snow in spring."[8] The German knitter followed excellent directions, but above all, she followed directions.

Upon moving to the United States, Zimmermann began to understand that her work had "suffered" under the German system; she had "lost the knitting independence" of her English youth, and come to "believe slavishly in any shop-dispensed or even printed directions."[9] Despite her realization that her knitting had improved technically under the German influence, she was distressed by what she considered a degeneration of her earlier design confidence in self-direction and personal agency in knitting into mere pattern following. But driven by her English soul to clothe her children in wool, Zimmermann persisted. While living amidst the immigrant and artist neighborhoods of the New York area, she wrote that "it occurred to me that one might experiment by using one's own brains, instead of picking those of others. The result was that our children gradually started to possess better-fitting sweaters (and stockings, and cute knitted shorts) . . . The designs were usually original with me."[10] Zimmermann's time on the East Coast was a rich period of integration between her technical skills and her creative ideas in rebuilding her own independence in critical knitting.

Zimmermann felt she first encountered American knitters only after her family moved to Wisconsin in 1949. On the East Coast, she had known other knitters but only those still working firmly out of their own immigrant traditions, not knitters raised up in the American culture of knitting. In Wisconsin, Zimmermann frequented the Shorewood Yarn Shop of Sophie Stefanski, sharing tips and ideas with local knitters. She wrote of her time there, "helping them with some of their puzzles and troubles . . . certainly taught me what a sad knitting life many knitters led, dependent on knitting instructions. These consisted chiefly of magazine articles which took for granted that their readers were familiar with technically-expressed and abbreviated 'directions' and were capable knitters to start with."[11] Zimmermann's first meeting with the American culture of pattern-dependent knitter left her alarmed.

Zimmermann's first public address to the American knitter set out to remedy this situation. In a relatively lengthy *Woman's Day* article on "Norwegian Sweaters the Easy Way," Zimmermann focused not on the production of a specific sweater, but instead on an underlying template of sweater structure and the options possible for sweater construction.[12] She presented a drop-shoulder design in wool with color patterning, and with discussions of practice and design options. She highlighted various unusual techniques such as circular knitting, steeking,[13] and the use of both hands for throwing the yarn in color knitting, and offered inspirational sources for color choices. While *Woman's Day* did provide standard directions for the specific sweaters offered in the article, Zimmermann's notes and copy encouraged the individual knitter to customize their work, to "make up" their own in color and fit.[14] She encouraged knitters to be critical and self-directive, offering them the techniques through which to take charge of their practice. Zimmermann's imagined knitter was a radically different knitter from the pattern-following knitter envisioned by industry.

The knitting industry was not the only avenue Zimmermann pursued for professional advancement. Wisconsin has had a long history of professional fine craftsmanship and the Wisconsin Designer Craftsman organization offered regular gallery-style exhibition opportunities to its members. Yet the identification of knitting itself as fine craft was problematic among professional craftspeople. Although Zimmermann's publications and design sales were growing, the Wisconsin Designer Craftsman organization rejected her application for membership for several years. Zimmermann's work was considered exhibition worthy in the domestic handwork category at the Wisconsin State Fair, an agricultural fair, where there was a far more porous boundary between professionalism and domesticity. Her sweaters were less acceptable to the Wisconsin Designer Craftsman in a period in which the organization was itself coming to grips with the evolving identity of professional craftsmanship.[15] Sandra Alfoldy's historical analysis of Canadian craft in *Crafting Identity* traces a developing professional craftsman identity based in exclusive professional knowledge and practices, and on the sharp differentiation between the creative-professional and the creative-domestic, and the archives of the Wisconsin Designer Craftsman show similar concerns.[16]

The Wisconsin Designer Craftsman initially resisted Zimmermann's application for membership and her eventual acceptance for membership and exhibition in 1958 went unremarked in the archives. Her debut in the 1958 Annual Exhibit occasioned a *Milwaukee Sentinel* review which exclaimed: "A blow for knitting as an aesthetic art was struck by Elizabeth Zimmermann who has an extremely handsome bulky, high-necked sweater in a Scandinavianish [sic] pattern of black on grey in the show. It's priced at $150 but anyone buying it could pass it on decades hence as an heirloom."[17] At least one reporter felt knitting belonged in the exhibit—despite the exhibition catalog listing Zimmermann's work under the category of weaving. In the ensuing decades, Zimmermann regularly exhibited, received awards, and kept pace with the highest levels of membership. Regardless of this success, and despite an exhibition and award record that spanned 1958 through 1971, her professional work seemed to never rest easily within the confines of the organization. No other knitter is identifiable in the record. Her interest in combining functionality with self-expression ran counter to the professional craft authority's growing prioritization of abstract conceptualism. Her celebration of domesticity as a productive site, displayed in numerous published stories of sweater designs developed while on canoe camping trips, or designing new buttonholes while Arnold, her husband, enjoyed the local ski-jumping events, were exactly the cozy domestic tone from which the professional craft organizations were attempting to distance themselves. She was deeply frustrated by the devaluation of technical excellence in producing domestic objects, and functional knitting as a professional studio craft would remain problematic for several decades.

"Dear Knitter": Dialogic Transformation in Personal and Institutional Identifications

Elizabeth Zimmermann sold designs steadily after 1955 to a wide variety of industry publications but she had limited ability to share her techniques and ideas on design, as she was confined by the industry standard of minutely detailed instructions and anonymous designer credit. Her frustration with the standard industry identity came to a head in 1958 over yarn manufacturer Bernat's heavily rewritten directions for her seamless yoke sweater. Having purchased her design, Bernat used the image of her sweater, but matched it with directions that would not produce the article. Her outrage at their disregard for both her intellectual work and their audience drove her to address knitters directly with her ideas. She began publication of a twice annual *Newsletter*,[18] outside the sphere of professional craft, as represented by the WDC, and the knitting industry. Formatted as a letter, directly addressed "Dear Knitter," and signed "Sincerely" or "Happy Knitting, Elizabeth," these newsletters began a dialogic exchange between knitters (Figure 3.1). They became an imagined space in which knitters could begin to represent themselves.

Zimmermann imagined her knitting audience as intelligent, curious, and willing to engage in self-expressive cultural work, though lacking the technical and material resources and the self-confidence for their practice. Her exhortations to use the best materials, to think independently, and to innovate were constant. Zimmermann offered options and resources, variations and templates, and requested reader feedback and ideas. Such signature designs as her circular knit, seamless yoke sweater, her color or texture patterned drop-shoulder ski sweaters, her Baby Surprise Jacket, or the Tomten jacket were provided as structural templates

Figure 3.1 The salutation "Dear Knitter," and her manuscript signature closings "Good Knitting" and "Sincerely-Elizabeth," emphasized the personal and direct address of Zimmermann's *Newsletters*. Image of Zimmermann's closing signature to *Newsletter* 11, Fall 1963. Published in *The Opinionated Knitter*, 61. Used by permission of Schoolhouse Press.

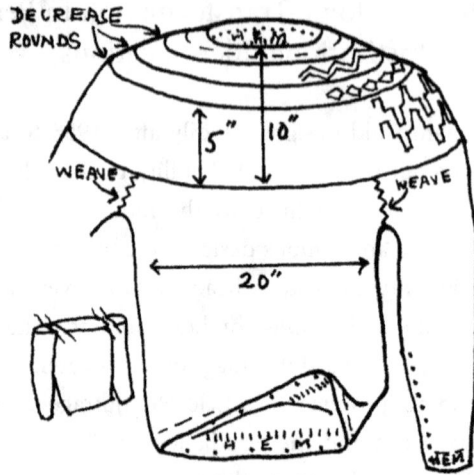

Figure 3.2 Zimmermann's Percentage System provided a method whereby the individual knitter could make custom fitting adjustments reflecting personal design choices. Sketch of the Percentage System for Icelandic Yoke Sweater, *Newsletter* 14, Spring 1965. Published in *The Opinionated Knitter*, 76. Used by permission of Schoolhouse Press.

upon which the individual knitter could improvise across significant design choices and create a unique garment. She offered an algorithmic template for customized fitting, known as Elizabeth's Percentage System (Figure 3.2). This system, and her explanations of knitting gauge, allowed the knitter to customize all aspects of fit in a sweater from length of sleeves and back to the shaping of neck and shoulders. Furthermore, she expounded on the various qualities and uses of wool yarns and made high-quality domestic and imported wools available to her correspondents. She believed in knitting as a craft worthy of serious study and maintained a curated, international, multi-lingual knitting book sales list. She worked back stage to bring important titles to the attention of Dover, the reprint publisher, and offered a free mail-order lending library for rare out-of-print books that continued for decades. And she mentioned other knitters by name and credited their input.

The *Newsletters* made the knitter visible, both to themselves in their own individual projects, and as part of the community of knitters. Whereas the knitting industry effectively disappeared the knitter, and the Wisconsin Designer Craftsman simply could not remember what knitting was, Zimmermann's readers quickly became visible to themselves in their customized work. Zimmermann's designs demanded the self-expressive participation of the critical knitter in choice of yarn, color, texture, fit, neckline and sleeve treatment, hemming, and closure choices. Zimmermann's knitter no longer produced a uniform commercial product but a uniquely personal one. In the dialogic process of the newsletters, they became aware of each other as part of a virtual social gathering of knitters, named and praised for queries and innovations, and mentioned as small businesses and charitable projects.

Initially a single page in 1958, by 1969, Zimmermann had expanded her publication, enlarged her community bulletin board section, and renamed it *Wool Gathering* (still in publication). Zimmermann continued her practice of sharing knitting as original craftsmanship throughout her thirty-four-year career as it expanded to include three national television series and four books, as well as multiple design publications and articles. Her mail-order yarn business expanded into publishing to become Schoolhouse Press, joining the overall explosion in knitting publishing of the early 1980s, with many of the new authors heavily influenced by Zimmermann. All of these publications spoke directly to the knitter in terms of his or her own independence of practice and design, exhorting knitters to resist the "blind follower" identity of the industry publications, and to generate their own innovations as self-expressive craftspeople, and to do so in whatever situation they found themselves.[19] Zimmermann's knitter was knowledgeable, innovative, independent, self-reliant, and often situated productively in the midst of his or her family and other knitters.

By the mid-1970s, Zimmermann had a great deal of company in her quest for craftsmanship, as the popular artisan fiber movement gathered national steam, and individual craftspeople began to generate craft communities and gatherings. Zimmermann herself was to turn an initial one-week adult education class of fourteen knitters at University of Wisconsin Shell Lake in 1974 into the nationally recognized and continuing institution of Knitter's Camp, a six-week series of camps for knitters of all levels in Marshfield, Wisconsin. The Oregon Black Sheep Gathering and the Maryland Sheep and Wool Festival on the opposite coast, despite small beginnings in the same year, eventually grew into significant and durable cultural institutions for the support of fiber craftsmanship. North American knitters were profoundly ready to take up the conceptualization of artisanship in popular fiber work.

North American knitters' response to Zimmermann's work was extensive both privately and publicly. The archival collection of Zimmermann's materials at Schoolhouse Press contains seventeen large scrapbooks of Zimmermann's fan mail expressing admiration and gratitude for the fundamental changes Zimmermann brought to both practice and identity. Letter after letter tells of beginners becoming proficient, experts learning new tricks, and of an explosion of creative work in knitting design. But more than simple excitement around knitting, the letters display critical knitting as an avenue of profound personal identity transformation, enabling their ability to think for themselves in inhabiting their work, and to gather with other knitters in pursuing their interests. Thousands of letters spoke of newfound independence and personal self-expression. One writer praised Zimmermann for having "a raised knitting consciousness" and further declared "My motto is recipes are for cowards."[20] Another noted that Zimmermann's "books are like an assertiveness training class in knitting. I get less timid with each article I knit."[21] Zimmermann's pleasure in this last remark was evident, as she hand copied the comment onto the inside front cover of her large scrapbook "Fanmail #6, April 1984."

Beyond individual transformation, communal transformation was underway as significant creative and social boundaries were eroded. Linda Ligon, founder of Interweave Press, recalled the effect of Zimmermann's teaching at a 1985 SOAR (Spin Off Autumn Retreat) gathering as astonishingly liberating:

> It's about knitting, but more than that, it's about thinking about knitting. It's about setting aside the rules, challenging the traditional assumptions … it's about sending those old line-by-line patterns up in flames! It's about being free! This is like nothing so much as an old-fashioned tent revival … She taught us to think like artists, like engineers, like sculptors, like plumbers; she taught us to "unvent," she taught us that knitting could be a slapstick adventure.[22]

Knitters became surer of their abilities to make innovative choices, and bring disparate ideas to bear in their practice of creative knitting.

The erosion of creative boundaries led to the erosion of longstanding social boundaries as well. Zimmermann received letters from across the social spectrum, but one Pennsylvania farmer wrote of her appreciation for Zimmermann's television program and related a story of a meeting across class boundaries in a local yarn shop:

> I thought city women didn't care for that kind of show but much to my surprise I discovered that's just not so. As I was buying some yarn … a very well dressed lady standing near me said how lovely the new colors were. And as things go we talked & she said she was watching you on TV & just loved it. Before you could shoo the cat out of the cream jar three more lady's [sic] stopped to talk. I never saw any of these women before but there we stood talking like old friends, about your knitting class.[23]

These descriptions of excitement, surprise, and an ensuing passion that created new commonalities are typical of the personal and communal disruption and transformation that resulted from Zimmermann's reconceptualization of knitting.

By the early 1980s, Zimmermann had achieved public institutional recognition in the pages of new national periodicals. In 1982, Butterick Publishing revived *Vogue Knitting*, and, in 1984, Golden Fleece Publications (later XRX Publishing) introduced a brand new periodical, *Knitter's*. The initial issues of *Vogue* hearkened back to the earlier *Vogue Knitting Book*, with a heavy emphasis on couture designs for an elite, or aspirational, audience. It featured designer knitting kits which reproduced couture design exactly, with no need to make choices in materials, technique, or color. It prioritized glossy high-fashion photo shoots, and highly abbreviated, detailed project directions were relegated to small print in a back section. Like its predecessors, *Vogue's* imagined knitter was an invisible and obedient pattern follower.

By contrast, the premier issue of *Knitter's* (late 1984) offered a very different product to a newly identified knitter and knitting community. It featured lengthy articles across a wide variety of process topics. Directions for individual projects were embedded as narrative into the feature articles, in standard-sized font, and with multiple design options discussed and debated. Designers and contributors were credited and visible in images and text. The list of advertisers ranged across North America and included a startling variety of small yarn shops featuring products for knitting, dyeing, spinning, and for studio organization and management. *Knitter's* was designed to appeal beyond the simple production of a fashion object into every aspect of craft knitting. Zimmermann was prominently placed with an interview, a column, and several of her designs featured. Furthermore, many of the contributors had connections to Zimmermann, and the editorials by Elaine Rowley and Alexis Xenakis specifically credited her as a driving principle in the genesis and organization of the publication.

An extraordinary April 1985 *Village Voice* review makes *Knitter's* distinction clear:

> Just when I was convinced that all glossy magazines ... have reached a state of unprecedented idiocy and crass hype, along comes the premier issue of *Knitter's*, which manages to be simultaneously intellectual (yes, I dare to use that term for a craft publication) and good-looking. ... *Knitter's* tone conveys love of the craft and concern for its practitioner. ... When they suggest a brand of yarn ... it's clearly just a suggestion and they give reasons ... editorial staff is composed of dedicated experts who know whereof they speak. ... If you are an experienced knitter, you'll adore this magazine. If you're a novice, it will set you on a sensible course.[24]

The publication of *Knitter's* marked a critical mass threshold of the new knitting identity as individuals gathered into new self-representing communities.

In contrast to *Knitter's* success, the general response to *Vogue's* initial issues was poor. Butterick's attempts to restructure the publication took place over several issues, and they invited Zimmermann to participate early on. She consulted with friends in the Madison Knitter's Guild who informed her that her participation at *Vogue* would "result in a negative image" for her.[25] However, *Vogue Knitting* had been the elite publication of her younger days, and she was flattered. Reasoning that she could be a better influence at *Vogue*, Zimmermann contributed an article on grafting and Kitchener stitch in an early 1984 issue. Recruiting Zimmermann as a regular guest columnist thereafter, *Vogue* expanded their feature articles concerning both technique and innovative process, and with bylines. Although *Vogue Knitting* remained an elite publication with strong connections to the New York fashion industry, and with an emphasis on beautiful photography of the finished object, its recognition of the new expectations of the independent knitting craftsperson was significant and enduring.

Intellectual Property: New Forms of Capital Among Knitters

The emerging communities of artisan knitters were enthusiastic in embracing new methods and presentations of information but this also generated serious tensions. As new structures of knitterly autonomy emerged, and individual knitters moved from an anonymous private tradition towards a traceable public history in design and publishing, knitters also created new forms of social and economic capital. The credit for these innovations and the ownership of that capital often came under dispute across an unevenly changing landscape and within a community with little common understanding of the forms of intellectual ownership.

In the earlier mid-century model, designers sold designs and remained largely anonymous to the knitting public. The majority of knitters knit, without financial recompense, for family or charity. Instruction was casually acquired by happenstance through friends and family, through inexpensive publications, or through a helpful yarn shopkeeper. Professional knitting tended to be poorly remunerated and informally arranged. Zimmermann's early work is a case in point. Her 1957 Aran Sweater for *Vogue Knitting* was commissioned and accomplished without any discussion regarding her remuneration, and though she was finally named at publication as the source for a suitable wool yarn, her knitting was unacknowledged.

Most design sales to publishers at this time tended to be "work for hire," which assigned all rights to the publication, and no copyright to the designer, though this was changing by the late 1980s.[26] Zimmermann's 1957 Seamless Yoke Sweater design exemplifies this issue. Sold to Bernat and heavily rewritten by the editors, Zimmermann had no recourse beyond redesigning and publishing the work herself. The knitting industry frankly devalued knitting as creative work in its focused drive for yarn sales. Editors and yarn manufacturers were largely harvesting, at little or no cost, the labor of an entire creative class, disregarded due to its domestic and female cultural space.

This state began to change as knitters began to exercise their autonomy, and understand their work as valuable creative capital. As textile writers and designers of the 1960s, 1970s, and 1980s gained name recognition, they came to realize that this branding could be turned to economic advantage through teaching workshops, article and design sales, and contracts for further books. Such fiber celebrities became highly sought after by the new local and regional gatherings with their rapidly increasing appetites for workshop teachers and speakers. The rise of the internet in the late 1980s opened up vast new horizons for name recognition and unmediated direct communication between knitters. Professional recognition in smaller gatherings could lead to celebrity status and economic benefit on the national and international stage. Yet even while the new communities achieved cultural durability, a resolution to the problem of the assignment of intellectual ownership remained elusive.

The Square Neck Pretzel Sweater illustrates this dynamic, as documented through the columns and letters of the 1989 issues of *Knitter's*. The Pretzel Sweater was hugely popular in 1988–89, and the pattern was available through Leisure Arts Publications ($2.50), but with no mention of the designer. A Meg Swansen Spring 1989 column on intellectual ownership mentioned the design as troubling in that, despite its huge popularity, there was no known origin or design history. A subsequent letter from Leisure Arts claimed the 1988 publication but explicitly disavowed any knowledge of the designer.[27] Chris Hyland, a yarn sales representative, finally revealed the designer to be Cheri Brown, a yarn shop owner. He had previously offered it to her for her shop and was horrified and embarrassed when she responded by claiming to be the original designer. It had been lifted from her by other sales representatives. Hyland's letter opined that Brown did not "mind if people have the designs she originated, but she would like to have the credit."[28] At mid-century, this thievery might have cost the designer the design fee of perhaps $150; however, by the 1980s, the loss would have been significant, and potentially amounting to several thousands of dollars in lost opportunities for article and pattern publication, and teaching positions. Leisure Arts certainly charged $2.50 for each leaflet despite having paid no designer for the work. This careless attitude towards intellectual ownership, particularly on the part of the yarn industry merely points out the continued devaluation of the labor of knitting and design on the part of actual knitters and designers. Despite knitters themselves moving towards self-representation and autonomy, the industry seemed to prefer the older model of the invisible knitter doing invisible work.

This single incident is but one of multiple examples of confusion around intellectual ownership which appear in both Zimmermann's own archives at Schoolhouse Press and in the issues of *Knitter's* Magazine. The nuts and bolts of intellectual ownership in knitting was muddied by misunderstanding over the difference between copyright, trademark, and patent; the ethics or legality of using published patterns in producing items for sale; and, an elusive definition of originality in design. The knitting community was generating new forms of value, yet was profoundly confused as to how those forms were assigned.

A specific, and recurring, point of confusion was the difference between a technique and the published description of that technique. Zimmermann introduced the common English technique of the knitted cord to American knitters and was constantly credited as the inventor of the technique, despite her frequent denial. Designers frequently requested permission to use "her" technique despite the legal principle that a technique could not be copyrighted. Another point of confusion was over plagiarism and the theft of intellectual property. One letter writer in the archives complained bitterly about a $500 per student workshop (with ten participants) in which the instructor taught Zimmermann's finishing techniques, having the students copy the material longhand from Zimmermann's books themselves.[29] Perhaps the instructor believed that hand copying exempted her from plagiarism charges, and she felt no compunction over pocketing several thousand dollars in teaching fees while using Zimmermann's intellectual material. The relatively minor ethical offense of plagiarism was possibly avoided while outright economic theft was perpetrated. The instructor could have asked the students to buy the Zimmermann texts.

Complete designs for garments presented another area for confusion, as there was no agreement on the crucial points in the continuum between an original, a derivation, or the transformation into a "new" original. The mid-century industry's desire for a sweater with absolutely specific directions, encouraged Zimmermann and other designers to duplicate structures and techniques with minimal changes in color or pattern and republish these as "new designs." For example,

Zimmermann sold a design for the original seamless yoke and Norwegian drop-shoulder sweater to industry, and also self-published a variation of it in the *Newsletter*. However, Zimmermann was not pleased when, in the later 1970s and 80s, other designers exercised similar options. Her scrapbooks show several instances of frustration over what seem to be derivative Zimmermann sweaters under the name of other designers. In most of these instances, it is clear that individuals were merely attempting to make their way amidst a mass of confusion in a dramatically changing paradigm that had not, nor has yet, found any real communal consensus on a fair or stable resolution of the issue. A few moments examination of ostensibly original patterns on the knitting social media site Ravelry makes clear that confusion over intellectual ownership rages on.[30]

Despite confusion over intellectual property rights, there was little confusion over Zimmermann's status among knitters in the early eighties. She was covered as a celebrity knitter by such disparate publications as *CoEvolution Quarterly* and the London *Sunday Times Magazine*.[31] Retiring from public life in 1989, her farewell note to Knitting Campers early in that year expressed Zimmermann's deep pleasure at the "acceptance of my knitting theories throughout the country," and how "looking at these rewarding evolvements happily and gratefully, it becomes much easier for me to ask you all for your blessing as I say farewell to you. My most heartfelt wishes and thoughts are with you—always. Good Knitting."[32] Zimmermann's long personal dialogue with knitters had ended. Her death in 1999 generated a four-column obituary in the *New York Times* which noted her introduction of new techniques to American knitters and quoted Joyce Williams: "She made me a thinking knitter."[33] It also included a diagram of EPS (Elizabeth's Percentage System), her custom fitting method.

Conclusion

Zimmermann's imagined "dear knitter" of the early newsletters, strengthened by her many publications, and the eagerness of North American knitters to take charge of their handwork, had achieved cultural durability, beyond the mere force of an individual personality, in new gatherings and institutions by the end of her career. Events such as the Black Sheep Gathering (Oregon), the Maryland Sheep and Wool Festival, and the Taos Sheep and Wool Festival, as well as new and evolving publications, allowed the identity of the visible and critical knitter to achieve an enduring institutionalization that would encompass multiple expressions and practices, surviving and developing far beyond any individual conceptualization of the knitter as creative craftsperson. In 1971, Zimmermann described her fantasy for American knitters:

> It is my heart's desire, that I imagine will remain but that, to gather together all the wonderful knitters I know for at least several days of knitting talk. Barbara Abbey, Peggy Chester, Dorothy Reade, Claire Keusch, Barbara Walker—what an elevating and erudite babble it would be. We should have to include Paula Simmons, who raises, shears, scours, cards, and spins her own wool, as well as all the intelligent and enquiring knitters known personally to us all, in my case starting with Martha Chace, Dorothy Case, Patty Smith, and going on for columns and columns of the names of those of you who knit for pleasure of the fingers *and* brain, who keep an open knitting mind, and do not hesitate to put things and theories to the test. We could tape the whole session, and have it available to knitters across the country, with all its argle-bargle, disagreement on whether to slip the first stitch, and exclamations of "You're PERFECTLY right; that's what I've always said." . . . My word! What a heart's desire, indeed.[34]

Zimmermann's dream of a community of engaged, creative, and enormously productive knitters, representing themselves and in productive dialogue with each other, was a reality, and it transformed knitting. Though the pattern following knitter of mid-century did not disappear, the self-directed knitter, thinking critically of her materials, techniques, and designs and participating in the communal dialogue of knitters, had achieved a permanent place in knitting culture and significantly influenced the institutions of traditional and digital publications. The social media site Ravelry is an excellent example of the heteroglossic quality of contemporary knitting, in contrast to the single voice of mid-century. With over 8 million registered users, and over 800,000 active in a thirty-day period, Ravelry allows knitters to represent their work, and their wider concerns and interests to their community all over the world.[35] The over 40,000 registered groups pursue a tremendous variety of topics of interest to knitters, from "the Victorians" historic knitting group to the "Lazy, Stupid, and Godless" group, and from the many groups following individual designers, to those representing small local guild gatherings. Zimmermann's direct address to knitters, her invitation to them to speak for themselves, and her encouragement to them to become critical knitters inhabiting their own work, is on wide display at Ravelry. Zimmermann's own interest group, "Zimmermaniacs," has over 11,000 members and other contemporary knitters recognize her contribution as well.[36] The designer Stephen West specializes in campy, queer, gender-bending knit-along videos to publicize his work. His 2015 Mystery Knit-Along featured West dancing in a polka-dotted onesie, and singing his own words to the music of Katy Perry's "Firework": "Like Lizzie Zimmermann, you must look within. Grab a glass of gin. / You just gotta cast-on. Be strong. Join my Knit-along. / Grab your needles and balls. It's a free-for-all."[37] Contemporary knitting is a heteroglossic free-for-all, in part due to Elizabeth Zimmermann. Far removed from its single voiced history, it has emerged as a self-expressive, and sometimes chaotic, exploration of individual creativity and innovation.

"Knitting is the saving of life; Adrian has taken it up too": Needlework, Gender, and the Bloomsbury Group

Joseph McBrinn

Richmond and Asheham: Loose Threads

In a highly dramatic scene in Stephen Daldry's acclaimed film adaption of Michael Cunningham's Pulitzer Prize-winning novel, *The Hours*, Leonard Woolf anxiously searches for his missing wife, the writer Virginia Woolf, finding her at the train station in Richmond, the leafy suburb south-west of London to which they had moved in October 1914 following her nervous breakdown a year or so earlier. In the scene Virginia pleads to return to living in central London: "I choose not the suffocating anaesthetic of the suburbs but the violent jolt of the capitol." During the exchange Leonard stresses that they moved to Richmond to escape the frenetic pace of the city and its impact on her health, and it was where they had set up the Hogarth Press, "[n]ot just purely for itself, but so that you may have a ready source of absorption and a remedy." "Like needlework?" Virginia replies.[1] In proffering a fictionalized account of the life of Virginia Woolf (that plays with the truth more than Cunningham's actual novel), the film unwittingly seizes upon "needlework" to represent Woolf's struggle against the suffocating constraints of the Victorian "feminine ideal."[2]

There are many other episodes in the annals of Bloomsbury that offer similar insights into the group's feelings about needlework and its relation to the construction of gendered identity. It is worth pointing out that these are not always about female subjectivity. For example, not long after the opening scene in Christopher Hampton's film *Carrington*, adapted from Michael Holroyd's celebrated biography of the writer Lytton Strachey, Woolf's close friend and conspirator, and possibly Bloomsbury's campest character, we see Strachey arriving at Asheham House in East Sussex, being greeted by Vanessa Bell, Woolf's sister. In the course of the evening's conversation, which drifts largely to conscription and the war, Strachey knits a red scarf. "Do you think knitting for the troops will be classified as essential war work?" he asks somewhat rhetorically.[3] Like the Woolfs' imagined exchange in Richmond station, which seeks to illuminate Virginia's resistance to repressive notions of femininity through her repudiation of needlework, this scene is a conceit to dramatize Strachey's queerness by visualizing his effeminacy through his appetite for it. For a woman to reject, or express ambivalence toward, needlework and for a man, in equal violation of prevailing social convention, to embrace it, may serve to highlight Bloomsbury's critical role in the modernizing of gender identity, by exposing its regulatory and performative underpinnings, but it also reminds us that Bloomsbury cannot be read as a complete disruption with the past. Analysis of Bloomsbury needlework reveals a closer correspondence between Victorian culture and modern art than has generally been acknowledged in canonical histories of modernism. And further, the subversion of Victorian notions of needlework, to undo repressive ideologies of idealized femininity and make public the presence of male effeminacy, reveals both Bloomsbury's progressive politics but also something of its playfulness.

Although I am beginning with two fictional scenes, two loose threads, the aim of this chapter is to unpick something of the hidden presence of needlework in the history of the Bloomsbury group, its context in contemporary debates about psychology and occupational therapy, and account for its use in the challenge Bloomsbury mounted to the dominance of Victorian gender and sexual stereotypes.[4]

"I find embroidery so soothing to the head": Bloomsbury Women, Convalescence, and Craft

For a woman of Woolf's generation, needlework offered a double bind. It was a pervasive pastime presented as an innocuous source of pleasure, relaxation, and even escapism. Yet, it was also loaded with negative stereotypes from its association with the crass commercialism of popular hobbyism, the sanctimony of church needlework guilds, and the cult of curative and philanthropic societies, to its reaffirmation of an all-pervasive "feminine ideal" that defined women as domesticated, passive, and subservient. The women of the Bloomsbury group were unconventional, progressive, and pioneers of cultural and intellectual modernism yet their complex feelings about needlework give some insight into how they navigated contemporary mores concerning gender identity and sexuality. As one critic has quite rightly pointed out, "when Virginia Woolf and her contemporaries rejected the work of the previous generation, the tenacious connection between femininity and domestic textile work still held."[5] Woolf's memories of her mother and sister, women she romanticized and who appeared less resistant (on the surface at least) to prevailing notions of idealized femininity, are bound up with images of their needlework: "I see her [Woolf's mother] sitting on the hall step knitting while we play cricket"—"Vanessa sat silent and did something mysterious with her needle and thread."[6] Even though we know relatively little about Woolf's actual stitching skills and practices, her lack of success, and lack of confidence, as a needleworker were well-known and reflect a deeper struggle with the social dynamics authorizing the "feminine" as a cultural construct. Her life-long housemaid Lottie Hope recalled, "she was not able to sew, although sometimes she liked to try," while her friend, the artist Barbara Bagenal recollected, "I had always thought that a hobby would have been a great help to Virginia, it would have given her a much-needed rest from her work. But she had no hobbies—other than the brief one of type-setting. She could not play the piano, or knit, or sew."[7] Similarly, Angus Davidson, one of the young men who worked at the Woolfs' Hogarth Press, recalled that the enterprise "had been started in Richmond—so I understood—as a sort of treatment, a sedative for Virginia, who enjoyed setting up type and found it soothing," but that Vanessa "sewed beautifully, she was a good driver, she could cook if required, whereas I don't believe Virginia did any of these things."[8]

From her earliest surviving letters to her last diary entries, Woolf talks about needlework as a form of relaxation, emphasizing its therapeutic role in times of stress, often from the anxiety-inducing process of writing. Most of these references are to embroidery. Knitting only really appears at the time of her severe breakdown before the First World War, and at the onset of her last severe depression c. 1940. "Knitting is also a help," Woolf noted in her diary almost exactly a year to the day before she took her own life.[9] There is one surviving portrait of Woolf (painted whilst she was still Virginia Stephen), by Vanessa Bell, that shows her sewing (Plate 4.1). It is believed to have been painted at Asheham in March 1912, almost six months before her marriage that August.[10] In early 1912 Woolf had been ill with the beginnings of the serious depression that would engulf her a year later. She was treated by Sir George Savage, the distinguished Victorian psychiatrist, who had long argued that "fancy work" could play a role in restoring female patients back to full health.[11] As she was forbidden to write during her convalescence, Woolf was probably encouraged to take up activities, such as knitting or sewing, as part of her "rest cure."

Writing to Leonard, from Asheham, after almost a month of silence, Virginia declared: "Knitting is the saving of life; Adrian has taken it up too."[12] Her younger brother Adrian had come to stay with her in Sussex as they had grown closer since their brother Thoby's death in November 1906, and Vanessa's marriage to Clive Bell the following February. Although "we were the most incompatible of people," they shared a house in Bloomsbury's Fitzroy Square, and later in Brunswick Square, until Woolf herself married.[13] Like Woolf, Adrian secretly struggled against contemporary sexual codes; he also lived in the shadow of an older sibling— Thoby, a paragon of Victorian manliness. Although Adrian married in 1914, qualified as a doctor, and retrained and practiced as a psychoanalyst after the First World War, when he first lived with Woolf he had had a love-affair with their friend, the artist Duncan Grant, and although Woolf seems not to have openly discussed his homosexuality, she did write somewhat tellingly, not only to Leonard, but to other friends of her brother's tacit effeminacy: "Adrian is very happy, and takes great care of me, and does my hair at night, and fastens my dress."[14]

It is in the context of new debates about the psychological development of gender and sexuality in the period, in which Adrian met leading Freudian psychoanalysts, including Ernest Jones and James Glover (under whom Adrian underwent analysis), that helps explain something of Woolf's own conflicted feelings about prevailing modes of "womanliness" and its attendant attributes such as needlework.[15] Through his work for the British Psychological Society, Adrian met Joan Riviere, who was working in the 1920s on an examination of femininity as a sort of self-constructed "masquerade," masking complex sexual feelings.[16] If Woolf, by her own admission, used needlework as a means to help create an acceptable "feminine" self, then Adrian Stephen's interest in knitting marked out his own sexual non-conformity, as needlework and femininity were so intertwined. Men of course did knit, but they became more conspicuous during the "knitting fever" ushered in by the war in which British manufacturers such as Weldon's, Leach's, and Patons flooded the market, shamelessly targeting female consumers, with patterns for mittens, socks, and, of course, mufflers for the troops. Indeed, it is hard to tell, when Lytton Strachey wrote to Clive Bell in October 1914 claiming, "I spend most of my time knitting mufflers for our soldier and sailor lads; but I expect that by the time I've finished them the war will be over, and they'll have to go to Henry [Lamb] and Duncan [Grant]," if he was being serious or lampooning the current needlework craze.[17] Strachey, in an earlier letter to his close friend Maynard Keynes, deliberately played with the image of himself as a "man" knitting a muffler "in navy blue wool for the *neck* of one of our sailor lads," adding, "I don't know which but I have my visions."[18] The tone of this letter is more sexualized and knowingly suggestive of both men's homosexuality.

As such, needlework was not entirely peripheral to writers such as Strachey or Woolf. Literary critics as diverse as Hermione Lee, Perry Meisel, Gayatri Chakravorty Spivak, Jane Marcus, Sayaka Okumura, and Elizabeth Goodwin Perry have all drawn attention (if often only cursorily) to how Woolf, for instance, employs textiles as a "critical metaphor," both technically and thematically, in her novels.[19] Yet few of Woolf's biographers, or indeed the authors of the numerous critical studies of her work, have paid much attention to her interest in needlework. Between 1913 and 1915, as she struggled through her debilitating breakdown, Woolf finished and published her first novel, *The Voyage Out*. Even if, about this time, she would write, "I try to paint and embroider, but these arts are so vapid after writing," needlework features as a recurring motif in the novel.[20] Images of "threads, fibers, meshes, fabrics, and networks" proliferate in her subsequent novels—from, Helen Ambrose's embroidery as a central motif in *The Voyage Out*, to Mary Datchet's needlework in *Night and Day* (1919), Mrs. Flanders's sewing in *Jacob's Room* (1922), Clarissa Dalloway's darning in *Mrs Dalloway* (1925), and Mrs. Ramsay's knitting in *To the Lighthouse* (1927).[21] Aside from her turn to embroidery and knitting in moments of crisis and convalescence, Woolf's diaries and letters further reveal the broad range of needlecraft activities she undertook from "making a patchwork quilt" to her excited declaration that "[a]fter an infinity of time, spent, now writing, now reading, my true gift has at last proved to be rug making."[22]

Although often conscious of her "disabilities as a needlewoman," Woolf remained committed to needlework and solicited designs from her sister.[23] In a letter to Vanessa, dated September 1925, which ends "I am practically recovered," clearly in reference to a bout of depression, Woolf asked her sister to design a "woolwork" project: "Would you have the great kindness to accept a small commission from me—to wit £1.1.—and do me a design for a chair cushion? We have got some new dining room chairs, and I find embroidery so soothing to the head that I want to work a cushion while I am here."[24] Woolf seems to have still been working on the embroidery a year later, as Vita Sackville-West wrote to her husband, Harold Nicolson, whilst staying with Virginia that "[s]he is sitting opposite me, embroidering a rose, a black lace fan, a box of matches, and four playing cards on a mauve canvas background, from a design by her sister."[25] This embroidery is now untraced and Woolf wrote to Vanessa in August 1927 admitting that:

I have an awful confession to make–really something ghastly: Either Nelly has thrown away the [embroidery] design you lent me, or the puppy has eaten it. It disappeared completely yesterday, after I had been working at it the night before. What am I to do to express my apologies? I had traced it exactly onto the canvas. Could you re-paint it if I brought this? [Raymond] Mortimer admired it so much that I half suspect him.[26]

The only known embroidery by Virginia Woolf to have survived is after a "woolwork" design by her niece Angelica Garnett (née Bell). In December 1940, Woolf sent Angelica a cheque, "part present, part—indeed, the greater part— payment for the new Leda at whom I'm working."[27] The design was for the seat of an ornate nineteenth-century wooden armchair, believed to be of Italian origin, in the sitting room of the Woolfs' home, Monk's House in Rodmell, East Sussex (Plate 4.2). Classical imagery had long occupied the artists of the Bloomsbury group, but *Leda and the Swan* is a curious choice of subject. It is one of sexual violence, a fantasy of the male imagination recalling "age-old patterns of sexual subjugation," and it may have been part of a series of designs by Angelica, as Woolf invited her, in the late summer of 1940, to come and "examine your naked boys—the embroidery I mean. I've picked out the private parts in bright red. But it's a bit of a muddle."[28] As her depression grew darker in those last months of her life, the symbolism of stitching the sexual assault of a woman, the "ravishing" of Leda, can hardly have been invisible to Woolf. The embroidery seems to have been left unfinished at the time of her death in March 1941, and it has been suggested by at least one critic that it was completed by either Ethel Grant, Duncan Grant's mother, or Angelica.[29]

Woolf was not the only member of the Bloomsbury group to explore the link between needlework and "the feminine ideal," as well as needlework and therapy. Ethel Grant became the principal embroiderer to the group before the First World War and continued stitching for them during the interwar decades even as they increasingly turned to professional fabricators. It is not clear when Ethel Grant started sewing her son's designs, nor what inspired his "particular affection for embroidery and wool-working," but it was certainly before Roger Fry had founded the Omega Workshops, in which embroidered textiles were to play an important role. Ethel Grant may well have been the catalyst in this. Vanessa Bell, Winifred Gill, Jessie Etchells, Nina Hamnett, Barbara Baganel (who was told by Henry Tonks at the Slade she should "take up sewing"[30]), "Mrs. Miles," the wife of the workshops' caretaker, patrons such as Lady Ottoline Morrell, "Mrs. Grant," and apparently even Virginia Woolf—indeed, nearly all the women associated with the Omega—were drawn into stitching its products. Here "needlework remained women's work."[31] Indeed, Paul Nash wrote, some years later, of the "Omega group" as "an exceptional species of sewing 'bee.'"[32] Although the male artist at the Omega could try his hand at different art forms, from printmaking to pottery, sewing, with all its gendered associations, seemed beyond him. Any exceptions were momentary—for example, Vanessa Bell recorded giving Duncan Grant "some crochet to do in an attempt to keep him quiet," and recalled Roger Fry "having spent his time virtuously crocheting hats to sell at the Omega."[33]

For a twenty-year period after the death of her husband Bartle Grant in 1924, Ethel Grant kept a list of the needlework she did for her son and his friends, and clearly understood the work as a kind of collaboration. These embroideries were often large and complex, and it seems that in the 1920s, and certainly after her husband's death, she also went through a period of emotional and psychological turbulence for which needlework was probably recommended as a therapy. Ethel was apparently "not too keen" at first to take on the position of embroiderer to her son, and circle, but after encountering the work of Dr. Emile Coué, a French psychologist whose promotion of "autosuggestion" and "positive affirmation" became popular in early 1920s Britain, she may have been more receptive to the role.[34] Coué's idea of repetition, of taking a thought and "rapidly and ritualistically repeat[ing] it twenty times, counting with a string of twenty knots which they slipped through their fingers one at a time," is not that removed from descriptions of craft processes, especially all sorts of needlework.[35]

Debates about the feminizing nature of needlework came to the fore during the First World War as it was prescribed to wounded soldiers returning from the front as a form of rehabilitative therapy. Medical and psychiatric authorities agreed that it could help restore physical dexterity, but more especially, soothe damaged nerves and minds. It had particular relevance to newly diagnosed conditions such as neurasthenia, or shell-shock, for which it was widely employed as a "rest cure"—as it had been in the treatment of "hysteria" in women since the nineteenth century.[36] As the interwar years drew to a close, crafts such as needlework, weaving, cord knotting, and even bookbinding, were promoted by the newly formed Association of Occupational Therapy and used widely as a treatment for injured combatants of the Second World War.[37] Ottoline Morrell, Bloomsbury's colorful society hostess, like Virginia Woolf and Ethel Grant, is also recorded as suffering from periods of emotional and psychological disturbance for which she was treated by doctors and psychiatrists in London and in Germany.[38] In 1924, Morrell exhibited an embroidery, after a design by the painter Henry Lamb, at an exhibition to raise funds for charity and to promote the Disabled Soldiers' Embroidery Industry, which had been established in 1918 to provide training and employment for returning ex-servicemen.[39] Morrell was to show her embroideries in several exhibitions throughout the 1920s and 1930s that included work by the Disabled Soldiers' Embroidery Industry and directed the public's gaze to the existence of "needlemen."[40] The workshop had been founded by aristocrat, artist, and actor, Ernest Thesiger, who was a well-known expert on embroidery, and who produced designs for this workshop in a style remarkably similar to that of the Omega. The promotion of needlework by the male artists, aristocrats, and celebrities in Thesiger's circle drew attention, like that of the Bloomsbury group, to men as producers as well as patrons of embroidery.[41]

"[D]eliberately vulgar and as idly pretentious": Bloomsbury Masculinity, Effeminacy, and Embroidery

If, in times of extreme emotional suffering, Virginia Woolf would deploy needlework as a mask to literally perform her femininity, what compelled her male counterparts to take it up? The men, as much as the women, of Bloomsbury grew increasingly committed to needlework in a period that saw it transformed from a woolly vestige of Victorian drawing rooms to a fashionable vehicle for modern art. In the wider history of Bloomsbury, the complex signification of textiles in general, and needlework in particular, has been much overlooked. The sexual division of labor has also drawn little comment. Think of Duncan Grant passing on his embroidery designs to Vanessa Bell or Ethel Grant to be worked up, or Carrington "tormented by her 'beastly femininity'" seeking "solace from her 'moods' of depression in pickling, sewing and tending to Lytton's cold, rather than in her art."[42] Yet Bloomsbury's men were far from unresponsive to needlework's potential attractions and applications. Lytton Strachey, like Virginia Woolf, admired, and purchased, English eighteenth-century embroidery.[43] Duncan Grant thought nothing of his painting style being described "as honest as needlework."[44] Roger Fry decorated the cover of his slim volume of travel writing, published by the Woolfs' Hogarth Press, with a design imitating Victorian cross-stitch.[45] And during the First World War, Fry briefly assisted his sisters on relief work in the Marne and Meuse region of France, where, under the aegis of the Friends' War Victims Relief Expedition, they encouraged refugees "to take up embroidery as therapy," providing both materials and designs.[46] The needlework that Fry, Bell, and Grant designed and exhibited during the interwar years, which was generally made by professional embroiderers such as the artist Mary Hogarth or Mary Symonds (editor of the popular *Needlecrafts* magazine), hardly differed in aesthetics or artistry from the homely therapeutic stitching of Woolf, that of the Belgian refugees, or even that of the Disabled Soldiers' Embroidery Industry.[47]

The presence of needlework in Bloomsbury stretches back to the group's earliest moments. Indeed, as a prelude to the opening of the Omega, Roger Fry organized a show of work by his circle in March 1913, under the title the Grafton Group. Aside from "paintings" by Fry, Grant, and Bell, the show contained embroidered "firescreens, bed-screens, woolwork chaircovers and tablecovers, all in the most approved modernist design."[48] The critic of the *Pall Mall Gazette* was less enthused: "Worst of all, the Grafton Group have begun to devote their attention to applied art—to furniture. All that can be said of it is, that it is 'gay.' The upholstery of a chair exhibited at the Alpine Club is as gay and as subtle in colouring and design as an Early Victorian beadwork bag."[49] Later, at the exhibition held to officially launch the Omega that July, Fry spoke to a journalist about the significance of the workshops' "Post-impressionist Berlin wool-work": "it seems quite a mid-Victorian idea, but it is not treated in a mid-Victorian manner. The colours and designs are full of colour and rhythm as the others were full of dullness and stiffness. I like Berlin wool-work. It is so durable and strong, and it is a particularly good medium for us."[50]

Just before the opening of the workshop, Fry visited his friend the architect and designer Charles Ashbee, who had moved his Guild and School of Handicraft from London to the Cotswolds in 1902. Fry's project was completely antithetical to Ashbee's arts and crafts idealism. When he saw the Omega's products Ashbee was compelled to write: "TOO AWFUL, simply a *crime* against truth and beauty ... *Berlin wool-work* mats and bags, ghastly cushions and curtains."[51] Fry himself had been highly critical of any design "as bad in taste, as deliberately vulgar and as idly pretentious as anything the mid-Victorian epoch discovered in its antimacassars and Berlin woolwork,"[52] yet he continued to describe Omega's embroideries, and later Bloomsbury textiles, in terms of "Victoriana," the "perfect flower of bourgeoisie" bad taste.[53] Indeed, the correspondence between Bloomsbury's search for "pure form" in abstract painting at this very point and cross-stitch and woolwork, which were essentially forms of commercial "stitch-by-numbers kits," is puzzling. But to explain its "so-bad-it's-good" meaning, we need perhaps to look to the emerging culture of "camp," around the time of the First World War, in which high art and popular culture, the serious and the frivolous, even painting and embroidery, could become conflated. The role of Bloomsbury in the period's emerging homosexual subculture is also an important critical context here, given that the gendered nature of stitched textiles would have marked men like Fry and Grant as effete aesthetes.[54] Effeminacy, in its explicit critique of the dynamics of Victorian heteropatriarchy was clearly, and consciously, deployed by the men (and women) of Bloomsbury.

After the Omega closed, Duncan Grant and Vanessa Bell continued to collaborate on interior decoration schemes that included needlework.[55] They produced interiors in Bloomsbury for the Stephens and the Stracheys, for the "bachelor" flats of Raymond Mortimer, Angus Davidson, and Maynard Keynes, as well as the Tavistock Square flat of Leonard and Virginia Woolf. They held exhibitions of their work such as the "Music Room" they designed, installed at the Lefèvre Gallery in King Street, St. James's in December 1932, the "fanciful exuberance" of which included several major pieces of needlework.[56] Virginia Woolf bought a screen by Vanessa and a carpet by Duncan from this exhibition.[57] A set of chairs that survive at Monk's House, in red painted beech wood with cane seats and embroidered backs (of simple vases of flowers) by Vanessa are believed to also have come from the "Music Room" exhibition (Figure 4.1). Woolf wanted to buy a large black screen with flower motifs (now in Portsmouth Museum and Art Gallery) and had earlier bought a firescreen from Duncan. This depicts a "still life of jug with flowers and lute and book with seascape in background," and had

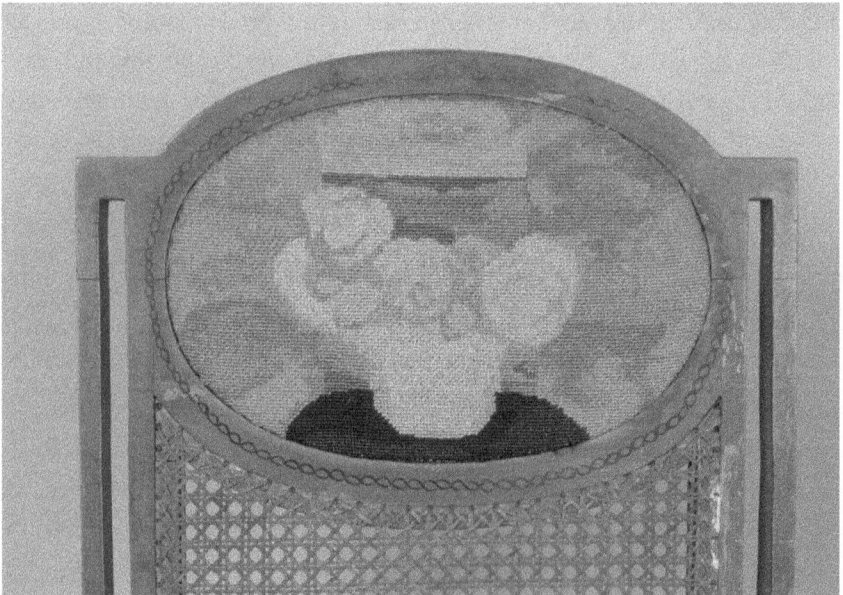

Figure 4.1 Vanessa Bell (designer) and Ethel Grant (embroiderer), *Chair cover*, 1932. Beech wood, paint, cane, needlework, 1070 × 515 × 530 mm. Monk's House, Rodmell, East Sussex, NT 768191.1. © Estate of Vanessa Bell. Image courtesy of Henrietta Garnett and The National Trust.

been stitched by his mother *c.* 1930 (Figure 4.2).[58] The designs of these seat covers and fire screen are in the Omega style and continue to evoke the aesthetics and techniques of Victorian cross-stitch and Berlin woolwork.

Throughout the interwar years Fry, as well as Bell and Grant, continued to design and exhibit embroidery as a group. When the Embroiderers' Guild reformed in 1920, they planned a large exhibition of contemporary work that was eventually

Figure 4.2 Duncan Grant (designer) and Ethel Grant (embroiderer), *Firescreen,* *c.* 1930. Canvas, gilt, wood, 1090 × 835 × 95 mm. Monk's House, Rodmell, East Sussex, NT 768212. © Estate of Duncan Grant. All Rights Reserved DACS, 2017. Image courtesy of The National Trust.

held three years later. It included work by Grant, Bell, and Fry, as well as a new artist associated with the group, Wyndham Tryon.[59] Enthusiasm about the work resulted, two years later, in a group show, entitled *Modern Designs in Needlework*, held at the Independent Gallery in London. Clive Bell, writing in *Vogue*, pointed out that the work was the "fruit of the seed sown in the Omega," yet the translation of modern art into wool, thread, and canvas applied to Victorian furniture remained perplexing; he referred to a "pre-Dieu" by Fry as "a piece of furniture in itself of surpassing repulsiveness."[60] As well as at the Embroiderers' Guild, Fry, Grant, and Tryon showed their embroideries at the Arts and Crafts Exhibition Society.[61] At the large exhibition of *Modern British Embroidery*, held at the Victoria and Albert Museum in the summer of 1932, Bell, Grant, and Tryon showed designs stitched by Ethel Grant and Mary Hogarth.[62] And at the *Exhibition of English Needlework (Past and Present)* in the spring of 1934, designs by Fry, Bell, Grant, Tryon, as well as Henry Lamb, were on display.[63] This was the largest display of Bloomsbury needlework since the 1925 exhibition.[64] The last major display of Bloomsbury needlework was the contributions of Grant and Tryon to the *Exhibition of 20th Century Needlework* held at the Leicester Galleries in January 1935.[65]

Clearly, Bloomsbury's men, in their pursuit of needlework, did not seek to forge a complete break with the past. Indeed, as Barbara Caine has suggested, their "rejection of Victorian heterosexual norms did not by any means entail a rejection of all forms of masculine privilege. On the contrary, female service from mothers, sisters, and women friends was deemed quite as much a masculine prerogative by both the homosexual and the heterosexual men of Bloomsbury as it had by their forebears."[66] Yet the "intense male friendships," the base of Bloomsbury, its tolerance, perhaps even valorization, of effeminacy, homosexuality, as the "Higher Sodomy," like its pursuit of needlework, can perhaps be read as evidence that such a "homosocial" group did contest, through the unexpected avenue of craft, repressive Victorian ideas of masculinity that were being revived and reinscribed following the devastation of the First World War. Bloomsbury needlework, therefore, may be read as a subversion of highly feminized Victorian cross-stitch and Berlin woolwork but also as a means to play with new cultural formations of effeminacy and camp.

Coda

This cursory analysis of Bloomsbury needlework, in the context of contemporary debates about gender identity, psychoanalysis and occupational therapy, as well as the wider revival of interest in embroidery, reveals that for Bloomsbury's women needlework offered a means to contest the "feminine ideal" whilst for its men it formed part of a critique of heteronormative masculinity, and for both sexes it was a means to construct a new sense of the queer self. Furthermore, Bloomsbury's eclectic admiration for aspects of Victorian culture, from Woolf donning her mother's crinoline dress for a photograph published in *Vogue,* to Strachey's literary *début* with a book undoing the "eminent Victorian," has long been seen as marginal to the group's role as agents of formalist modernism. Yet Simon Watney has argued that such incongruities were "one of the defining characteristics of Bloomsbury modernism [in] that it contained no sense of avant-gardist rupture with the past," and Alexandra Harris has similarly speculated that "[f]or the early Victorians, ornament had functioned as a release from austerity, and a century later it did the same for modernists tired of asceticism."[67] Christopher Reed has further suggested that "modern" for the artists and writers of Bloomsbury, as for a range of avant-garde as well as middlebrow groups in Edwardian and interwar Britain, made "new meanings from old forms," and it was the very pleasure and amusement (what Reed terms "the Amusing style") following on from the darkness of the First World War and its aftermath, that was a central motivation to Bloomsbury's revival of Victorian needlework's aesthetics and techniques—as Reed succinctly puts it: "[n]o phenomenon better exemplifies the Amusing ideal of blending Victorian and vanguard aesthetics than in the now-forgotten vogue for modernist embroidery."[68]

Part Two

Elaborating Identity: Expressing Ideology, Crafting Community

Whig's Defeat: Stitching Settler Culture, Politics, and Identity

Lisa Binkley

Introduction

The *Whig's Defeat* quilt (Plate 5.1), made *c*.1860 by Jessie Campbell (b. 1834) in Huntingdon County, Canada East (present day Quebec), is a red and green appliqué quilt of the type often made in commemoration of special occasions and, in this case, would have been made in anticipation of its maker's marriage as a symbol of her gentility and readiness to manage a household interior.[1] While quilts were often made for display on the matrimonial bed, the pattern of this quilt suggests an alternative meaning. In 1866, at the age of thirty, Campbell married Andrew McPherson, her aunt Marjorie Leslie's widower, facilitating the continued relationship between two Scottish Highland families united at the Battle of Culloden (1745). Through investigation of the coverlet's making and use, and eventual display, analysis of its materiality and the material culture reveals its maker's emerging identity from a young unwed daughter of Highland immigrants, searching to find a better life in the colonies, to the wife of a Scottish-Canadian landowner, required to serve on behalf of the British colonial government. From the selection of its pattern and textiles to its methods of stitching, and its eventual display on the maker's matrimonial bed, *Whig's Defeat* reveals the identity of its maker as she rose to meet pressures of the changing social, cultural, and political life around her.

Defining *Whig's Defeat*: Red and Green, and Organic Appliqué

As a decorative coverlet, *Whig's Defeat* is an excellent example of a style of handmade coverlet popular between 1840 and 1880 in Canada and the United

States, with its red and green aesthetic, abundant hand quilting, complex patterning, and, in this example, decorative fringe. It was customary for young women to learn practical needle skills as part of their education and, in some cases, prepare as many as a dozen utilitarian quilts for everyday use and one decorative quilt for display on the matrimonial bed.[2] This particular example, with its combination of intricate curved patchwork and organic appliqué would have been complicated and time-consuming to make, illustrating the maker's expertise as a quiltmaker. The quilt includes twelve sixteen-inch blocks, each incorporating four curved bands of diamonds in red, framing a concaved green square and embellished by finely stitched appliqué feathers in the form of a coxcomb, intended as representation of the American Whig political party's emblematic rooster.[3] The center blocks are framed with a border in red and green that has been described as a poinsettia motif[4] and resembles the detailed organic borders common on other contemporaneous red and green quilts, and other similar appliqué coverlets, popular between the 1840s and 1880s in North America.

Inspired by the late-eighteenth and early-nineteenth-century Indian palampore, and the discovery of the Turkey red dyeing process, the popularity of the red and green aesthetic coincides with a period in North American quiltmaking where "quiltmakers were consciously striving to create new styles."[5] From the palampore, quiltmakers were moved to cut out and apply printed organic shapes, such as birds, flowers, and most popularly, a tree of life, onto a light-colored background—usually white or unbleached muslin or silk. By the second quarter of the nineteenth century, when red and green quiltmaking had gained momentum, quiltmakers were cutting out their own designs from the array of new boldly colored and printed cotton textiles available from manufacturers. From their designs, quiltmakers could express their own creativity, especially when the supply of palampores became scarce or too expensive. In 1840, the highly guarded technique of producing vibrant and colorfast red was discovered, and from this point Turkey red became a common feature in many patchwork and appliqué quilt designs.[6] As Stana Nenadic and Sally Tuckett explain:

> For centuries, British and European dyers had been seeking a bright red dye, which could withstand strong sunlight and frequent washing without fading, and knowing of the Turkey red process, they were keen to reproduce it. Using the most common variation of the madder root—the *Rubia Tinctorum*—dyers could achieve a vibrant, dark, and colourfast red; making Turkey red was complex, repetitive, and expensive, taking up to two weeks, and required almost constant attention from the workforce.[7]

The combination of rich red textiles, produced through this exhaustive process, coupled with the labor-intensity of hand appliqué, demonstrated the skill of its makers, in a striking red and green aesthetic that became a hallmark of personal and, at times political, expression for quiltmakers during the middle decades of the nineteenth century.

Campbell's articulation of the *Whig's Defeat* pattern is the only known historical example of its kind in Canada and alludes to her interest in the craft of quiltmaking and needlework as an expression of her political awareness. Other examples held by the National Museum of History at the Smithsonian Institution, Washington D.C., the Kansas State University Historic Costume and Textile Museum in Manhattan, Kansas, and the Spencer Museum of Art at the University of Kansas, Lawrence, Kansas are clearly identifiable as similar in their patterning to Campbell's coverlet, yet present variations in design with altered dimensions, layout, and textile selections. Some of the other examples have alternative names to *Whig's Defeat*, including *Democrat's Fancy*, *Fanny's Favorite*, and *Richmond Beauty*, all of which suggest political undercurrents in the design.

In the red and green style, the *Whig's Defeat* pattern was first developed in the southern United States by an unknown quiltmaker in reference to the defeat of the leader of the American Whig Party and Kentucky representative Henry Clay (1777–1852), following his failed 1844 bid for President of the United States.[8] Once viewed as a great statesman and negotiator by Abraham Lincoln, Clay was also considered "hot-headed, utterly inexperienced, and ignorant, yet vehemently patriotic and recognized for his contribution of instigating the War of 1812."[9] Committed in his politics, Clay represented the Whig platform that refused to rest on either side of the abolitionist movement and sought the right for new frontier states to make their own decisions about slavery.[10] With the intricate patterning of *Whig's Defeat*, quiltmakers expressed their creativity through various articulations that, although the dimensions of the design were changed by its makers, the distinct combination of sharp points and the coxcomb embellishments distinguished this pattern from other red and green quilts (Figure 5.1).

During the nineteenth century, with the advent of women's periodicals, needlework patterns of a wide variety circulated across the United States and Canada. The possibility that *Whig's Defeat* appeared in one of several magazines, such as *Godey's Lady's Book* or *Peterson's Lady's Magazine*, might offer one possibility of how the pattern made its way to Canada. Other explanations for its dissemination might lie with the quiltmakers themselves, who were creative and innovative in how they copied and shared patterns. While some might have

Figure 5.1 Maker unknown, *Whig's Defeat,* date unknown. Once displayed at Henry Francis du Pont's summer home. Image courtesy of Winterthur Museum, Delaware. Note: Two of the blocks feature printed fabric of George Washington and Henry Clay's images. Quilt in Private Collection.

drafted a design to paper by tracing the shapes directly from a coverlet or copied designs from printed patterns, others drew their design ideas freehand. It is possible that Campbell might have received printed patterns in the form of periodicals upon her father's return from his frequent travels to the United States, which were likely for work.[11]

Between the 1840s and 1860s, *Whig's Defeat* was not the only politically influenced quilt design circulating in North America. In the United States in particular, political quilts were popular creations among the middle class. A more detailed interpretation of the predominantly red and green style, the highly popular *Baltimore Album* quilts, were made by women living within the city limits of Baltimore in the decade leading up to the Civil War. In Baltimore, during that decade, residents were concerned about several issues, including the loss of manufactories that had been removed to the southern states in an effort to avoid the additional shipping costs incurred by their distance from the cotton fields, and distress on the area's residents caused by the influx of immigrants, especially the famine Irish, who were willing to work in the region's remaining manufactories for a fraction of the current wage.[12] Noted for their politically inspired symbols and vignettes, organic appliqué designs, and elaborate stitching were distinctive elements of the *Baltimore Album* style to be recognized for their messaged undertones. In several of the coverlets from the *Baltimore Album* series, held by various museums across the United States and Britain, blocks commonly referenced the two dominant American political party symbols, an elephant for the Republican party and a donkey for the Democratic party. In addition, many of the blocks featured in the *Baltimore Album* quilts also included signs of club affiliations, such as the Daughters of Rebekah, a branch of the International Order of Odd Fellows for female participants. Other symbols such as the Phrygian cap, a symbol of the abolitionist movement frequently appeared in blocks and in conjunction with the American emblem, the eagle. Through the appliqué of political symbols, quiltmakers were able to identify their political affiliations in a form of subversive resistance and through a voice mostly recognized by fellow needle artists.

Middle-class Sensibilities and Victorian Femininity

To make her coverlet, Jessie Campbell selected textiles that would have been a reflection of her family's personal economy, education, and political awareness. For the surface and backing of the coverlet, Campbell would have purchased new cotton textiles in solid-colors of red, green, and white from a local merchant, signaling her intention of making a commemorative coverlet that displayed her skill with the needle. Although it is unknown if she purchased her textiles from the local merchant in Dundee or from a merchant in Glengarry County, Ontario, where she travelled during the late 1850s to serve as a housekeeper for relatives,[13] the incorporation of new textiles attests to the importance of the making of this quilt. According to my calculations, the maker required approximately fourteen yards of cloth to complete the surface and backing of her coverlet. At the time when cotton was priced at between thirteen and twenty-five cents per yard, it would have cost the maker between $1.82 and $3.50 to purchase fabric for the entire coverlet. If solid and printed cotton were compared at today's rate (2019), the purchase of solid cotton would have been approximately half the cost of printed cloth.[14] Since both Campbell and her father travelled outside their home county for work, the deliberate purchase of new cloth for this quilt signifies the importance of such a coverlet for young unmarried women. Because the purchase of cloth represents a significant event in the life of a young woman, the careful consideration for the type of cloth she purchased would have been made with an awareness of the contemporaneous cloth industry, heavily influenced by an American textile market in transition under the influence of abolitionism.[15]

To complete her coverlet, Campbell incorporated her most-practiced needle skills, carefully hand stitching each of the diamond bands, piece-by-piece, sewing them to the green concave square, and then appliquéing a total of two-hundred and forty coxcombs to the center panel along with the fourteen floral sprays that make up the coverlet's outer border. Once she completed the overall surface design, Campbell quilted a cross-hatch pattern in with ten to twelve stiches per inch by a rocker stitch, a practical and effective method of stitching for such a fine quilt. By stitching with white thread against a ground of white cloth, she created a shadowy effect that emphasized the coverlet's patchwork and appliqué, creating a second dimension of design.[16] This extensive amount of quilting is common to decorative quilts, further displaying the artistry and skill of its maker, and emphasizing the dedication required to complete a special coverlet.

As an added embellishment, Campbell framed her coverlet with an elaborate cotton knotted-fringe border, accentuating the quilt's decorative aspect, and engaging in conventions of Victorian design (Figure 5.2).[17] The fringe on *Whig's Defeat* is made from two-ply cotton yarn and has been knotted in diamond patterning, echoing the forms stitched in red and white on the surface of the coverlet. When displayed on a bed, this decorative detail emphasizes the drape of the quilt over the bed frame and would have likely coordinated with "other contemporaneous Victorian design elements, such as mantelpieces, drapes, and bed curtains."[18] As noted by nineteenth-century designer Lucy Orrinsmith in *The Drawing-Room: Its Decorations and Furniture* (1878), fringe was considered "a quintessential element of the lower middle-class Victorian home."[19]

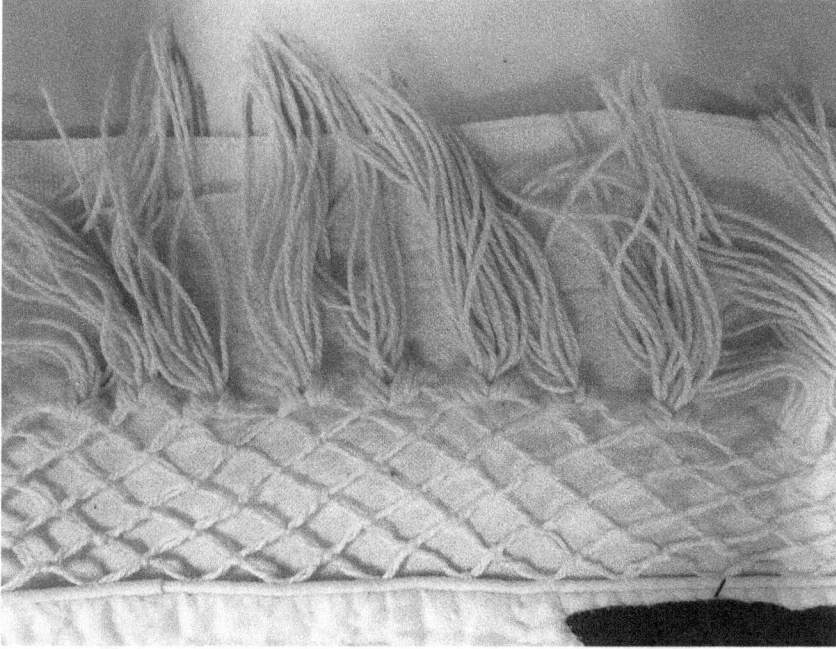

Figure 5.2 *Whig's Defeat* detail, fringed edging. Author's photograph.

Whig's Defeat as the McPherson Wedding Quilt

In 1866, when Campbell married Andrew McPherson (b. 1803) (Figure 5.3), the widower of her deceased aunt Marjorie Leslie (d. 1864), the display of *Whig's Defeat* on the matrimonial bed in commemoration of their marriage would have served as a device through which the maker claimed her own space in her new surroundings. While on the couple's bed, within the confines of the private area of the home, the quilt would have been viewed only by members of the immediate family, the three youngest children of Marjorie and Andrew McPherson, who still lived in the family home. It is evident from the coverlet's current-day condition that it was rarely used, only presented for special occasions, and highly cherished by the family, before it was passed on to the couple's oldest daughter Margaret McPherson. The coverlet was eventually passed on to the Agnes Etherington Art Centre by Margaret's son C. Ross Anderson.

Furthermore, the quilt served as representation of the continuing relationship between two Highland families, the Leslies and the McPhersons. In 1866, when Campbell married McPherson (b. 1803), she would have been expected to step

Figure 5.3 Andrew McPherson, Lorneville, ON, *c.*1880. Photograph courtesy of Bonnie Harwood.

into the role of wife and mother. To marry Campbell, McPherson travelled over four-hundred miles from his home in Eldon Township, Victoria County, near present-day Peterborough, Ontario, to Huntingdon County, Quebec to meet with Campbell and request her hand in marriage. According to family history, "[McPherson] travelled the long distance for the specific purpose of marrying another descendent of the Leslie clan as an ongoing gesture of commitment between the two families that began at the Battle of Culloden."[20] In Eldon Township, Campbell encountered a "close-knit Highland community," similar to the one she left behind in Huntingdon and Glengarry. By 1866, Eldon Township was comprised of over seventy-five percent Scottish Presbyterians and had a relatively long history of immigration from the Highlands.[21] Three initial waves of Highlanders arrived between 1825 and 1827: the first group of Scottish settlers, originally from Argyll, came up from North Carolina in 1825; a second group of settlers followed land speculator James Cameron from the Duke of Argyll's estates in Iona and Mull;[22] and the third wave that arrived in 1829, included Andrew McPherson and his two brothers Duncan and James.[23]

In addition to the quilt's association with domesticity and its significance as a commemorative family object, once in the McPherson home, *Whig's Defeat* became further imbued with political meaning through its connection to Andrew McPherson, who, as a land-grant recipient, was required by the British colonial government to participate in the local militia for the purpose of protecting the colony's borders. "In Victoria County (within which Eldon Township was located), all able-bodied men between eighteen and sixty years of age were required to establish a local militia and provide himself with arms and ammunition."[24] As part of the requirement to receive land grants in the colony, many settlers had been called to arms to represent the British during the American War of Independence, the Seven Years War, and the War of 1812 for the purpose of protecting the border that divided British North America and the United States. Revered by the British for their military effectiveness and resilience extending back to the Battle of Culloden, Highland settlers had been granted land in strategic locations, such as along the north shore of the St. Lawrence River, the long body of water that effectively divided the United States of America and Canada. Ironically, the British government, which forced the mass clearing of Highlanders from their lands in Scotland relied on Highlanders to protect the colonies in North America.

Once displayed on the matrimonial bed of Jessie and Andrew, the coverlet embodied all that represented the married couple and their individual identities before the marriage. Now associated to Andrew, the coverlet symbolized his life in Victoria County since his arrival, including the challenges of settling uncleared land and his duties as part of the militia. Between 1829, when Andrew arrived in Victoria County with his brother and 1866, the year Campbell and McPherson were united in matrimony, the year prior to Canada's Confederation, the local militia was called into service three times on behalf of the British colonial government. The first call to service was in response to the Rebellions of Upper and Lower Canada (1837–38), where settlers stood in opposition to elite ideologies and the rule of absentee landlords in exchange for local leadership that understood the needs of the newcomer population. The 6th Peterborough Battalion, for which McPherson served as Captain, was again called to duty during the Oregon Boundary Dispute of 1846, which ended in agreement between the United States and the British colonial government with the establishment of the border at the 49th parallel before troops became involved.

Thus, the coverlet became a symbol of the legacy of the Scottish Highlanders that settled in the region and its connection to the celebration of the defeat of the British Whigs.

Articulating her Politics: Campbell's *Whig's Defeat*

Sentiments of British elitism in Canada were present during the settling of Quebec and Ontario during the second and third quarters of the nineteenth century and would indeed have been amplified for Scottish settlers, whose families had left the Highlands at various stages under the devastating conditions of the Jacobite Risings and the Battle of Culloden (1745),[25] the Highland Clearances (1750–1815),[26] and the Highlands' subsequent economic downturn (1780–1820).[27] The Rising at Culloden represents a period in which the Highlanders acted in defense of their homeland as they fought for self-rule and democracy. When tensions arising from religious difference, increasing population, and food shortages (1740, 1751, and 1756) motivated the Royal Navy to commit a series of regular attacks on Inverness communities, even those loyal to the Crown, opposed the monarchy on political and religious grounds chose to ban together to fight for Scotland.[28]

In North America, when a similar demonstration of solidarity for democracy manifested under the banner of republicanism,[29] between 33,000 and 55,000 Canadian troops enlisted on the side of the Union.[30] Since many of these troops were descendants of Highlanders, some of whom had been brought to Canada during the late-eighteenth and early-nineteenth centuries to fight on the side of the British during the Seven Years War (1756–63) and the War of 1812 (1812–14), the idea of fighting for the American North was considered a sense of duty,[31] an opportunity based in cultural cohesion and nostalgia. The compelling political undertones of the *Whig's Defeat* pattern would have appealed to Campbell at a moment when political tensions were percolating south of the Canada–United States border, located within ten kilometers of her family's farm. In fact, the threat of an American Civil War was on the minds of many Canadians: many had ventured south of the border for employment, and, during the 1850s, as tensions over the ownership of slaves migrated north, often reuniting with their former countryfolk.[32] At the Canadian market town of Dundee, Quebec, located ten kilometers south of the Campbell farm and directly across the border from the American military installation at Fort Covington, citizens of the two states would have indeed engaged in discussion over the threat of war.[33]

For those living in the southwestern region of Quebec, the values of republicanism and democracy would have weighed heavily on their minds, especially for those who were present in Upper and Lower Canada for the Rebellions of 1837–38. During the Rebellions, citizens of Upper and Lower Canada sought responsible representation of elected officials from the colonies, rather than elitist legislators appointed by colonial government. Existing representatives, referred to as the Family Compact (Upper Canada) and the Château Cliques (Lower Canada), were tied to the British elite and proved to be disconnected from the issues facing most settlers.[34]

For many of the Scottish immigrants from Canada who participated in the Civil War, knowledge of the role of the British Whigs in the destruction of Highland culture and society was entrenched in their North American experiences. Tom Devine highlights how the British government set forth in an overt demonstration of military presence toward Highland culture, ensuring the Jacobite clans would never "rise again to menace Protestant succession":[35]

> Through the passage of a series of Acts of Parliament, an attack was launched on the culture of the Gael and the system of clanship: Highland dress and the playing of the pipes were proscribed as the symbols of militarism; heritable jurisdictions, the private courts held by the landowners were abolished; and the carrying of weapons was forbidden and the estates of rebels declared forfeit to the crown. The thinking was that Protestantism would induce ideological conformity while prosperity would remove the alienation, which had caused rebellion.[36]

Although in 1760, with the defeat of the British Whig party, which sought the weakening of clans and sat in opposition to the Crown and the Catholic Church, Highlanders anticipated reprieve from the British authorities, the return to power of the British Whigs in 1763 set in motion the decades-long demolition of Highland society. Under newly elected prime minister Charles James Fox, Whig politics returned to power under the new banner of the Tory party.[37] Even under the brief hiatus from Whig control, the long process from clan society to capitalism was well underway; clan gentry had begun to take on characteristics resembling landlords rather than clan chieftains, raising rents and making it almost impossible for tenants to survive.[38] Under this new system, many tenant farmers migrated to the Lowlands in search of work on smaller crofts or in the growing industrial sector of Glasgow and Edinburgh. In his tour of the Highlands in 1773, Samuel Johnson wrote about the decline of clan culture and how the clans retained little of their original character: "Their ferocity of temper is softened, their military ardor is extinguished, their dignity of independence is depressed, their contempt for government subdued, and their reverence for their chiefs abated."[39]

Educated at home by her grandmother, Campbell would have been well-aware of her family's history in the Highlands, especially since the legacy of the relationship between two Highland clans, one Catholic and one Protestant, was deeply rooted in her own personal family history. When Jessie Campbell's grandparents, Alexander (b. 1752) and Marjorie Leslie (b. *c.* 1770), arrived at Montreal in 1825, they were accompanied by their immediate family and also members of the McPherson clan from Inverness with whom they had formed a tightly woven relationship extending back to a time before the Battle of Culloden (1745).[40] Prior to the Rising, as agricultural conditions worsened in Inverness,[41] Jacobite Clan Chief Ewan McPherson invited members of the Leslie clan, who were Hanoverian supporters, to teach the McPherson clan how to improve soil conditions for farming.[42] When word came that British and Highland troops were meeting on the battleground at Culloden, the Leslies, despite religious differences, marched alongside the McPhersons in what could be viewed as a show of solidarity for Highland culture. Following the defeat at Culloden, which resulted in the deaths of thousands of Highlanders, Ewan McPherson went into hiding, and was later found guilty of High Treason.[43] According to family oral history, while in hiding, McPherson was sheltered by his clansfolk for the next nine years before going into exile. While in exile, only four people were aware of his whereabouts and continued to provide him with food and shelter; two of the four people that secured McPherson were Leslies, establishing an ongoing bond between the two clans.[44]

Campbell's appropriation of the *Whig's Defeat* pattern from its original association to the defeat of the American Whig political party, which stood on the side of states' rights and did not take a side on the slavery issue, reveals the quiltmaker's understanding of America's political environment, but also alludes to her position of her family's Highland heritage, which rested on the side of the emancipation from British rule—a side sympathetic to the developing Canadian psyche. As Campbell settled in her new role as matriarch of the McPherson clan, Canada as a nation was also emerging in its new role as an independent state, released from under the direct governance of Britain. As though Campbell was responding in her own way to Samuel Johnson's observations of the changing characteristics of clan life, her coverlet served as a political device; its contrast in design, soft organic shapes, and distinguished and exacting points in the patchwork, intimate the shifting nature of clan culture to settler identity. As the only historical coverlet of this design currently held by any Canadian museum,

Campbell's *Whig's Defeat* represents the cross-cultural political philosophies and emerging cultural identities forming in the colonies. While the coverlet's name and design reflect Campbell's interest in displaying her femininity, her selection of the *Whig's Defeat* pattern as a commemorative coverlet, one for which she would have dedicated considerable time, attests to her understanding of her family's legacy, her emerging middle-class sensibilities, and her awareness of the political climate in which she lived.

Conclusion

Whig's Defeat was made in commemoration of marriage and displayed upon the McPherson's matrimonial bed, embodying its maker's emerging identity as a wife and a mother, and eventually as a Canadian citizen of Scottish descent. Originally made six years prior to her marriage and seven years before Canada became recognized as an independent nation-state, Campbell committed to completing the coverlet, as did many other young women in Victorian Canada, as a symbol of her upbringing, education, and gentility, and her ability to manage her household interior. With the aspiration of one day marrying, she stitched her quilt, committed to following a design which she appropriated from American political culture and applied her expert needle skills, taking time to complete this superb example.

Once displayed on the bed she shared with Andrew McPherson, the coverlet became a symbol of the continued commitment between two Highland families, the Leslies and the McPhersons, and the legacy of Highland culture that enriched the lives and strengthened the communities of Scottish newcomers to Canada. Following the coverlet as it passed through time and space, and alongside Campbell as she married and relocated her home from Quebec to Ontario, the coverlet adopted new meaning. The making of the coverlet could be viewed as representation of the relationship between North American and British politics, and as a symbol of the changing politics of colony and Empire. The display of the coverlet takes on an alternative meaning, one that reflects Samuel Johnson's observations of declining clan culture during his travels through Scotland in 1773: while clan culture may have been in decline under the oppressive powers of the British Whig political system in the Highlands, the emerging political state in North America brought forth new forms of political, cultural, and social identity that became part of Canada's Scottish-settler community.

The analysis of decorative needlework serves an integral purpose in recouping the lives of young women in settlement Canada. An absence of personal diaries or day-to-day accounts by settler women reflect how women were either too busy to write about their daily experiences or that many simply did not read or write. In this case, Campbell was educated and would have been able to keep a written account of her daily life; however, the only known record of her life exists within the stitches of her quilt, and through the selection of pattern and choice of textiles.

"From Prison to Citizenship," 1910: The Making and Display of a Suffragist Banner

Janice Helland

The Museum of London's permanent People's City gallery, 1850s–1940s, includes a section dedicated to the militant Suffragette campaign of the early-twentieth century. The collection of memorabilia related to the movement includes still photographs and a continuous loop video featuring people and events, along with footage from the violent "Black Friday" demonstration of November 1910.[1] In the midst of the smaller displays hangs a large embroidered banner designed at the Glasgow School of Art by instructor Ann Macbeth (1875–1948) and made collaboratively with her students.[2] The banner is composed of eighty rectangular pieces of white linen, each containing the embroidered signature of a woman imprisoned for participation in protests against the government's refusal to grant women the vote.[3] The white rectangles are sewn together and bordered by green and purple panels—green, white, and purple were the "signature" colors of the militant Women's Social and Political Union (WSPU) (Plate 6.1).[4] The preservation of the banner and its signatures within the museum is, to borrow a term from Raphael Samuel, a form of "memory keeping."[5]

Memories and Meanings

Heather Pristash, Inez Schaechterle, and Sue Carter Wood in their essay, "The Needle as the Pen," discuss the "rhetorical meaning of needlework—and thus, its coded meaning."[6] They contend that an object "made in the colours of a specific organization," in this case the WSPU, "can, in itself, carry a message of support for that organization, or even serve an educational purpose, if it is displayed in a place where viewers could 'read the code' it contains."[7] According to Diane Atkinson, the "purple, white and green scheme was heavily marketed and merchandised by the suffragette leadership."[8] "No political campaign," contends Atkinson, "before or since the WSPU has used a colour scheme so comprehensively and so effectively."[9] The banner's "coded meaning" certainly was understood when first exhibited in Glasgow's suffrage bazaar in April 1910 and again when it was carried in London's "From Prison to Citizenship" procession in June 1910. Within the museum context, however, the significance of the colors may not be apparent to all viewers, particularly those with little knowledge of the WSPU. Nevertheless, the colors, along with the totality of the banner, signify historical memory waiting to achieve relevance for those viewers who pause to contemplate it. As Clive Edwards suggests, objects "facilitate memory," and are "part of a life-story"; they "bear specific memories, and are reminders as to when and where they were produced or acquired."[10]

Within and around the memories and reminders, it is important to contextualize the moment and the object in British history and acknowledge, as Lynne Walker so astutely reminds us, that "the abuse and imprisonment of suffragettes and even their own violent destruction of property need to be contextualized and reread within the wider global politics and power relations of the British empire, where local resistances of oppressed people were asserted in the face of the imperial government's vast might and capacity for enforcement and control."[11] While the banner commemorates one group of women—all white, mostly English and Scottish, and from a range of social backgrounds—it also represents an important moment in the broader movement for women's rights.[12]

At the top of the banner, the name of the organization is stitched in large, bold letters that are surrounded by the names of four WSPU leaders, two on either side: Emmeline Pethick Lawrence, Christabel Pankhurst, and Emmeline Pankhurst, Annie Kenney. Each of the rectangles that form the dominant central panel are embroidered in violet with the names "in their own handwriting—of all the hunger strikers," imprisoned suffragists who used hunger strike as protest.[13] These women insisted they were political prisoners: "The women who have been sent to prison in connection with Woman Suffrage disturbances have, from the beginning, demanded treatment as political prisoners."[14] Despite appeals to the Home Secretary "to accord them the rights and privileges to which political prisoners are entitled in every part of the world," they continued to be treated as criminals.[15] In making the protest, *Votes for Women* declared: "the treatment which the Suffragettes receive in Holloway is worse than that which was accorded to political prisoners in the Bastille and is inferior, in some respects, to that which Russian political prisoners are receiving today."[16] Thus, in July 1909, the first woman to hunger strike, Scottish artist Marion Wallace Dunlop

(1864–1942), began a protest that would culminate in the hunger striking and forcible feeding of over 200 women. The banner commemorates eighty of those women (Table 6.1).[17]

Table 6.1 Banner signatures. In certain instances the signatures are difficult to decipher; one signature remains unknown. Square brackets indicate full or alternate names; some women signed using a pseudonym.

Lucy Burns	Constance Craig or Bray	Jane Warton [Lady Constance Lytton]	Jane Esdon Malloch Brailsford
Mabel Kirby	Dora Marsden	Georgina Healiss	Leslie Hall [Letitia Withall]
Ellen Pitfield	Florence Clarkson	Mabel Capper	Hannah Shepherd
Agnes Corson	Margaret West	Dorothy Pethick	Edith Hudson
Kitty Marion [Katherina Maria Schafer]	Helen Tolson	Helen Gordon Liddell	Alice Hawkins
Mary Leigh	Sarah Carwin	Elsie Roe-Brown	Bertha Brewster
Jessie Lawes	[illegible]	Selina Martin	Lilian Dove-Willcox
Violet Mary Jones	Grace Cameron-Swann	Adela Pankhurst	Kathleen Brown
Fannie [Fanny] Halliwell	Winifred Jones	Theresa Garnett	Nellie Godfrey
Helen A[lexander] Archdale	E[lizabeth] E[llen] Hesmondhaugh	Vera Wentworth	Nora Dunlop
Ellen Barnwell	Eugenia Bouvier	CAL Marsh [Charlotte Augusta Leopoldine Marsh]	Lillian Norbury
Lilgard Atheling	Elsie N. Howey	Mary Phillips	G. Holtwhite Simmons
Ethel Slade	Catherine Worthington	Helen K. Watts	Maud Joachim
Ada Wright	Violet O'Brien	Rona Robinson	Florence Sprong
Kathleen Jarvis	Nellie Crocker	Dorothy Shallard	Edith Davies
Elsie Mackenzie	Edith New	Alice Paul	Emily Wilding Davison
Isabel Kelley	Caro B[ray] Jolly	Florence Cook	Catherine Tolson
Marion Wallace Dunlop	Rosamund Massy	Laura Ainsworth	Violet Bryant
Gladys Roberts	Edith Rigby	Jenny Baines [sometimes Jennie Baines]	Helen Burkitt
Mary Allen	Ellen Pitman	Annie Bell	Grace Chappelo[n?]

Making the Banner: Ann Macbeth and the Glasgow School of Art

Macbeth began her studies at the GSA in 1897, and by 1901 was working as "assistant instructress" to her teacher and mentor, Jessie Newbery (1864–1948).[18] She and Newbery became members of the Glasgow and West of Scotland Association for Women's Suffrage in 1902, the year the association formed, and later were affiliated with the WSPU.[19] The School itself provided a convivial venue in which progressive ideas could form and develop. Both Jessie and her husband Francis (Principal of the School) were advocates of William Morris and the Arts and Crafts Exhibition Society, and they were socialists, concerned for equality. Furthermore, as Liz Arthur observes, Jessie Newbery "frequently used the women's suffrage colours of green, white and violet" in her textile art.[20] Janet Rae, in her recent study of Scottish textiles, maintains that "GSA teaching colleagues and embroidery students" shared Newbery and Macbeth's support for the WSPU, and "often spent studio time making suffrage banners."[21]

Macbeth was an exceptionally talented and innovative embroiderer as well as a lecturer "on the teaching of needlework," and the author of a number of books on textiles.[22] Her innovative work was celebrated at home and abroad with notices appearing in British and European art journals. In 1902, for example, Francis Newbery (1855–1946) published a lengthy article in *Studio*, a leading British art journal, in which he lauded Macbeth's accomplishments with the needle.[23] That same year Macbeth was recognized internationally when she won a silver medal for her appliqued and embroidered textile hanging, *The Sleeping Beauty*, at the Turin International Exhibition for Modern Decorative Art.[24] By 1908, she was head of the Embroidery Department at the GSA, replacing her mentor and sometimes collaborator, Jessie Newbery.[25] Together they had designed and embroidered a banner, "Let Glasgow Flourish," commissioned by the Glasgow local committee of the British Association for the Advancement of Science (1901). The lettering on the banner, displayed during the annual meeting of the association held that year at Glasgow University, has the same geometrically linear and bold characteristic that appears on the suffrage banner.[26]

Macbeth, after she succeeded Newbery, continued to advocate a collaborative approach in her teaching and art production and, significantly, she did not sign her name to the banner.[27] This may have been because, at that time, she had not been on hunger strike, or because of the collaborative nature of the making, which included the "stitching of the self" by eighty women.[28] Moreover, the production of the 1910 suffrage banner undoubtedly involved collaboration with the WSPU itself. The attribution of Macbeth as designer is known only because of a short mention in *Votes for Women*: "A suffrage linen quilt with a beautiful design in colours by the well-known artist Ann Macbeth, and containing the embroidered names of hunger strikers, forms an interesting memento, and will be sold for £10" at a suffrage bazaar in Glasgow.[29] Because Marion Wallace Dunlop was the first woman to engage in a hunger strike in July 1909, and the banner was exhibited in Glasgow's suffrage bazaar in April 1910,[30] the making of the rectangles, the embroidery on the green panel, and the assemblage must have taken no more than nine months.

Although there is no documentary evidence, it is probable that members of the WSPU, possibly including Emmeline Pethick Lawrence (1867–1954), who later purchased the banner, assisted with the distribution of the white rectangles upon which women embroidered their names. The design of the banner and the fabric would have been selected by Macbeth; the size of the object, including the size of the rectangles, also would have been determined as part of the overall design. The rectangles themselves, however, and the violet silk thread used to embroider them, would have had to have been distributed to women who lived in various parts of England and Scotland along with the request for an embroidered signature.

Obviously, detailed planning and meticulous organization both for dissemination and collecting would have been necessary. Some pieces may not have been returned. For example, in July 1909, twelve women were arrested for a "raid on the House of Commons" and "stonethrowing"; they were sentenced and imprisoned in Holloway (London). All twelve undertook hunger strike and all twelve embroidered their names for the banner.[31] The following month, ten women were imprisoned in Holloway; yet only eight signed the banner.[32] Although some extant textiles were embroidered in prison, it is likely the banner signatures were done outside of prison, which may account for "missing" names; some hunger strikers may have been in prison when the requests went out.

The green and violet silk of the banner, with its elegant silk stitching across the top of the green panel and carefully stitched borders which mark the transitions between white and green, green and purple, attests to technical competence. The style itself and the carefully thought-out design, however, indicate Macbeth's enthusiasm for and understanding of the specific linear style that grew out of the Glasgow School of Art beginning in the 1890s, nurtured by Jessie and Francis Newbery. As Elizabeth Cumming declares in her study of the arts and crafts movement in Scotland, the "Newberys were as much theorists as artists, designers and educators" and the "new Glasgow design," which developed amongst faculty and students in the school, "was unique to that city and the result of the city having a focused art school."[33] Critics and viewers alike recognized the "unique" style by 1896, when the London Arts and Crafts Exhibition included a large contingent of Glasgow artist/designers and, by 1900, with their acclaimed participation in the eighth exhibition of the Viennese Secession, they moved on to the international stage.[34] The banner's distinctive style also differs significantly from many suffrage banners that included what might be called "feminine" stitching and content. Lisa Tickner, for example, suggests that imagery of the "ethereal feminine," with which artists were familiar and which was incorporated into banners by some groups, was "adapted with difficulty to the needs of a militant campaign."[35] Alternatively, Macbeth's banner had been designed with a non-figurative, bold and arguably more modern style. It would have stood out dramatically amongst the other textiles when first displayed in Glasgow, and then, later, when it was carried in procession in London.

The Banner on Display: Glasgow and London

Precisely when the banner design was finalized and how the signatures were obtained remains speculative; nevertheless, it appeared completed and ready for display in the three-day suffrage exhibition which opened in Glasgow on 28 April 1910, the first such exhibition in Scotland, and the second in Britain.[36] It was to be, according to *Votes for Women*, "another great triumph for the women who are demanding political enfranchisement."[37] Press accounts point to the significance of two aspects: an intent to highlight the prison conditions for suffragists and a demonstration of "women's work." Mrs. Pankhurst, during her opening-day speech, reminded viewers that although political and "active in militant work," woman continued to "devote a great part of her time to that kind of work which was considered to be essentially women's work."[38] According to Pankhurst, "one good result of the bazaar would be that they would allay any fears in their brothers' minds that if they got the vote they would give up being women."[39]

One of the highlights of the exhibition, certainly not feminine, was the faux prison cells, each of which was inhabited by a woman who had experienced incarceration. One represented the type of confinement reserved for political prisoners, a designation insisted upon by suffrage advocates and one that was consistently refused them: the "so-called political prisoner has a comfortable room with a fireplace, his own furniture, food of his own ordering, books, newspapers, and letters."[40] The other, a "second division cell," represented the space in which suffrage women "served their sentence."[41] Caro Jolly, who assumed a role as prisoner in one of the faux cells at the exhibition, signed the banner.[42]

While the reconstructed cells demonstrated the spaces inhabited by and petitioned for, another "small modelled group" illustrated "the horrors of forcible feeding,"[43] accounts of which can be found on the pages of *Votes for Women* as well as in many newspapers, though it is doubtful the model was able to capture the women's experience as effectively as the textual accounts related by the women themselves. Selina Martin, for example, who signed the banner, gave a poignant account of the spaces in which she was confined after being arrested and incarcerated in Walton Green Gaol (Liverpool). Martin and Leslie Hall, another signatory, were arrested together for "disorderly conduct" during Prime Minister Asquith's visit to Liverpool.[44] Later, *Votes for Women* published Martin's account of her ordeal: the doctor "ordered me to be dressed in my own wet clothes, and I was taken to a cold, damp cell without ventilation, and was handcuffed behind and left on the floor. At night I was taken to a larger cell and kept in irons."[45] Martin also detailed when and how she was forcibly fed: "Thursday night I was thrown down, and frog-marched up some steps, letting my head bump on the steps as I was carried. I was then forcibly fed, after which I was dragged to the top of the steps and thrown down."[46]

Unlike the reconstructed cells, the banner signaled camaraderie and shared experience, as well as a reification of the subversive act in which the signers had engaged. Like nineteenth-century friendship or signature quilts, it combines "a multiplicity of voices to create a statement of solidarity."[47] It is doubtful, however, that it was ever meant to be a quilt, despite the reference in *Votes for Women*; to my knowledge, Macbeth never designed or executed a quilt. The term "quilt" may have been used because of the "pieced" nature of the signed rectangles. Furthermore, by the time Macbeth exhibited the textile panel, preparation for a "great demonstration" had already begun;[48] and, Macbeth and her students had produced at least one other suffrage banner.[49] Significantly, it was Pethick Lawrence who purchased the banner from the Scottish suffrage exhibition: "Members will be pleased to hear that the quilt embroidered with the names—in their own handwriting—of all the hunger strikers, which is the interesting souvenir of an epoch in the history of our country, has been bought by one of the leaders, Mrs Pethick Lawrence."[50] Most important, those able to attend the exhibition and view the completed object would have interacted with the community represented by the collection of signatures and recognized the significance of the act of signing.

Figure 6.1 WSPU "From Prison to Citizenship" banner procession, 18 June 1910. © Museum of London.

Slightly less than two months later, in June 1910, the textile once again appeared in public, this time as a highly visible banner in the procession, "From Prison to Citizenship" (Figure 6.1). The imposingly organized "vast" procession, according to *The Scotsman*, included "nearly ten thousand women" and stretched "two miles"; "every class was represented, a number of well-known members of society marching with their humbler sisters."[51] The marchers carried 700 banners and were accompanied by forty bands.[52] The Glasgow banner, which became known as the "Hunger Strikers' Banner," appears to have been the largest and would have had to have been carried by at least two poles, if not three.[53] Guidelines for size suggested that a double-pole banner should measure no more than 127 × 183 centimeters; the Glasgow banner measured 222 × 248 centimeters.[54] Carried by WSPU members, it must have made a striking and memorable impression on protesters as well as those who lined the streets.

Stitching the Self

While viewing the banner as a collective whole, this section highlights selected signatures—not to separate them out in any orderly way, but rather to seek examples of the varying "stories" produced by the act of reading the signature as well as by considering the significance of signing. The banner, for example, differs from the 1912 Suffrage Signature Handkerchief (Museum of London, ref. 50.82/1496) embroidered by Janie Terrero from signatures collected in prison "during chapel or in the exercise yard."[55] Rozsika Parker, in her discussion of the handkerchief, maintained the signatures were "gestures of solidarity and protest," and as such combined the "political tradition of petition with the social tradition of embroidered signatures as mementoes to mark special occasions."[56] Her observation could be applied equally to the banner, as could Maureen Daly Goggin's assertion that Terrero's collection of signatures represented a subversive act.[57] The Glasgow banner required more thought and preparation than the handkerchief, but it too represented a subversive act. Both exemplify the significance of signatures, which, as Goggin contends, "were, and still are, tangible representations of the self."[58] Three banner signatures reappear on the handkerchief, a grim reminder of how many times, and over how many years, some of the protesters were arrested and engaged in hunger strike.[59]

Reasons for the arrests of the banner's eighty women varied from throwing stones at Winston Churchill's motor car, to smashing windows of properties from department stores to government buildings, to "disorderly conduct." Ages varied, professions varied, social class varied, although many of the signatures are those of women from the educated classes. As Joy Kay reminds us, "one of the inevitable distortions of research into women's suffrage has been the emphasis on the leaders and personalities of the major societies."[60] The reason for this, as Kay writes, was "understandable as they were the speechmakers, the headline grabbers and, perhaps most significantly, the women who left memoirs or some record of their lives."[61] Significantly, the women who contributed to the banner did not all fit this demographic.

Nellie Godfrey, for example, charged for hurling an iron "missile" wrapped in paper with the words, "thrown by a woman of England as a protest against the Government's treatment of political prisoners," was a thirty-year old baker's assistant from Essex.[62] Her name does not appear in accounts of the more well-known members of the movement but her signature, neatly and clearly stitched on the banner, asserts her place as an advocate and safeguards her identity as memory. Similarly, information about Violet O'Brien remains elusive; her signature is on the banner, but I could find only one mention of her in a local newspaper that listed the names of 106 women and eight men arrested when they attempted "to force an entry to the House of Commons."[63] Contrary to the information in this local publication, the major national newspaper, *The Times*, focused only on Mrs. Pankhurst and, near the end of its version of the same event, listed a few names of "well-connected" women such as Maud Joachim, "niece of the violinist," and "the Hon. Mrs Haverfield, daughter of Lord Abinger."[64] Local newspapers, many now available digitally on British Newspaper Archive (British Library), frequently provide more information about individual women, arrested and released, than major papers such as *The Times* or *Votes for Women*, which tended to report on the "celebration" held upon release of prisoners, particularly if many women were released together. The WSPU paper consistently placed its emphasis upon the well-known WSPU activists or upon the speeches given at the celebration of release. Thus, in certain cases it seems the signatures on the banner are the most visible memory of historical women activists. Information about other relatively unknown hunger strikers emerges in often lengthy accounts, again mainly in local newspapers, and rarely in major papers.

Edith Hudson and Elsie Roe-Brown, for example, were arrested about the same time as Godfrey and for similar offences, albeit in a different location and protesting the visit of a different politician: for causing a "disturbance at Leith [Edinburgh] in connection with Sir Edward Grey's visit."[65] Sentenced to thirty days, they engaged in hunger strike but Scottish authorities proved reluctant to forcibly feed; newspaper accounts, however, made it clear the option was under consideration.[66] Roe-Brown was a nurse, a working woman like Godfrey; she was dismissed from her position at an Edinburgh nursing home after her arrest.[67] Also like Godfrey, Roe-Brown and Hudson were, as was the case with many who signed the banner, the "rank and file" of the movement.

Hudson and Roe-Brown were not the only Scottish women to add their signatures to the banner. Scottish-born artist Marion Wallace Dunlop, the celebrated first hunger striker, claimed ancestry from Scotland's thirteenth-century warrior, William Wallace, giving her own resistance an exalted pedigree. She had been arrested for "imprinting on one of the walls of the House of Commons an extract from the Bill of Rights."[68] Because the authorities refused to treat her as a political prisoner, "she determined to carry into effect that most terrible weapon of political prisoners, the hunger strike"; she fasted for ninety-one hours before being released.[69] Glaswegian Mary Phillips (1880–1969), a "keen socialist" and paid organizer for the WSPU, was arrested in July 1909 for disturbances at a meeting in Exeter and, like Dunlop, went on hunger strike to protest lack of recognition as a political prisoner.[70] Helen Archdale, along with four English colleagues, was arrested in Dundee in October 1909 for "creating a disturbance during the progress of Mr Winston Churchill's Dundee meeting."[71] They were on hunger strike for four days but not forcibly fed. Forcible feeding had not been "adopted in Dundee although it is believed to be the intention of the Scottish Prison Commission to 'feed' on the next repetition of a strike in Scotland."[72]

A number of women who signed the banner were leading members of the WSPU. Mary Phillips, as mentioned, was a paid organizer, first for the Glasgow and West of Scotland Association for Women's Suffrage, and later for the WSPU.[73] Ada Wright "worked continuously, voluntarily, for the WSPU, speaking at meetings all over the country."[74] Mary Leigh, in 1909, was "drum-major of the newly-founded WSPU drum and fife band."[75] Rosamund Massy (1870–1947) was a "veteran WSPU campaigner" whose prominent family, as well as her husband, fully supported her political activities.[76] A celebratory contingent of WSPU members and public supporters greeted Lilian Dove-Wilcox and Mary Allen, prominent Bristol activists, upon their release and return to the city. Dove-Wilcox recounted her prison experiences to the press: "Most of us had a month [in Holloway] ... but as soon as we were in prison we mutinied. We refused to wear prison dress, and broke windows because the cells were so close and stuffy." She went on to tell reporters that they were "sentenced to eight days' close confinement in the punishment cells, and that was really awful."[77] The hunger strike began during the confinement. Upon release both women were presented with a gift: "a leather belt with silver buckle, enclosed in a handsome case,"[78] and both prepared signatures to be included with the Glasgow banner. Significantly, Annie Kenney (1879–1953), the much-admired working-class member/activist of the WSPU and one of its "most popular speakers and charismatic figures," whose name appears at the top of the banner below that of Mrs. Pankhurst, "took the chair" at the reception held for the Bristol women.[79] From Manchester but based in Bristol, Kenney illustrates the touring activities of leading members of the WSPU; they literally traversed the country, engaged in public speaking and lectures in numbers of different venues, and represented the mobile community of which the women were part. This kind of movement may also suggest how white rectangles and violet threads were distributed and collected for inclusion on the banner.

Elsie Howey and Vera Wentworth, again prominent members, were arrested along with Mary Phillips in July 1909: Phillips was from Glasgow, Howey from Nottinghamshire (she attended St Andrews University in Scotland), and Wentworth, whose name is also embroidered on the prisoners' handkerchief, was a Londoner.[80] According to Votes for Women, they were released from prison at Exeter, where they had been incarcerated for leading "the tremendous protest of citizens against Lord Carrington when he came to address a great meeting there."[81] Another example of the mobility and community of the women, American activist Alice Paul, was arrested in London along with Emily Davison, Mary Leigh, Mabel Capper, Dorothy Shallard, and Kathleen Jarvis; all signed the banner.[82]

While many of those who provided signatures for the banner were active members of the WSPU, and are remembered as such, two have achieved prominence in historical accounts of the movement: Emily Wilding Davison (1872–1913) and Lady Constance Lytton (1869–1923). Davison's imprisonment in October 1909, prior to embroidering her name for the banner, was particularly brutal. In January 1910, she "threatened action against six Manchester Justices" because of an incident at Strangeways Gaol [Manchester] where she suffered a broken tooth, bleeding mouth, was hosed with icy water and left in general poor health; she sought £100 damages.[83] According to the justices, there was no firm evidence: "it was not denied that the defendants had been party to an assault on the plaintiff though they contended their action was justified."[84] Additionally, it was determined that the "conduct of a plaintiff that led up to the assault must always be taken into account in assessing damages"; as a result, damages were "nominal" and assessed at 40s.[85]

It is Davison's death, however, the result of her foray onto the Derby race course only to be struck by the King's horse, that, as Jane Purvis recently maintained, "has become a defining moment in British political history."[86] The incident was "reported by all the main newspapers, captured by Pathé news and relayed around the world," and, as a result, Purvis contends, "Emily Davison has been perpetuated in popular culture as an unbalanced, suicidal fanatic."[87] In her reassessment of Davison's life and activism, Purvis contemplates a more nuanced examination of her alleged and sensationalized suicide. She writes that Davison was a "sensible woman with a coherent philosophy who deliberately undertook her final militant act, knowing it might have fatal consequences." Although she was a "risk-taker," acknowledges Purvis, "Emily probably did not intend to die."[88]

Lytton's historical fame rests largely on her masquerade as working-class "Jane Warton" when she was arrested in 1910, and her subsequent exposure of the class-based treatment of female prisoners. A contemporary account of her imprisonment was published in a local newspaper: "She describes the operation of forcible feeding as simply suffocation. Each time after the operation she vomited, and during the operation suffered horrible torture. Lady Constance was released on the grounds of health. She alleges that this decision was not arrived at until her identity became known."[89] Purposefully, she signed the banner as "Jane Warton," thereby stitching on to the panel the memory of her alternate identity.

Recent accounts of the activities of both women have revised the narrow and limited analysis of their activism and commitment to suffrage. Michelle Myall's

1998 article provides an interrogation of the histories of women's roles in the suffrage movement, beginning with new approaches taken in the late 1980s which "reveal the intricacies and complexity" of the WSPU and, with that, Lytton's campaign activities.[90] In retrospect, it is not coincidental that three of the most written-about activists signed the banner: Lytton, Davison, and Wallace Dunlop. Like some of the other embroiderers, it may have been easier to collect signed rectangles from organizers and high-profile members because of their accessibility or from those related to organizers such as Dorothy Pethick (Emmeline Pethick Lawrence's sister) or Jessie Lawes and Nellie Crocker (cousins of Pethick Lawrence).[91] The banner, however, still binds these women to their lesser known campaigners.

Conclusion

The signatures of the WSPU banner draw attention to the less well-known members of the suffrage movement, and remind us of the diverse activities of the more famous members while, at the same time, it is equally relevant to view the eighty signatures as a collective whole. The collective affirms the mutual aims and objectives, the willingness to put one's self in harm's way for belief in a cause, and shared activism. Each signature, as Goggin reminds us, represents the self;[92] each woman knew she was stitching her name to commemorate her own incarceration and commitment to a cause. Beyond the individual, however, each "stitching of the self" was connected to others, resulting in a shared space that reverberated with the call to "give women votes." The collaborative process required to produce the banner complements and enhances the shared experiences of the women who protested, demonstrated, and were arrested. It is a signifier for specific historical moments: a moment when women requested the right to vote, a moment that when arrested they requested treatment as political prisoners, a moment when they were denied that right and a moment when, collectively, they engaged in a strategy to protest their treatment. The banner's preservation in the museum, as mentioned above, facilitates remembrance of those moments, educates viewers, and acts as a "memory keeper."

Our Lady of the Snows: Settlement, Empire, and "The Children of Canada" in the Needlework of Mary Seton Watts (1848–1938)

Elaine Cheasley Paterson

In her diary of 29 July 1906, London art-school educated, Scottish-born designer Mary Seton Watts (Plate 7.1) explained how Rudyard Kipling's poem "Our Lady of the Snows" was "at the heart" of her design for a spectacular embroidered silk banner commissioned by Lord Grey, then Governor General of Canada (1904–1911).[1] Our Lady of the Snows (1906) was one of two large silk banners designed and worked by Watts, as part of a series given by Grey to educational institutions across Canada. While most of these banners depict a St. George theme—this was requested by Grey for the "principle training Schools and Institutes" in Canada where he believed it "was the duty of every individual, after the fashion of Saint George, to kill the Dragon of evil everywhere it may be found; and it may be found everywhere"[2]—Mary Seton Watts's banner offered instead symbols of peace, faith, and love. Nevertheless, her banner was presented in 1907 by Grey, on behalf of Queen Alexandra, to McGill University's prestigious Royal Victoria College for women in Montréal. While the designer could not attend the ceremony herself, Mary Seton Watts's ward and daughter Lilian Chapman went on her behalf to Montréal.[3]

Rather than viewing this "Canadian banner" as an outlier in a creative life, this chapter is an attempt to mobilize Mary Seton Watts's needlework for what it may reveal about the role of education in the settlement of Canada at this time. The designer's own aspirations from the imperial center, as well as those of government decision-makers, philanthropists, and educational institutions may be understood as "stitched" into the banner Our Lady of the Snows. This chapter maps the making of this needlework banner—from its inception within the creative practice and voluntary social reform work of its designer Mary Seton Watts, through its role within the imperial politics of education and settlement envisioned by Canada's Governor General Lord Grey, to its reception at an elite educational institution in Montréal, McGill University. To do so, I take feminist scholar Liz Stanley's kaleidoscopic approach to create a cultural biography of the banner that explores its "complexity and mosaic patterning" from different angles and perspectives, where "each time you look you see something different."[4]

From this microhistory of a banner and Mary Seton Watts's needlework practice, broader concerns emerge.[5] These are knit together here in order to consider how the cultural work of designing, making, and gifting this elaborate banner may be seen as part of the same impulse in nineteenth-century Britain toward social welfare, colonial settlement, imperial citizenship, and belonging that underwrote London's "child savers" movement and its child migration schemes. I propose these are two strands of the same, much larger imperial project of developing citizens of empire. My goal is to lend new meaning and continued relevance to the banners by pointing to these broader concerns for citizenship, education, and settlement shared between center and periphery of empire, and embedded within Mary Seton Watts's *Our Lady of the Snows*.

Material Belonging

Currently on display in a hallway of the Royal Victoria College, *Our Lady of the Snows* includes an angelic needleworked figure, with elaborate goldwork and delicate appliqué of pearl, crystal, garnet, and aquamarine (Plate 7.2). The complex and subtle textural effects of the banner are enhanced by its intricate design, delicate appliqué, and detailed needlework. In her diary of 1902, Mary Seton Watts mentions "doing her needlework," suggesting she might have worked on the two banners for Grey herself, although the banners' size (approx. 8.5 × 4 feet), varied materials and techniques, complex design, and quick completion make it unlikely she worked the pieces alone. It is more likely these banners were made by a group of women, perhaps those of the Royal School of Art Needlework (est. 1872), whose founders were known to Mary Seton Watts.[6] Yet the seraph motif of the central figure, worked in silk and velvet applied to a satin ground and embroidered with gold and silver thread, is arguably her signature motif, and appears across many media—most notably, on the interior gesso and exterior terracotta work of the Watts Mortuary Chapel in Compton, Surrey, designed and worked by Mary Seton Watts with her Home Arts and Industries Association (HAIA) initiative, the Compton Potters' Arts Guild.[7]

Mary Seton Watts's personal investment in the banner is clear; as she writes, "I want to put *everything* into the banner design that can possibly be thought out."[8] Yet this "thinking out" of Canada reflected her perception of the country as a northern dominion of imperial Britain, reproducing the "great white North" of Kipling's poem. The poet's stereotyped depiction of a snow-covered wasteland was one the Canadian Government's policies of settlement and education were trying desperately to dispel.[9] Indeed, Kipling's perception of Canada and his views on British imperial policy there made it an interesting design source for a banner presented to the first women's college at a Canadian university. Kipling, believing himself a "responsible imperialist," sought to substantiate British imperial duty and validate its "civilising mission" in the colonies.[10] Yet the poet's expansive nationalism meant love of one's country included an enthusiastic affection for the entire British Empire, what historians have called "Greater Britain." Similarly, an early account of Lord Grey's life in Canada explained how his "imperial idealism" had led to the commission of a "series of silken banners," of which *Our Lady of the Snows* was the first to be completed, designed to "hang in colleges and schools of the country, proclaiming the mission of the British Empire."[11]

Using the arts to promote this sense of imperial belonging and expansive nationalism, Grey explained that these banners were most beneficial for "making an impression upon the mind of the rising generation."[12] Canadian craft historian Jennifer Salahub explains that Grey was a "staunch imperialist whose term of office was marked by numerous projects intended to shape Canadian identity within the framework of empire."[13] In a letter of 1945, Lord Grey's son explains that while in Canada his father was continually "trying to get Canadian Schools to look on themselves as part of the Empire, [to make] all schools Imperial Minded with such slogans as 'Ottawa/Winnipeg/Calgary/Montreal is my home and Empire my Country.'"[14] Kipling and Grey's formulation of empire marks a shift toward what Australian scholars Helen Gilbert and Chris Tifflin refer to as a humane or benevolent notion of empire: "a conception that acts not for itself but for the controlled, and a notion of dominance that is not oppressive but libertarian."[15] Benevolence in this context encompasses philanthropy as well as forms of public, municipal, and humanitarian responsibility across Greater Britain.

In her catalogue *Raise the Banners High*, curator Helen Clark claims that banners, such as those presented by Grey to Canadian institutions, "speak to us of history and tradition, of theatre and spectacle; of causes that have been won and those still to be fought for; of optimism and a sense of expectation; of a world to win."[16] In this instance, the "world to win" was Canada and education was central to its settlement and colonization. Thus, within a broad consideration of the role of education in the settlement of the dominion of Canada, Lord Grey's gift of Mary Seton Watts's *Our Lady of the Snows* evokes the spectacle and expectation of empire. Of particular interest is the context for women's higher education at the Royal Victoria College, where *Our Lady of the Snows* has been hanging for over a century in the hope of inspiring and reminding its viewers, Grey's "rising generations," of their duties as citizens of empire.

Our Lady of the Snows was presented as a gift to the College in the same year that McGill University conferred an honorary degree on Rudyard Kipling. The honor was presented to him by Lord Grey during Convocation and would have been bestowed in the large Assembly Hall of the Royal Victoria College, under Watts's hanging banner which had pride of place.[17] These close social connections have been traced by Shurlee Swain in her transnational history of child welfare where she contends reformers and politicians in the colonies moved in the same familial and social circles making change possible in ways that would take far longer in the metropole.[18]

McGill University's Royal Victoria College, for instance, was a purpose-built women's residential college opened in Montréal, Quebec, Canada in 1899, paid for by Lord Strathcona as a gift to the University. The central role and prestigious urban location of the College, at the juncture of Union and Sherbrooke Streets, coupled with its status as collective housing and an educational space for women, signaled elegance and prominence, convenience, and connectedness. The women of Montréal's English-speaking middle class had been welcomed as students at the university since 1884.[19] Architectural historians have suggested this college was built to segregate women students within the University setting, consolidating and gendering their institutional spaces.[20] Yet the Assembly Hall in the women's building kept a steady flow of visitors streaming into the college, for it was the largest gathering space at the University. The Hall regularly served as the site of the University's most ceremonious occasions, including Convocation, at which point the Royal Victoria College became the center of the University.[21]

While conjuring images of femininity and social class in its needlework and precious materials as well as location, *Our Lady of the Snows,* in its title and design, offers a political stance taken to the settler colonial society to which it was gifted. To understand fully how this stance is layered within this exquisite banner, I look to Mary Seton Watts's earlier philanthropy as an active social worker in London's east end.

Voluntary Social Action

By the late-nineteenth century, modern industrial nations realized that they could no longer leave the well-being of the individual to the laissez-faire market mechanisms which had presumably been responsible for Britain's earlier economic success. The importance of gender in the history of philanthropy and the role women played in the development of local and national social-welfare institutions at this time is documented in scholarship across the arts, history, and politics.[22] Middle-class women were not only practitioners of philanthropy, according to historian Sarah Richardson, they also made a critical contribution to the intellectual arguments that prompted and sustained such work. Philanthropy and benevolence, then, should be understood as more than a strategy for middle-class women to participate in public affairs, and rather as one of the ways they *shaped* these affairs too.[23] Women also played a significant role within transnational manifestations of cultural philanthropy, education, and social welfare as these were deployed throughout the "commonwealth" as humanitarian efforts in support of the idea of a "benevolent empire" of Greater Britain.

One such initiative was the Cottage Arts Association founded in 1884 by Irish-born Eglantyne Jebb and renamed the more comprehensive Home Arts and Industries Association (HAIA) in 1885. The primary purpose of this Association was to cast a network of organized philanthropic craft education throughout the English countryside to sustain economic development in rural areas. Headquartered in London's east end, the HAIA was propelled forward by a combination of arts and crafts socialism, and the concern among cultivated classes to encourage the "improvement" of working classes.[24] As a social worker in East London at this time, Mary Seton Watts taught an evening class in clay modelling to "shoeblacks" (mainly young boys shining shoes on the city's streets) at the newly opened Toynbee Hall (1884). This was among the first university settlements to offer education and social welfare services in the poor Whitechapel district, and was organized by reformers Samuel and Henrietta Barnett. Founded with the goal of facilitating "close relationships between settlement workers and neighborhood residents," Toynbee Hall created a vast educational network of lectures, classes, clubs, organizations, and projects.[25]

Through this voluntary social work, Mary Seton Watts met Jebb and within two years of starting her work in Whitechapel had been unanimously elected to the HAIA Council headquartered there (by 1886) and asked to serve on its design committee. Through her work with both Toynbee Hall and the HAIA

Council, Watts gained a realistic understanding of the finances involved in running a craft workshop, and received a broad exposure to current design innovations and theories, as well as developments in approaches to social welfare. All of this helped prepare her to run a branch of the Association in rural Compton where she and her husband were living by 1890. The most substantial project she undertook in Compton was the Watts Mortuary Chapel; this emerged from evening classes in clay modelling taught in her home to upwards of forty regular adult students. That Mary Seton Watts was inspired by Jebb is clear from her dedication of the Chapel to Jebb in her book *The Word in the Pattern* (1904), which details the design symbolism and lists all the craftworkers involved in the Chapel build.[26]

Both the Toynbee Hall settlement and the central council of the HAIA were part of an explosion of voluntary social welfare initiatives in the 1880s emanating from London's east end, intended to benefit poor working families, and whose reach extended across the Empire. Within this context, a generation of women discovered that voluntary work and social action could be a way of expressing profound personal convictions, talent, and intelligence, and of embracing charity and politics as methods of social criticism and social reform.[27] The evening classes in Whitechapel and later in Compton, and the work on the Chapel or at the pottery, offered alternative educational routes for those unable to easily access the education system and labor market, notably women of the middle classes and those people on low incomes. Children were also frequently the targets of these supplementary educational opportunities. British craft historian Stephen Knott claims the evening class is one of the most important structures to shape twentieth-century craft, contributing to the development of a more craft-aware social consciousness, primarily through skill mobility, that is, the ability to add skills learned at evening classes to those already learned through one's primary occupation.[28] The evening classes taught by settlement and HAIA men and women left a significant pedagogical and social welfare legacy.

Artisanal Training

Certainly, the social reform circles Mary Seton Watts worked within held education, particularly artisanal education, as central to the success of their voluntary social welfare projects with London's working poor. At a time of intensifying labor unrest in the 1880s, these reformers largely ignored the history of protest by artisans in the 1840s to envision them as "respectable individuals contributing to their communities and strengthening the national and economic order."[29] By offering skilled training to poor youths, these reformers "strove to recapture a preindustrial ideal of self-sufficiency, craftsmanship, and social harmony" in line with many of the design and labor reforms sought by advocates of the HAIA, the arts and crafts movement, and Garden City initiatives.[30] Education was similarly instrumental to other voluntary settlement initiatives concerned for the children of poor families, specifically the "child saving" movement occurring in and around Whitechapel and which included British child migration programs to the colonies.[31] As such, Mary Seton Watts's voluntary social reform work in the 1880s may be set within a larger picture of imperial philanthropy, one which included the "child saving" movement's migration schemes. These "child rescue" workers also included doctors, teachers, social workers, and the police surveilling British working-class children. Indeed, London's most influential children's charities were launched in this period, including Barnardo's.

As part of the wider discourse about achieving the "good life" as imagined by late-nineteenth-century cultural and social reformers, the "child saving" movement's migration programs gained considerable traction at this time among upper-class and aristocratic donors, many of whom also supported the social and cultural reforms of the HAIA, Toynbee Hall, and other settlements.[32] By the 1880s, the implicit goal of many children's institutions was to create an alternative world to the existing culture, which was rife with industrial class conflict. Within children's model villages and settlement workshops, boys and girls trained to become skilled workers who were meant to experience a sense of pride in their work, an identification with artisanal values, and a family-like affection for their social superiors. These qualities were thought to transform "waifs and strays" into recognized individuals and citizens.

Rather than working in isolation, children's charities were part of an ecology of reform which included Poor Law services as well as social settlement and cultural philanthropy and which influenced one another on numerous issues, ranging from architectural design to craft training programs. Within this "mixed economy" of state services, charity, and self-help organizations, Poor Law officers often worked in tandem with private charitable organizations, and both with parents.[33] In her book *Imagined Orphans*, Lydia Murdoch explains how, at their best, relations between parents and these institutions demonstrated cooperation and negotiation in the face of extreme hardship.[34] Yet historian Gordon Lynch's work seeks to understand how these seemingly unimpeachable moral sentiments often *contributed* to suffering while claiming to alleviate it.

British Child Migration Movement: The Child-citizen

Historian Ellen Boucher claims that voluntary campaigns were frequently hierarchical but they could also offer a space for working-class men and women to participate in civil society, to engage in the culture of respectability, and to advocate for the needs of their communities at a time when many remained excluded from active citizenship in Britain.[35] Indeed, one of the most well-known Victorian philanthropists and "child savers," Irish-born Dr. Thomas Barnardo (1845–1905), offered the promise of "the good life" (advocated most famously by arts and crafts reformer and socialist William Morris) to the children of London's working poor through education, skill training, and emigration to the idyllic settings of rural Canada.[36] This Victorian vision of the settler empire opened up new ways of thinking about the potential of poor children, as colonial class structure was seen as more socially fluid than that in Britain.

The "child savers" migration of British children raised awareness of the colonies in the metropolitan center and points to the reciprocal effects of imperialism, demonstrating how the empire influenced British institutions, British class relations, and even British notions of national identity. In the context of building up the nation, the British child migration schemes made sense to their advocates because British colonies were understood as an extension of the borders of "Greater Britain." To move a child from Britain to Canada or Australia, according to Lynch, was therefore a significant physical journey, but the child was still seen as residing within the imagined shared space of the British world.[37] In 1884, Dr. Barnardo's Homes magazine, *Night and Day*, put it this way: "the colonies are not merely possessions but part of England ... we must cease to think that emigrants when they go to the colonies leave England, or are lost to England and ... contemplate the whole Empire together and call it England."[38]

The child migration movement, of which Barnardo was a part (there were many other sending agencies), was at its height in Canada at the time Lord Grey's banners were given to the nation. Migration and resettlement in Canada were viewed by many as initially holding out the promise of a better life through education and agrarian labor for Britain's "waifs and strays," the children of those same working poor offered reskilling at settlements like Toynbee Hall by voluntary social workers, perhaps even the "shoeblacks" taught by Mary Seton Watts. Similarly, the ideals of imperial Britishness found institutional expression in the training and educational programs provided to child migrants in London, prior to their journey from center to periphery of empire and were touted as cementing the foundations of empire for generations to come (Figure 7.1). This

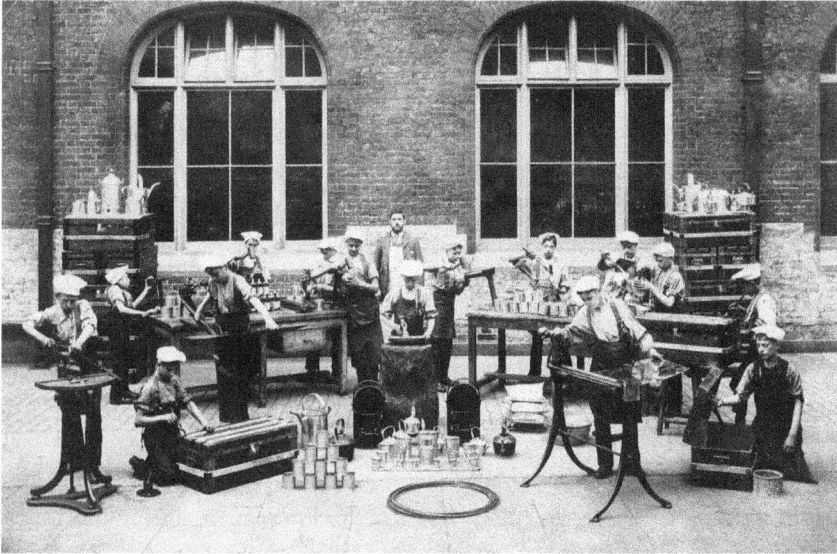

Figure 7.1 Children at work in the Tinsmith's Shop of Barnardo's Stepney Home, *c.* 1910. © Barnardo's Archive [Arc2001].

ideal of the artisan as a model working-class citizen remained important into the early-twentieth century.[39]

Indeed, welfare officials and reformers, like Thomas Barnardo, initially conceived of their institutions primarily as professional training centers. Lynch claims public advocacy for these schemes was most commonly made on the basis of moral grounds such as alleviating the suffering of needy children, rescuing them from corruption, and building up a better nation or empire. In practice, however, institutional training was much more a process of cooperation and bargaining among parents, children, and welfare officials. These judgements about morality were rarely "made with a strong appreciation of the affectional bonds that *did* exist between the children and parents undergoing difficult circumstance."[40] Structural pressures placed severe strains on interpersonal relations: overcrowded housing, unemployment, and the struggle for financial survival made the care of children much harder. The failure of welfare systems to provide support to enable families to maintain care of their children within the home, along with legislative failures on slum housing, created conditions that drew humanitarian laments and philanthropic action. Parents turned to public and private institutions partly because they provided professional and educational instruction for children.[41] This situation existed in rural Compton as well where as many as eighty children attended Mary Seton Watts's clay modelling classes held on Saturday mornings.[42]

The British child migration schemes were seen as practical attempts to help children deemed to be "deprived of a normal family life" through poverty, parental ill-health or death, or family breakdown. These social reform workers and supporters represented "child saving" or "child rescue" as removing children from the perceived moral dangers of corrupting family environments. They argued that in Canada and the other colonies, children would flourish not just emotionally and materially, but in personal, civic, and spiritual virtues as well. The reception in Canada was not always welcoming, yet criticism was rebutted by arguments about the moral importance of the work and the rectitude of those involved in it.[43]

Thomas Barnardo took great interest in children living in destitute areas of urban Britain, opening his first residential "Home" for destitute boys in 1870 at Stepney causeway in east London (which combined a residence with school and workshop) and establishing a mass child migration scheme during the 1880s, which continued long after his death.[44] According to social historian Seth Koven, the array of child rescue institutions, vocational training workshops, and child migrant programs laid the foundations for the philanthropic empire of the charity known simply as Barnardo's in the century after his death and currently one of the largest charitable organizations in Britain.[45]

Child migration schemes like that of Barnardo and other metropolitan reformers were presented as a vision of mutual development: of needy children made whole and the settler empire fulfilled. Underscoring British child migration was "an emphasis on the settler empire as a redemptive space for these child-citizens."[46] Though hard to imagine now, in an era of growing concern that chronic, industrial poverty was stifling the potential of thousands of British children, the vision of a more wholesome life to be found in the farmlands of Greater Britain appealed widely, from the elevated tier of elite reformers to the most struggling of poor parents. In their *Child, Nation, Race and Empire: Child Rescue Discourse, England, Canada and Australia, 1850–1915*, Swain and Hillel suggest that the image of the lonely, abandoned, or at risk child was constructed upon a denial or victimization of the family and kin who, they contend, if properly supported, were most likely to ensure the child's safety. And, it was this image, one used masterfully by Barnardo, that supported the "naturalisation of child removal" which seeped into discourses of child rescue and subsequent institutional practices of child welfare throughout empire.[47]

Thus, Britain had already developed practices for dealing with children in need of "social discipline" and these practices—separation and institutionalization—laid the basis for colonial provision. In its colonies, authorities initially borrowed from British models. This process of cultural borrowing continued throughout the nineteenth century with charitable organizations in the dominions replicating many British philanthropic practices and colonial legislatures following the shifting British trends in child-welfare law which arose out of the child-rescue movement. This process of cultural transmission continued well into the twentieth century.[48]

The purportedly benevolent movement of thousands of children from metropole to periphery of empire reveals much about the parallel movement of philanthropic social and educational ideals espoused by the social workers and "child savers" of London's east end to colonial dominions. Mary Seton Watts's philanthropy, when viewed through this transnational lens, is a productive point of entry from which to explore educational opportunities available in Canada. It may also offer insight into the ways education was, as Grey believed, instrumental in developing imperial subjects, "the children of Canada" to whom Mary Seton Watts dedicated her banner (Figure 7.2). The voluntary social reform ethos that travelled with these British child migrants is also expressed in the gift of the silken embroidered banner hanging in McGill University.

Figure 7.2 "Group of boys," British Home Children at receiving home in Ontario, Canada. National Library and Archives of Canada. [C-034837]. In the public domain.

Conclusion

On display, hanging within a complex site of women's university education in Canada, Mary Seton Watts's activist and philanthropic social reform views of home and empire may be understood as stitched into her gift to the Royal Victoria College. Through a recognition and unearthing of seemingly invisible colonial narratives embedded within the banner designed to educate the "children of Canada," I think about this beautifully shimmering and complex material object as participating in the history of settler colonialism—a history which, in Canada, includes, among others, the royal gift of banners to Canadian schools and universities by a Governor General, the educational opportunities and institutions for middle-class English-speaking women, the migration of thousands of British children indentured to farmers to be educated and trained as productive farm laborers and good citizens in Canada.[49] I acknowledge the privilege this history affords me and seek to use it as a catalyst for change—settlement, migration, child welfare and education, historical truth and reconciliation, are all pressing discussions in Canada deserving of sustained critical enquiry and reflection in order to posit ways forward toward a future Canada.

And so, in light of this, I have begun to map the making of this banner from its inception within Mary Seton Watts's creative practice and voluntary social reform work, through its role within the imperial politics of education and settlement envisioned by Grey, to its reception at an elite educational institution in Canada. I turn to the embroidered banner as way of unravelling the histories entwined within this gift. This chapter is *one* attempt to think through, to unsettle, assumptions about Canada and to ask: What "silent sermon" (to quote Grey) might Mary Seton Watts's banner "impress upon the character" of those young women, and now men, passing it in the halls of Royal Victoria College at one of Canada's most prestigious universities? What duties and responsibilities do they imagine for themselves as citizens of this settler nation?

Part Three

Recovering Identity: Locating the Self Through Needlework

"Je me declare Dieu-Mère, Femme Créateur": Johanna Wintsch's Needlework at the Swiss Psychiatric Asylums Burghölzli and Rheinau, 1922–1925

Sabine Wieber

The 54th Venice Biennale "ILLUMI*nations*" (4 June to 27 November 2011) was curated by the Swiss art historian Bice Curiger, who embraced a bold vision for this iconic exhibition and juxtaposed contemporary art with historical works. Curiger intended for this exchange to uncover art's potential to reshape contemporary culture and question rigid national boundaries.[1] Upon entering the Giardini's Central Pavilion, for example, visitors first encountered three large canvases by the Venetian Mannerist painter Jacobo Tintoretto (1518/9–1594) before they were exposed to any modern art. This curatorial strategy continued throughout the Central Pavilion and included a beautiful room dedicated to text-based works by the contemporary artists Karl Holmqvist and Guy de Cointet (1934–1983) that were hung alongside seven embroideries by the early-twentieth-century "outsider artist" Johanna Natalie Wintsch (1871–1944).

Curiger's selection for this space was intriguing, not least because it presented three individuals who worked across very different, and historically disconnected, institutional contexts and media. Holmqvist and Cointet are post-conceptual artists with firm roots in the contemporary art world. Wintsch, on the other hand, had no artistic training and made her embroideries while confined at two Swiss mental asylums during the early 1920s. This fascinating dialogue between "old and new" introduced a surprising discovery from art history's dusty vaults—the work of Johanna Wintsch—and generated new meanings for all three artists' work. In Wintsch's case, Curiger lifted her beautiful embroideries out of their typical exhibition contexts of outsider art or textile history and encouraged viewers to reconsider preconceived notions of aesthetic merit and/or critical potential.

Wintsch's semi-abstract embroideries include letters and words that bleed into fantastical representations of structures, animals and sea-life, arabesques and geometric patterns (Figure 8.1). Her embroideries are striking in terms of their visual composition because they feature a lot of "empty" space. Her geometric shapes and floral motifs are clearly delineated, but they are rarely filled with stitch work. Wintsch liked to work with silk thread (four and two strands) and used either cotton or linen fabric as her support. Her embroideries are relatively intimate in scale because she used standard-sized canvases intended for more conventional needlework such as samplers (31 × 31 cm). Wintsch occasionally conceived her more ambitious pictorial programs such as *Aragon—RE/ICH* (Plate 8.1) across two supports, but she did not sew them together to form a single picture space.

Wintsch preferred primary colors and achieved gorgeous tonal variations by carefully aligning and/or juxtaposing individual threads. Her embroidery

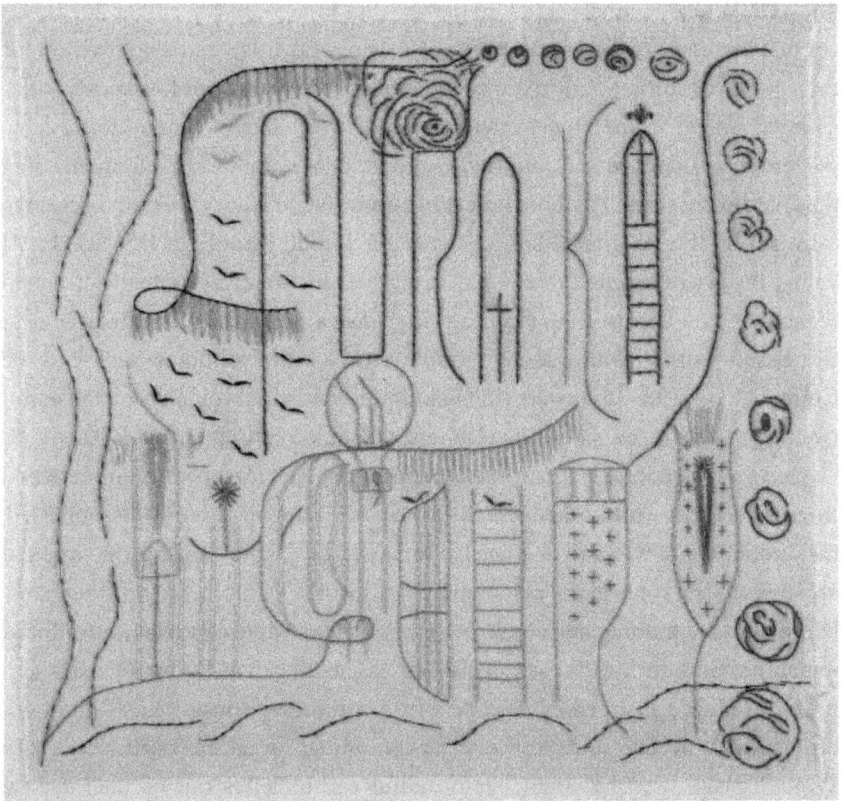

Figure 8.1 Johanna Natalie Wintsch, *Dr. Gehry,* 1923. Silk on cotton, 31 × 31 cm. Prinzhorn Collection, Heidelberg, Inv. Nr. 6039–2.

techniques are sophisticated and evidence a high degree of competence. As most women of her class and generation, Wintsch acquired her needlework skills in school where *Handarbeiten* (handicraft) formed an essential part of the curriculum for young girls and introduced pupils to the whole gamut of textile work from embroidery and sewing to knitting, lacework, and crochet.[2] A total of thirty embroideries by Johanna Wintsch are currently in public collections.[3] They were all produced during her three-year stay at two separate mental asylums on the outskirts of Zurich, Switzerland: The University of Zurich's Psychiatric Clinic Burghölzli and the Mental Asylum Rheinau. After her release in 1925, Wintsch earned a living as an embroidery teacher, but none of her later work survives.

Crafting in the Asylum

Wintsch dedicated several embroideries to some of her favorite psychiatrists as well as fellow patients at Rheinau. An early piece, for example, spells out the name "Dr GEHRY" in green embroidery thread across the bottom register (Figure 8.1). The letter "R" is shaded with crosses in lilac thread and the letter "Y" metamorphoses into a sea anemone-like creature featuring a vaginal-like opening. Dr. Karl Gehry was Rheinau's deputy medical director during Wintsch's institutionalization and he encouraged his patients to occupy their time with creative endeavors because he advocated the therapeutic potential of keeping busy.[4] Wintsch stitched the word *"Jura"* (Law) above Gehry's name, but she inverted the letter "J." An isolated letter "K" is embroidered in a different color and might refer to Gehry's first name. Wintsch surrounded her enigmatic text with a frame of abstracted roses of varying sizes, waves at the bottom of the canvas, and green blades of grass or seaweed that gently sway in an imagined breeze. Birds in flight are stitched in blue and yellow and carefully delineated fringes form the letters "G" and, possibly, "L." Wintsch's whimsical birds and fringes animate the picture space and direct the viewer's gaze. Wintsch further emphasized the embroidery's wonderful sense of rhythm through her subtle yet powerful application of color and delicate yet confident stitch work.

Wintsch's embroideries were well-suited for Curiger's room at the Biennale because their formal qualities could easily be subsumed into an art historical discourse of modernism. But Wintsch's iconography was deeply personal and cannot be divorced from her experience as a patient in a psychiatric asylum. This chapter departs from Curiger's curatorial narrative of "outsider art" that celebrated the unadulterated creative potential of the untrained "artist" working outside of the art world's institutional framework. What follows instead, is a narrative that attempts to recover Wintsch's historical agency in what can only be described as severely confined circumstances. Viewed from this critical perspective, Wintsch's needlework practice functioned as a means through which she tried to recover a sense of her former (i.e. non-institutionalized) self. Wintsch's completed embroideries thus represent powerful material traces of her tireless efforts to position herself against the institution's confining therapeutic regimes and hierarchies. Put simply, this chapter suggests that Wintsch employed the power of her needle and thread to transgress the asylum's subjugation and carve out a space of her own, one stitch at a time.[5]

Early Signs of Mental Illness and Institutionalization

Johanna Natalie Wintsch was born in Warsaw in 1871. Her parents were from the Swiss village of Illnau (Canton Zurich) but moved to Poland for better employment opportunities. The family returned to Switzerland in 1882 because Johanna's father exhibited symptoms of tertiary syphilis. Sadly, he died at the same mental asylum into which his daughter would be admitted forty years later (Burghölzli). By 1885, Johanna had lost her father and her two older brothers to syphilis. Her mother moved the remaining family to Lausanne where she hoped to find employment as a seamstress. The family finances soon spiraled into a hand-to-mouth existence and Johanna was forced to leave school and subsidize the family income with piano and French lessons.[6] Switzerland was one of central Europe's first countries to allow women to matriculate and Wintsch was keen to attended university.[7] But traditional gender roles condemned her to subsidize her two younger brothers' education instead (both became doctors). The family's challenging financial circumstances were compounded by strenuous interpersonal dynamics. Wintsch's brother later observed that their mother was "very authoritarian and thwarted many of her daughter's ambitions, which compelled [Johanna] to keep to herself a lot."[8] When Wintsch wanted to marry a blind suitor, for example, her mother forbade the union in no uncertain terms: "you will birth idiots and blind children with this blind man."[9]

Medical records indicate that Wintsch had her first psychotic episode in 1917 (age 46) when she heard voices and accused her mother of being the devil.[10] Her behavior became increasingly irrational and triggered Wintsch's admission into the Psychiatric Hospital Cery on the outskirts of Lausanne the same year.

Wintsch spent several months at Cery before she was released into "family care" (*Familienpflege*) at a local farm. Wintsch returned home in 1922 but soon exhibited mania and religious delusions. This led to her second institutionalization in October of that year.[11] Wintsch was admitted into the University of Zurich's psychiatric clinic Burghölzli, which was one of Europe's first hospitals to embrace Sigmund Freud's (1856–1939) psychoanalysis. Here, Wintsch was diagnosed with paranoid schizophrenia by Paul Eugen Bleuler (1857–1939) who was an important figure in the history of psychiatry because he coined the term schizophrenia in 1911.[12] The symptoms described in her patient records align with our current clinical picture of this mental disorder, namely, paranoid delusions accompanied by disturbances of perception, such as delusions of persecution, exalted birth or a special mission; hallucinatory voices giving commands; whistling, humming, laughing; and hallucinations of sexual or other bodily sensations.[13] Paranoid schizophrenia can be episodic (with partial or complete remissions) or chronic. Wintsch probably fell into the first category because she was not readmitted into a psychiatric asylum until 1944 where she died that year at the age of 73.[14]

Burghhölzli and Rheinau (1922–1925)

Wintsch arrived at Burghölzli with few worldly possessions, but she brought with her an ornately embroidered nightdress. This caught the attention of her doctors and prompted Wintsch's presentation before a group of clinicians at the University of Zurich.[15] It is not known if Wintsch wore the nightdress or brought it as an example of her needlework. Either way, she was immensely proud of her achievement and launched into a lengthy explanation of her embroidered signs and symbols. Bleuler, whom Wintsch would soon come to detest, dismissed her needlework: "in terms of content and form [they were] entirely divorced from experience-based thinking."[16] But for Wintsch, her embroideries presented a series of complex codes that only she could unlock, and she was incensed at Bleuler's arrogance and ignorance.[17] This confrontation did not bode well for Wintsch's future within the regimented structure of a psychiatric unit, and she would spend only a short time at Burghölzli. Ultimately, the clinic was not set up for long-term patients and Wintsch's schizophrenia diagnosis essentially designated her as "incurable."

Wintsch was soon moved to Burghölzli's "sister" institution, the "Cantonal Psychiatric and Care Asylum Rheinau" (*Kantonale Irren- und Versorgungsanstalt*

Rheinau) with space for up to 1000 patients. Rheinau was designed as a custodial asylum in the business of looking after chronic patients with little hope for a cure. It is worth noting that in the early 1920s, psychopharmacology was in its infancy and the symptoms of serious mental illness were managed through a series of "mechanical" interventions, including bedrest, bath-therapy, sedation, isolation, physical restraint, and work therapy.[18] Wintsch must have been aware of Rheinau's reputation as a last-stop facility because her patient file recorded that "she created a scene when she was supposed to get into the car to Rheinau and [declared] she was God and curses this place."[19]

Unsurprisingly, Wintsch's volatile conduct persisted at Rheinau. She perpetually struggled with the constraints imposed upon her by the asylum's strict daily regimes and her many battles are well documented in her patient records.[20] Patients were expected to submit to the asylum's rigorous control of their every movement from sunrise to sunset. The asylum's forcefully imposed regulations did not sit well with Wintsch, who, despite living with a dominant mother and in constant worry over finances, had experienced a certain autonomy before her first psychotic episodes in 1917. Wintsch was unmarried and acted as her family's head of household in terms of domestic matters. Her pre-institutional habitus combined with her symptoms of paranoid schizophrenia posed serious challenges to Wintsch's integration into Rheinau's rigid institutional regime.

An Unruly Patient

One of the earliest entries in her Rheinau patient file described her as prone to "grandiose gestures . . . and with a loud and excited manner of speaking."[21] It goes on to describe that Wintsch regularly provoked confrontations with wardens and nurses, whom she accused of gratuitous violence towards other patients. In a letter of complaint deposited in her patient file, Wintsch recalled the following episode at Burghölzli: "I ask you, Director Bleuler, to not be so harsh with this fragile, old lady, Anna S. She told me . . . 'He hit me on the stomach—I find this misguided.' The angels like Anna S., they don't scream with indignation. They only blush."[22] Wintsch saw Bleuler as "Satan."[23] Fellow patients and even treating physicians were defenseless children and angels or subjects of adoration respectively.[24]

Wintsch's written complaints were regularly dismissed as unruly behavior and disappeared into her patient file rather than being forwarded to their intended recipients. She was labelled as errant (*störend*), fretful (*unruhig*), abrasive (*abweisend*), petulant (*bockig*), demanding (*anspruchsvoll*), and bad-tempered (*zänkisch*).[25] In other words, she was seen to disrupt virtually every single normative behavior expected of a woman of her age and class.[26] The German language terms employed by psychiatrists to describe Wintsch's behavior patterns signal deeply troubling gender biases rife in early-twentieth-century psychiatry. These anxieties over "aberrant female behavior" can be traced back to early modern witch trials, but they also had more historically specific roots in late-nineteenth-century capitalism and modernity.[27]

Needlework and Discipline

For asylum authorities, Wintsch's needlework represented a welcome means to manage a patient who was labelled as unstable and troublesome. Wintsch was calm and focused whilst embroidering even if she tended to get overly excited when showing off her latest efforts. Wintsch received materials from visiting family members as well as the asylum's sewing workshop. This was a privilege because patients often had to make do with whatever materials they could find for their creative endeavors, including their own bed linens, their hair, twigs, etc. Since doctors viewed Wintsch's needlework practice as part of her therapeutic regime, she was encouraged and supported in her endeavors. Her needlework thus formed part of "work therapy"—a precursor of today's occupational therapy—and accommodated a wide range of activities from needlework to agricultural labor. Psychiatric discourse of the day promoted these activities as therapy, but they were equally driven by the asylum's economics.[28] Aside from their economic benefits, these measures were primarily designed to tire patients and make them more amenable to institutional control.

It is impossible to consider these psychiatric discourses and institutional realities without acknowledging Michel Foucault's paradigm-shifting analysis on modern "disciplinary" society.[29] Foucault's astute critique of the furtive collusions of knowledge and power forced medical historians to dismantle the rhetoric of early-twentieth-century psychiatric discourse of institutional reform and expose mental asylums as perpetual sites of control and oppression. Rheinau, for example, cultivated a public image of a progressive asylum that strove to accommodate patients in light-filled interiors surrounded by generous parklands and implemented the latest psychiatric knowledge to care for their long-term patients. But the day-to-day realities of managing an overcrowded institution with insufficient public funds engendered a very different experience for its patients and staff.

Patient Experience

Foucault's defiantly anti-authoritarian scrutiny of the history of madness "from above" has not been without criticism. Buoyed by the social sciences' "cultural turn," medical historians began to look at ways in which patient experiences of the asylum's disciplinary structure and regimes could be reconstituted.[30] Roy Porter's iconic essay "The Patient's View: Doing Medical History from Below" (1985), advocated a patient-centered "history of healing" that shifted medical history's perspective from institutional narratives and doctors' accounts towards hitherto neglected archival material such as patient files.[31] Even though patient files were compiled and used by the asylum's administrative and medical branches, they reveal so much more than a patient's disease pattern and symptoms. Fourteen of Wintsch's embroideries, for example, were hidden in her patient files until 2008.[32] Patient files therefore offer rich archival depositories of diverse material (letters, biographies, texts, drawings, artefacts, photographs, textiles, etc., in addition to the extensive medical documentation and surveillance) that document every minute detail of a patient's day-to-day life, and also offer invaluable insights into lived experience when read "against the grain."[33]

Focusing on patient experience in no way negates the fact that Rheinau operated a suppressive regime of control and surveillance that shaped Wintsch's life on all levels. But if the "cultural turn" has taught us anything, then it is the insight that historical subjects are never passive, even if their agency has been curtailed by circumstances beyond their control, as was the case for Wintsch through mental illness and institutionalization. The historian and cultural theorist Michel de Certeau convincingly argued that historical actors continually appropriated society's infrastructures of discipline and control. Contrary to Foucault, he suggested an open-ended negotiation between normative strategies and subversive practices, which he called tactics:

> In the technocratically constructed, written, and functionalised spaces in which the consumers [in this case, patients] move about, their trajectories form unforeseeable sentences, partly unreadable paths across space. Although they are composed with the vocabularies of established language ... and although they remain subordinate to the prescribed syntactical forms (temporal modes of

schedules, paradigmatic orders of spaces, etc.), the trajectories trace out the ruses of other interests and desires that are neither determined nor captured by the system in which they develop.[34]

Wintsch's needlework can be viewed as materializing precisely this kind of a trajectory. On a most basic level, the actual making of embroideries offered Wintsch mental, and maybe even physical, reprieve from the tightly controlled regimes of the asylum. During these hours of complete absorption in her task at hand, Wintsch escaped the asylum's habitus and established a fragile link to her daily life as she knew it before Rheinau. Wintsch's creative practice could set this abscondment in motion because needle- and textile work had been part of her entire life. She grew up in a family whose income was derived from textile work and she taught embroidery as an adult. Needlework was deeply familiar and comforting to Wintsch and her embroideries became a powerful material connection to her old life. The sharpness of her needle, the tactile qualities of her silk threads and the repetitive motion of moving the thread in and out of the linen or cotton canvas directly tapped into Wintsch's kinetic and sensory memories.

Material Agency

Wintsch produced at least twenty of her thirty known embroideries at Rheinau. This is a remarkable achievement given their complex iconographies and painstaking techniques. As previously mentioned, she was proud of her work and readily showed it to fellow patients and examining psychiatrists.[35] She was equally keen to explain her embroideries' iconography and one of her primary care psychiatrists, the young *Oberarzt* Dr. O. Pfister (1899–1982), dutifully recorded her often convoluted and long-winded interpretations in her patient file.[36] In 1923, Wintsch produced an embroidery for a fellow patient named Albertine Schenk entitled "*L'ange unique/TITUS*" (Plate 8.2). Schenk's name is prominently stitched into the two outer leaves of a lotus-like flower in the center of this piece. This central image is surrounded by the same stylized roses seen in her Dr. Gehry embroidery (Figure 8.1). The letters for spelling out "*L'ange unique/ TITUS*" are much more difficult to decipher because Wintsch used Greek symbols and mirror images. Why Wintsch referred to Titus, the Roman Emperor notorious for conquering Jerusalem, remains unclear, but calling Schenk a "unique angel" corroborates Wintsch's aforementioned perception of fellow patients as innocent victims. Pfister took Wintsch's needlework seriously from the get-go and eventually argued for her release based on her "intensive visual occupation and engagement with the content of her hallucinations."[37] This observation reveals that Pfister viewed Wintsch's needlework as a curative activity rather than an exclusively occupational one.

Against all odds, Wintsch was released into the care of her younger brother Jean-François in 1925.[38] Pfister's persistent lobbying on behalf of Wintsch had finally paid off. He strongly believed that Wintsch's needlework provided a tangible sphere of action (*Handlungsraum*) that helped her to articulate, materialize, and eventually discard her delusions. However, Wintsch herself played a crucial part in her release because she cunningly deployed her finished embroideries to favorably position herself in relation to Rheinau's institutional structures and hierarchies. Wintsch dedicated and gifted several pieces to specific doctors (Dr. Gehry, Dr. Pfister), and endeavored to ingratiate herself with these young psychiatrists. Wintsch's use of material culture to declare her effusive affection for certain individuals might be considered a symptom of her mental illness, but she had been in the system for long enough to know that her examining psychiatrists were ultimately responsible for making recommendations about her socio-medical progress. Wintsch recognized that Rheinau was a care asylum for incurable patients, but she never gave up petitioning for her release— in words and stitches. Viewed from this perspective, Wintsch used her embroideries to not only configure a rich inner life, but to simultaneously orchestrate her complicated relationships with doctors, nurses, and fellow patients to her advantage. Wintsch deployed the "power of the needle"[39] to favorably position herself within the mental asylum's hierarchies and to appropriate institutional protocol to her advantage. This must be viewed as a shrewdly conceived tactic in de Certeau's sense of the word.

Needlework as Solace

Aragon—RE/ICH (Plate 8.1) is one of Wintsch's most ambitious and well-known embroideries. Its iconography is complex and unfolds over two separate, but visually linked, linen canvases. Wintsch often incorporated the date of completion into her visual programs and, in this instance, a church bell rings in 1 November 1923. The two sides of her image are linked by a rainbow that emanates orange and yellow flames and connects two bird or angel wings striated with pulsating green veins. What might initially be read as a heart shape directly underneath the rainbow turns into the abstracted body of a bird with large vacant eyes and two superimposed feet with talons. Two words are faintly stitched into the heart-cum-bird shape: "Jesus" on the left and "Maria" on the right. Drops of blood pour out of Maria's half of the heart, which might signal Wintsch's identification with this biblical figure. The night is illuminated by dark blue stars and a crescent moon. The landscape over which this mythical bird/angel creature hovers is abstracted but includes many of Wintsch's typical motifs such as a church spire morphing into rockets, an all-seeing eye, flowers (in this instance forget-me-nots rather than roses), and playful iterations of plant and sea life.

As ever, Wintsch's needlework technique is meticulous and her silk thread matches the primary colors she liked to use. Wintsch stitched the title "Aragon" into a simplified mandala (the spiritual symbol in Hinduism and Buddhism for the universe) and placed it directly above a page of sheet music. The music sheet's clef mutates into a cat's tail that draws life-force from a body of water, potentially a reference to the wetlands of the river Rhine on whose shores the Rheinau asylum was located. Lastly, the name Octave Samuel Rochat is prominently stitched into two red circles surrounded and filled by forget-me-nots. Rochat regularly appears in Wintsch's needlework albeit under different guises: Jehovah, Jesus, Father, God, or simply Octave. Wintsch boldly positioned herself as "dieu-mère, femme créateur"[40] that is the female creative counterpart to Rochat's identity as God/Father. Rochat was a real person with whom Wintsch had a very brief encounter before her institutionalization,[41] but in her embroideries, he becomes the receptacle for many unfulfilled desires.

Wintsch's surviving embroideries offer material traces of one individual's deeply personal journey through several Swiss asylums during a moment in time when the diagnosis of a mental illness heralded a complete rupture of life as she knew it. Wintsch experienced every aspect of her daily routine in the mental asylum as an infringement of her autonomy—from the doctors' invasive medical gazes to her wardens' constant surveillance, as well as her severely restricted freedom of movement. Her institutionalization represented a traumatic break: her world literally shrank, her domestic space was reconfigured, and her agency curtailed. But she was allowed, even encouraged, to continue her needlework practice. Whilst absorbed in the minutiae and regularity of her handicraft, Wintsch was able to block out the asylum's harsh realities and temporarily conjure up a pre-institutional sense of self.

Wintsch's needlework practice offered her a space of solace from the asylum's constant surveillance and control. Her stitching was the only experiential link to her old self and/or her "normal" (i.e., pre-institutional) existence. Textile historians have long argued that needlework offers a "form of rhetoric with the potential to shape identity, form community, and prompt engagement with social action."[42] This certainly holds true for Wintsch's embroidery practice, yet Wintsch's needlework did not actually represent the making of a new self. Instead, it reconstituted a former self that, in Wintsch's case, had been shattered by her first psychotic episode in 1917. It is difficult to support these complex dynamics of subjectivity-formation with concrete evidence but Wintsch's treating psychiatrists undoubtedly believed in the restorative powers of her needlework because she was released in 1925 as "socially healed"[43]— meaning that she exhibited social competence and could be reintegrated into society.

Needlework as Bargaining Chip

Wintsch's needlework not only facilitated her temporary escape from the harsh institutional realities at Rheinau but also intervened in the asylum's disciplinary regimes. As previously mentioned, Wintsch often gave her embroideries away to flatter her treating physicians—most notably Dr. Pfister who was the recipient of fourteen embroideries.[44] The making and gifting of these objects recalibrated Wintsch's position within the institution's tightly patrolled hierarchies. In Arjun Appadurai's words, Wintsch used material culture to define and (re)inscribe socio-medical relations.[45] Since Wintsch was in control of the production and dissemination of her embroideries, she attained agency in an environment where patients were prohibited from making even the most basic decisions (e.g., when and what to eat) whilst enduring the most invasive "treatments" (isolation, sedation, bath-therapy that placed patients into bathtubs for hours and days on end).

Although Wintsch's embroideries emerged from a context of "work therapy" and were thus anchored within the asylum's disciplinary structures, their iconographic programs could not be policed quite as easily. Wintsch used a coded system of symbols and letters that could be dismissed as the ravings of a madwoman. But her iconography also offered a subversive critique of named individuals and the asylum as a whole. The spatial, structural and discursive configuration of the institution configured Wintsch's day-to-day life but these strategies "from above" were met with her tactics "from below," through which she carved out ephemeral moments of agency and maybe even resistance. Wintsch's embroideries offer a captivating material trace of her efforts to reconstitute a sense of self, which the institution tried so desperately to erase, and to position herself favorably in relation to those in immediate positions of power, such as Dr. Pfister.

Hans Prinzhorn and Patient Art

A diagnosis of mental illness represented a huge stigma for the patient and her family in the early-twentieth century. The mentally ill were literally erased from family genealogies and their material traces were discarded. Wintsch's embroideries largely survived these common erasures because asylum authorities considered her needlework worthy to keep instead of returning it to her family after her death. This time period was marked by an unprecedented interest in the creative output of mental patients. Psychiatrists and lay-people alike were fascinated by the material traces—drawings, paintings, writings, collages, needlework, and "ready-mades"—left by these otherwise unseen and unheard members of society. In 1898, for example, an exhibition dedicated to the "Care of the Mentally Ill" (*Irrenpflegeausstellung*) took place in Vienna and featured a large selection of art and handicraft by psychiatric patients from asylums across the Habsburg Empire.[46]

The Vienna exhibition's popular success and positive critical reception encouraged asylum directors and psychiatrists throughout Europe to start collecting objects of artistic value from their respective patient populations. These artefacts initially formed the nucleus of teaching collections and they were primarily valued for their diagnostic and instructional potential more so than for their artistic merit.[47] However, this collecting ethos underwent a major revision in 1919, when the German art historian and psychiatrist Hans Prinzhorn (1886–1933) was tasked with expanding the Heidelberg University's Psychiatric Clinic's small collection of patient artefacts that was started by the prominent German psychiatrist Emil Kraepelin (1856–1926) in 1896.

Prinzhorn asked mental asylums across central Europe for any type of visual and/or material objects made by patients that manifested "expressions of their personal experience."[48] He was fascinated by their outputs because he believed that patients could spontaneously unleash their creative potential without being (self-)censored by social norms, conventions, and inhibitions.[49] As a result of this belief system, he encouraged psychiatrists and asylum directors to collect and foster their patients' creative impulses. His efforts instigated a critical paradigm shift in the history of medicine and art history that engendered a growing valuation of "patient art" and eventually culminated in Jean Dubuffet's "art brut" and today's "outsider art."[50]

Prinzhorn received approximately 5000 artefacts by 450 individual patients (80 percent men, 20 percent women) over the course of only two years (1919–21).[51] They covered a wide range of media and techniques but were often very fragile because, unlike Wintsch, most patients had to make do with everyday materials they could stash away, such as newspapers, fruit-wrappers (exotic fruits such as oranges were always wrapped in wax paper), paper bags, clothing, etc.[52] Prinzhorn's efforts directly impacted the survival of Wintsch's embroideries since Pfister happily sent her embroidered gifts to Heidelberg. Wintsch's needlework was exhibited as early as 1929 when her work was included in a travelling exhibition organized by the Prinzhorn Collection on "Art of the Mentally Ill."[53]

Conclusion

Johanna Natalie Wintsch left a rare archival footprint that includes her enigmatic embroideries as well as her patient records. It is very difficult to connect "patient art" objects with historical personae and it has taken painstaking research by curators and historians to match the two in Wintsch's case.[54] Foucault argued that historical actors only become visible through their encounters with authority because these instances leave a physical trace of an otherwise fleeting existence.[55] This observation holds true for Wintsch. We know her through her needlework, which was only later linked to her patient file. Without this material trace, her patient file would have disappeared into the ether of history alongside thousands of other patient files that currently wile away in archives across the world. Wintsch engaged in needlework all through her life, but the only embroideries come from her years in the asylum. Nothing else survived. Sadly, Wintsch only comes into view because of her encounter with two Swiss mental asylums.

A photograph taken in the early 1920s shows Wintsch busy at work on one of her embroideries. She poses with her ambitious composition *Aragon—RE/ICH* in her lap and an unidentified book in her left hand. She is sitting outdoors on a simple park bench in Rheinau's carefully landscaped institutional grounds. There is no trace of any confinement and none of the mental institution's buildings are in sight. This photograph represents an extraordinary visual record because mental patients were rarely photographed. We might see an occasional identification photo in their admission records, but Wintsch's "in situ" shot is exceptional. The photograph was obviously carefully staged but it speaks volumes about the value that was already ascribed to Wintsch's needlework whilst she was still in the asylum.

The Swiss art historian Katrin Luchsinger recently described the complex deployment of visual and material culture by mental patients as marking an intervention and participation in the institution's course of events (*Zeitgeschehen*).[56] On first encounter, Wintsch's embroideries might be dismissed as the beautiful yet strange manifestations of a fractured mind that might never be fully integrated into gender-specific, socio-cultural norms operating in early-twentieth-century Switzerland. But her embroideries actually offer a rare glimpse into the ways in which a female patient, who had been admitted into a mental asylum against her will and who had been diagnosed with an "incurable" disorder, used her needlework to reclaim a sense of agency and position herself against the asylum's all-encompassing disciplinary regimes one stitch at a time.

Hybrid Language: The Interstitial Stitches of Anna Torma's Embroideries

Anne Koval

The stitching itself must be my language, the first—the cosy one—similar to my Hungarian.

Anna Torma[1]

. . . a space in which to stitch not only a seam, but also a self.

Heather Pristash, Inez Schaechterle, Sue Carter Wood[2]

The Hungarian-Canadian artist Anna Torma creates elaborate, large-scale textile-work that incorporates time-honored techniques such as quilting, appliqué, and embroidery, and uses hand-dyed silks and cotton thread, and a multitude of fabrics (Plate 9.1). She explains: "Technically, I use hand embroidery, this old, time-consuming, well-known textile patterning technique. I am always fascinated by the challenge to fill this medium with contemporary meaning. Working in a large scale, I compose hangings that are rooted in this heritage, but are also equally related to other visual art mediums like painting and drawing."[3] In acknowledging this long history of textile art, Torma sees her practice as "a segment of something larger, as part of the surrounding social fabric."[4] Despite using these traditional approaches, her work resists normative classification and instead occupies an interstitial space—as insider and outsider, contemporary and traditionalist, feminist and post-feminist—all explored within the diverse language of stitchery. The social theorist Homi Bhabha positions the "interstitial" as the overlap and displacement of domains of difference: "These 'in-between' spaces provide the terrain for elaborating strategies of selfhood—singular or communal—that initiate new signs of identity, and innovative sites of collaboration, and contestation, in the act of defining the idea of society itself."[5] Arguably these interstitial spaces have long been a strategy employed by women artists, but in the case of textile artists like Torma, the chosen language of needlework is—by its very nature—interstitial.

As an immigrant to Canada, Torma has confronted the challenges of difference, from the displacement of family to the re-establishment of her professional status as a contemporary artist in a new country. With her husband, the artist Istvan Zsako, and their two young children, Torma fled socialist Hungary for Germany, where they lived as temporary residents before their official emigration to Canada in 1988. As part of a shifting cultural diaspora, Torma's identity is intimately tied to her politics and her history, to the reality of her family's spatial dislocation and relocation, and to migration and resettlement. As African diaspora scholar Carole Boyce Davies writes of this renegotiation of identity with place, "Migration creates the desire for home, which in turn produces the rewriting of home."[6] Notably, in Torma's work, the familial remains an integral aspect of her work and practice where the domestic has served as a continual theme, and personal and family histories become a means for accessing a larger cultural memory.

As the record-keeper of her family and her own life, Torma approaches embroidery in a manner that strongly echoes the notion of "stitching the self," where needlework becomes an assertion of selfhood. As noted by a number of feminist writers, including Elaine Showalter, whose essay "Piecing and Writing" links the process of quilt piecing with the pen, comparing textile production to textual production, a quilt can be viewed as an analogy for women's lives.[7] Lucy Lippard's well-known metaphor of quilting and women's lives further extends this thinking. She states that "Since the new wave of feminist art began around 1970, the quilt has become the prime visual metaphor for women's lives, for women's culture," defining the physical embodiment of quilting as "a diary of touch."[8] Lippard views the quilt not only as loaded metaphor, embodying the "personal as the political," but also as a material diary of women's interrupted lives. Pristash, Schaechterle, and Wood's framing of the needle as a rhetorical tool recalls this earlier feminist thinking about the relationship between writing and textile-based practices. They argue that "the needle has been a vehicle for women's own construction of alternative discourses, discourses with the potential to expand women's discursive worlds and the power they wield over their own lives."[9] In their assertion that needlework is not just an alternative discourse but, rather, *the form* of discourse, they maintain that the needle itself can serve as a "powerful rhetorical tool" to help shape identity and community.[10] In Torma's art, her needle acts as both an artistic "tool," and as a rhetorical device to narrate the complexity of her world, as seen in the diversity and inclusivity of her source-material from children's art, outsider art, Art Brut, folk art, history, Hungarian politics, and popular culture.

In writing this essay I am aware of the writer/quilter's task of sourcing varied and numerous materials, of cutting and piecing them together, and then inscribing/stitching them into a whole. Writing, like quilting, often takes the form of the collective with many voices shaping the final work. As Adrienne Rich suggests, "Re-vision—the act of looking back, of seeing with fresh eyes, of entering an old text from a new critical direction—is for us more than a chapter in cultural history: it is an act of survival."[11] This chapter will revisit earlier feminist writers such as Elaine Showalter, Hélène Cixous, and others, as well as the theories of *l'écriture féminine*, haptic visuality, the aesthetics of excess, and collecting as a female fetish in order to connect Torma to a broader feminist discourse. Drawing on the materiality of the quilt, this chapter is shaped out of a multitude of feminist voices, pieced together to position Torma's needlework as a "space in which to stitch not only a seam, but also a self."[12]

Feminisms

Rozsika Parker's *The Subversive Stitch: Embroidery and the Making of the Feminine* (1984) signaled a new feminist departure for examining the much-neglected history of embroidery. Drawing upon the social history of women, Parker traced how shifting notions of femininity and its construction have been ascribed to artists working within the medium. In her concluding remarks Parker stressed the importance of continuing this inquiry into how contemporary artists use the medium in new and subversive ways: "For women today, the contradictory and complex history of embroidery is important because it reveals that definitions of sexual difference, and the definitions of art and artist so weighted against women, are not fixed."[13] Although Parker's critical examination is largely historical, her message is equally applicable to contemporary women artists, particularly those, who have struggled within patriarchal systems on both political and personal levels, such as Torma.

Born in 1952 socialist Hungary, Torma received her degree in textiles from the Budapest Hungarian University of Applied Arts in 1979. At that time Hungarians had little access to contemporary American and Western European debates on feminism as an artistic and political tool. Instead, many artists were pressured to reflect the values and belief system of the communist state. As Torma recounts:

Hungary was very closed then. We were very much longing to see even a small piece of information from the West. We were tuned into it, and tried to learn what was going on somehow. We managed to go around the official art and somehow sneak out of that little box. For this reason textile was really a good area to be working in.[14]

Under communism textile art was considered a "low art," and, as a result, this medium was somewhat ignored. Consequently, Torma was mentored in an experimental and fertile atmosphere when textile art was undergoing a *quiet* revolution. Margit Szilvitzky, one of Torma's art professors, was critical to the development of her art, as Torma recounts: "She gave us a broader view than official aesthetics of the late socialist state [Hungary]."[15] The art historian Katalin Keserü affirms this cultural dichotomy:

It must be remembered that the textile revolution in Hungary (part of the Central and Eastern European '68 revolution), was, with one or two exceptions, achieved by women. Bound up with the ideas of equal status for free art, for textiles, and indeed for women artists, it started as an avant-garde movement, and later based itself on textile-making, cultural and historical traditions as a female occupation.[16]

The art historian and critic Edit András corroborates this history of avant-garde textile art as it emerged in early 1970's Budapest, stating: "On the one hand it served as a valve, which enabled the unofficial art scene to pulse together with the international scene; on the other hand it provided a platform for experiencing a relative sense of creative freedom of expression, since the field was not as closely monitored as the leading genres, painting and sculpture."[17] András points to Zsuzsa Szenes' *Against the Cold in General* (1978), a multi-colored, knitted guardhouse or "checkpoint," as an example of an early feminist work that materially undermined the era's heavy military presence, and demonstrated how politically subversive the textile revolution could be.

Torma graduated from this creative environment of the Applied Arts program in 1979 to work as a professional textile designer in Budapest. She soon became pregnant with her first son, Balint, and motherhood necessitated that she work from home. Torma speaks of a significant shift in her artistic practice at this time: "At art school I specialized in print design, but after my first son was born I realized I needed to change the way I worked. I remembered how my mother and grandmother did their embroidery when they had bits of spare time. So the ancient patterns suddenly and unexpectedly surfaced."[18] She admits that as a child, and later as a student, she had largely avoided this practice:

In Hungary, when I was a child, the women in almost every household embroidered. They embellished objects for everyday use. I did it reluctantly; I wanted to be out playing. I have very fond memories of the process, though—the mood on a quiet afternoon, usually after very hard work in the fields. It was nice to sit with clean hands and in better clothes, and stitch.[19]

This piecework method embraced by Torma, not only served as a coping mechanism for motherhood, but also radically changed her art.

L'écriture feminine

Significantly, this return to embroidery became part of Torma's maternal inheritance, her chosen artistic dialect. She acknowledges: "I use stitches as my first language of self-expression. I feel fluent and articulate using stitches instead of trying to paint or draw. The stitching itself must be my language, the first—the cosy one—similar to my Hungarian."[20] Such embodiment of language, an inherited "mother-tongue" passed down from grandmother to mother, recalls Hélène Cixous's theories on *l'écriture feminine*. For Cixous, "language is itself a bodily function,"[21] and the physicality of embroidery echoes this theory. Cixous's literary concept of "writing the body"—in Torma's hands—becomes an extension of her embroidery, an embodiment of her life.

As Cixous articulates in *The Newly Born Woman*, the feminine writer, "like a mother, looks with the look that recognizes, studies, respects, doesn't take, doesn't claw, but attentively, with gentle relentlessness, contemplates and reads, caresses, bathes and makes the other shine. Brings back to light the life that's been buried, fugitive, made too prudent. *Illuminates it and sings its name.*"[22] Cixous's emphasis on the role of the mother's body in feminine writing can be applied to Torma's diary-like motifs where, as record keeper of her children's words and art, the mother is ever present. The cultural theorist Julia Kristeva further situates this motherly impulse as the "flow of *jouissance* into language" where the semiotic *chora* is bound with the maternal in art.[23] Translated into the language of Torma's silk embroidery, the *chora* becomes the chorus, as she allows her work to sing "the other." Her inclusivity allows for multiple narratives where stitching becomes a physical language of self-expression. Cixous says of the writer (which I redefine here as artist): "She lets the other speak—the language of 1,000 tongues which knows neither enclosure nor death ... Her language does not contain, it carries; it does not hold back, it makes possible."[24] This embodied voice is present in much of Torma's work where she translates and rewrites her political and domestic worlds, painstakingly transcribing the images and words of her children, her husband, of outsider artists, to give them a voice to speak.

In Torma's *Encyclopaedia Domestica* (2012/16), a series on long cotton panels, the accumulation of these many voices, or *chora,* is made tangible in the richly embroidered and appliquéd surfaces. As a veritable encyclopedia of discarded, hand-worked textiles (many made by women), Torma has stitched together these found objects into a narrative that speaks of domestic, folk, and kitschy pop cultures. Kristy Bell, in an essay on Torma, observes, "The connection between Torma and these women of the past is carried by the fabric and by the desire to make something beautiful, so much so that Torma notes there are 'vibrations' in her compositions."[25] The musical analogy of singing "the other" becomes implicit in Torma's practice. This work evolved from earlier pieces with musical titles such as *Blues, Serenade,* and *Rondo,* where she collected the textiles of anonymous amateur artists, alongside photo-transfers of art by her adult artist sons, in an intentional randomness or improvisation that speaks inherently of her inclusivity: a "singing in chorus" of these disparate voices. This attempt to sing "the other" is intrinsic to Torma's art.

Cixous's understanding of *l'écriture féminine* as a means of "writing the body" can be applied to a number of women artists whose work with textiles attest to this bodily inheritance of sewing, in particular the work of Louise Bourgeois and Ann Hamilton. Bourgeois has worked extensively with textiles from her childhood and claims, like Torma, a matrilineal lineage: "When I was growing up, all the women in my house were using needles. I've always had a fascination with the needle, the magic power of the needle. The needle is used to repair damage. It's a claim to forgiveness."[26] For Bourgeois sewing facilitated a form of psychic healing, "I always had the fear of being separated and abandoned. The sewing is my attempt to keep things together and make things whole."[27] Although Torma's use of stitchery is different from Bourgeois—she works largely on flat surfaces with an extensive vocabulary of embroidery and appliqué at her fingertips—she would agree there is a sense as an artist of making whole in her own work.

This bodily link to art is equally intrinsic to Hamilton who claims: "My first hand is my sewing hand. A line of thread drawn up and down through cloth influences how I think about the confluence and rhythms of space and time."[28] Hamilton, like Torma, confesses to this direct line to creativity through sewing. Significantly, all three artists use text in their work, with Bourgeois and Torma employing thread to write their words, whereas Hamilton often uses a more literal text, often sourced from literature. This play of text/textile is most evident in the work of Torma who appropriates her text from a variety of sources including her children's written words, school primers, textbooks, dictionaries, encyclopedias, pedagogical charts, and popular culture. This multitude of voices allows Torma to sing "the other." Her work is not about the essential body, but towards a new conception of the body. In this way, Torma's work embodies *l'écriture feminine* as an exchange, or translation of perception, operating as an extension of the notion of the interstitial, in her representation of these domains of difference.

Embodied Touch

In her essay "Castration or Decapitation," Cixous writes that "A feminine textual body is recognized by the fact that it is always endless, without ending: there is no closure. . . . There's tactility in the feminine text, there's touch, and this touch passes through the ear."[29] In Torma's textile work, embodiment is both in the *act of viewing* within the gallery and in the *act of making*. This privileged touch of the artist, can only be re-enacted by the viewer through a form of haptic visuality.[30] Film theorist Laura Marks explains that: "In haptic *visuality*, the eyes themselves function like organs of touch."[31] In visual culture, if our sense of touch is deferred, we can seemingly experience the pleasure of the sensation from which it derives. Marks specifically addresses how haptic visuality operates in film where the "close-up" acts as a form of embodied spectatorship. In Torma's work the viewers' haptic reading replaces the sense of touch normally affiliated with fabric, either as worn against the skin as in clothing, or within the domestic realm, such as bedding. This affective-looking requires a shift of sensibility from one realm of association to another as the viewer's sense of self becomes one with the fabricated "other" within Torma's work.

Kristy Bell writes of this embodied or affective viewership: "When I consider Torma's embroideries, I wonder: what would this work look like if I could lift its veils and enter it—if I could slip into this world of thread and silk that is so appealing to the senses?"[32] She elaborates, "It is a desire both to enter the imaginative realm of the artworks and to feel the full richness of the materials that create this universe—in other words, to personally experience the beguiling worlds of lived reality and myth that Torma constructs."[33] On viewing the work in person, you find the need to get close to read the details, to revel in the mark-making and stitchery.

In Torma's immersive installation of *Bagatelles* (Plate 9.2), this experience of embodied touch is implicit with these six richly embroidered and painted silk panels. This work, developed during a Canada Council artists' residency in Paris in 2007, was inspired by her visit to the Bagatelles Garden in the Bois de Boulogne.[34] The French term "bagatelle" refers to a short light-hearted piece of music and links to Torma's earlier work with musical titles. "Bagatelle" can also mean "a thing of little importance," as Torma acknowledges: "I advocate for small things, out of mainstream, the overlooked and fragile. I feel I can orchestrate those elements into an organic, breathing tableaux that represents a lot more than the bagatelles, the small building elements themselves."[35] She draws on the rich panoply of source material from *Liste de familles de la vegetation,* to her "Dictionary of Fabulous Beasts," where two mythical "Gatekeepers" act as guardians of these fantastical gardens. Many of these beasts are compiled from her inventory of her children's drawings, those small building elements, often overlooked. The embroidered text playfully reads: "Who, may I ask, is the BEAST?" Within these gardens of plenty, flowers and figures run riot alongside more historical taxonomies.

While in Paris, Torma discovered the historical color merchant Sennelier, where she sourced specialized paint for silk and began to plan *Bagatelles,* painting directly onto the silk, and layering this with embroidery. This painterly gesture was new to Torma's work and suggests a French sensibility that recalls Claude Monet's late series *Les Nymphéas,* as well as the Renaissance textiles in the Musée de Cluny and Parisian *haute couture* fashion. This interpretation is reinforced with Torma's various installations of *Bagatelles,* where the six silk panels envelope the viewer, similar to Monet's series of curved canvases depicting water lilies installed at the Musée de l'Orangerie (Paris). In both series the viewer is surrounded by the artist's impression of a garden. We do not so much as *see* the garden topographically, rather we *experience* the garden, as an immersive act. This is something akin to *jouissance*—an intense pleasure all at once—as our eyes implore us to reach out to touch the richly embellished surfaces. As a gallery viewer, we can only *look,* yet seem to experience the pleasure of looking with *all* of our senses, thus enabling a haptic sensuality.

The sensuality of touch is integral to both the viewer's interpretation of Torma's work and the artist's connectedness with each piece. As Bell has noted, "Torma's contact with her art is deeply physical: touch governs each and every gesture."[36] As embroiderer, Torma has the privilege of "touch," her touch is everywhere.[37] She admits that "The work is very sensuous. When I touch silk, I think: 'Ohh, it came from China, and they raised the silk worms; it was probably a family business.' There are endless stories in a little piece of fabric."[38]

Such tactile intimacies suggest another feminist strategy where the finite needlework and richly embellished surfaces can, arguably, be coded feminine.

The feminist Naomi Schor in *Reading in Detail: Aesthetics and the Feminine* poses a critical question: "Is the detail gendered?"[39] To Schor the detail is both "gendered and doubly gendered as feminine," and "rooted in the domestic sphere of social life presided over by women," in the everyday, and the prosaic.[40] It is this close attention to detail in Torma's work that helps to pull us in; we need to get close to read the language of her stitches, and to delight in the multiple narratives that emerge.[41]

Torma admits to being drawn to the aesthetic of excess in her art, as seen in her use of a multiplicity of fabrics and threads, in the abundance of texture and color, and in her rich sourcing of materials. Janis Jefferies has written that with textile art, "Once released [from the constraints of modernism], detail and pattern become excessively magnified and erupted, even exceeding the borders which once tried to contain them."[42] This feminist strategy of excessiveness typifies the work of a number of textile artists including Sheila Hicks and Allyson Mitchell, the latter who defines herself as a "maximalist artist." Both Hicks and Mitchell enlarge and use multiples in their practice. Mitchell, like Torma, often appropriates found textiles to incorporate into a larger, often subversive, narrative. Art historians Bridget Elliot and Janice Helland regard the strategy of excess as implicit with textile art practices, stating, "The gendered conflation of textiles—particularly embroidery—with the feminine suggest that somewhere within the softness of fabric and the intricacy of stitching lies an inherent relationship that cannot be signified or secured: it is always 'excess' and therefore external to more easily and rigorously defined concepts."[43] As such, textile art is often without bounds, remaining on the margins and, as Jefferies also indicates, disrupts dominant discourses.

Collecting as Female Fetish

In keeping with excess theory is the excess of collecting. Torma describes herself as a "spiritual keeper of memories" and acknowledges that her work acts as a tangible repository for remembered moments, "as a private diary of pages on fabric, with drawings, pictures and visual fragments from my past and present."[44] In many of her embroideries these memories are not represented in a linear fashion, nor is there a narrative center to her work. Rather, the ordering of words, plants, objects, and lists—a kind of housekeeping—keeps her world in harmony. Motifs are often culled from her children's drawings and interspersed with their written narratives, meticulously copied and transcribed into her colorful embroideries. Sensitive to her children's authorship, she records their unrestrained drawings and words with a careful accuracy. The artist reflects: "I loved that early age when they were *languageless* ... where communication was based on signs, drawings, body language, guessing and empathy."[45] She comments on this impetus for borrowing from their youthful work:

> I use their decaying childhood drawings because I want to steal the intensity behind them. They drew quickly and powerfully. Embroidery is very much the opposite of that way of working. But I wanted to make something powerful, not just decadent and pretty. Children draw because the desire is there. With embroidery, I can save the desire in this format; it's forever.[46]

This maternal appropriation of her children's drawings (both now adult artists), and her use of embroidery as a means to embed or "save the desire" forever, evokes a form of female fetish where the mother's desire for the child to remain in her domain is reenacted. In *Feminizing the Fetish*, Emily Apter critiques Freud's notion of the fetish as only applied to the male and always sexual. She argues that the female fetish exists and is frequently discovered in the obsessive collecting of the mother.[47] Mary Kelly's early feminist series *Post-Partum Document* (1973–79) plays on this accumulative pattern where diary-like entries and child-objects—the child's handwriting, footprints, a fragment of a diaper— become part of the mother's fetish for remembering the child. As Apter observes in a later essay on Kelly, "*Post-Partum* documents the museological mania of a maternal collector/fetishist with a gently manic sympathy."[48] She maintains that the fetish can be visual and related directly to the sense of touch. In Torma's work, embroidery, with its tactile fabric and thread, is a play on a doubling of making and remaking of memory through the artist's touch.

In Torma's *Monster Spirit* (Figure 9.1), this diary-like motif is used throughout with the artist recording in stitches her son's punishment for talking as a boy at school. Torma recalls: "This is a found school text, from David's early years in elementary. 'Write down 60 times I will not talk' type of exercise, you probably remember. When I found these school exercises, I mused, how many meanings there can be if you read it differently: poetic, sarcastic, etc." She notes that, as an immigrant, this was particularly poignant, "Especially, if you have a different school routine than the Canadian, in English."[49] Throughout this work text and image play off each other. The stitching has a staccato quality, embellishing the cotton backing with energetic colors and narratives.

The theme of collecting as a form of female fetish is already present in earlier work by Torma, as seen in the companion pieces *Essential Elements* and *Man's Island* (1996), where she appropriates found clothing to emphasize gender

Figure 9.1 Anna Torma, *Monster Spirit,* 2008. Silk thread embroidery on cotton fabric, 45.7 × 35.6 cm. Photo credit: Anna Torma.

differences. The discarded clothing acts as a surrogate for the feminine/masculine aspect of each work. Using a crazy-quilt aesthetic, where she combines a random pattern determined by each piece of clothing, the artist gives more value to the worn out fabrics, suggesting the trace of the body is inherently present in the work. In *Essential Elements* a nostalgic gaze rests on a delicate antique ladies' blouse and elegant gloves, lace collars, discrete black beading, and a monogrammed "M." Such intimate details conjure up the uncanny, where objects that are at once familiar, are somehow displaced. Art historian Carol Mavor, in her book *Becoming*, writes on this residual memory that is associated with clothing: "It is a knowingness that encourages coming closer, turning around, feeling fabric (Is it silk? Is it old?), feeling buttons, feeling beads, smelling a perfume … in order to take in every detail."[50]

Torma's collecting activities have long included the work of her immediate family and, more recently, have extended to the work of her mother-in-law, as seen in her series *Red Fragments I* (2017).[51] The title is both literal and conceptual in its allusion to aging, illness, and migration. For this piece, the artist sought a means to connect with her mother-in-law, a gifted needlewoman, who had suffered a stroke. Torma encouraged her to make new pieces using the traditional Hungarian cross-stitch patterns in red yarn, as a means to rehabilitate her mental and emotional health.[52] She explains:

> My installation work, *RED FRAGMENTS*, records this collaboration and also revisits my immigrant past through my folk art heritage. I want to point out with this installation the tension between coherent designs and fragmented pieces, the beauty of unfinished works. The embroidery fragments clearly show the persistence and try-again attitude until the prepared small canvas [fabric] with the red-threaded needle runs empty, unable to be touched by her hands anymore.[53]

As her mother-in-law gradually lost the ability to embroider these time-honored patterns, the resulting absence of stitches alludes to her vulnerability and an acute sense of loss for both artists. Torma's specific adoption of the North American quilt pattern for this work befits her cultural assimilation, which serves as a backdrop to the appliquéd patterns of her mother-in-law's traditional Hungarian embroidery. As in so much of Torma's work, family is central, both conceptually and emotionally. She has previously commented that: "As an artist I always felt that my mother and family were all behind me, a part of my life, and a part of my activities when I make art. It is a conscious thing. It is about inclusivity, about sharing and gathering from many sources, deep and large."[54] Again Cixous's concept of "singing the other" is implied in this complex narrative that includes the work of her mother-in-law, Hungarian cross-stitch embroidery, a record-keeping of declining health, and Torma's overarching inclusiveness.

Stitching the Self

These multiple narratives are a continual form of discourse in Torma's work, but also contribute more specifically to the notion of stitching herself into her own work. Returning to Bhabha's concept of the "interstitial" as those "in-between" spaces that provide strategies of selfhood, nowhere is this more apparent in Torma's work than in her series *Vanitas I* and *II* (2011), where she literally sews a photo-appliqué portrait of herself as a tiger into the first silk panel.

Vanitas I (Figure 9.2) shows a humorous self-portrait of Torma surrounded by all things culturally inscribed as "feminine," an imaginary world, drawn from her childhood. In this work she recalls her early play with handmade paper dolls

Figure 9.2 Anna Torma, detail of *Vanitas I*, 2011. Silk thread embroidery and appliqué on silk fabric. Photo credit: Anna Torma.

with flowery names such as *Rose*, *Lily* and *Iris*—a child's world—remembered by way of stitches. The silk backing and fleshy color suggest old lingerie from the past. Viewers are drawn into the narratives, as various codes of fashion are deciphered from comic book villains to elegant fashion plates. Torma employs her needlework strategically as the subject requires, more crudely, in her childlike recollections, or with great skill as she appropriates magazine illustrations, and deliberately mixes her metaphors with multiple narratives, as though layering memory. She further complicates this reading by using what she terms a "soft collage" or appliqué technique that has roots in Miriam Schapiro's femmages, woman-centered fabric collages. Torma has long used her own method of "soft collage" with its implications of modernism as a mode of introducing three-dimensionality to her work.

The series, created for the group exhibition *Paper Doll*, was inspired by Torma's recollections of playing with paper dolls as a child.[55] This exhibition also included an archival collection of handmade paper dolls and juvenile diaries of Sylvia Plath that served as a focal point for seven contemporary artists whose work explored the materiality of the cut-out and the ephemerality of play.[56] Torma read Plath's *The Bell Jar* as a student in the seventies and reflects that: "the voice of the book matched with my melancholy and helped me to question the meaning of life, art, and womanhood."[57] This inquisitive tone is more pervasive in *Vanitas II* where a meticulously embroidered anatomical figure, sourced from an old anatomical chart, serves as an index for the body, while the *skin* of the silk backing acts as *momento mori*—a reminder of our human frailty. As *vanitas* we are made aware of our own histories and mortality. The work is layered with color transfers of old photographs and documents that narrate the fragmented history of her family.

Torma, as the record-keeper of family and her own life, uses her needle both as an integral part of her practice, but also as a rhetorical tool for shaping the complexity of identity, both collective and singular. In keeping with both the notion of stitching the self and the complexity of working within a practice that can be interpreted as interstitial, in its recognition of difference, Torma speaks to a multitude of feminisms that have shaped the politics of women's lives and art. Her work is replete with imagery that navigates a complexity of themes, from the domestic to popular culture, to the politics of migration. Using well-known feminist strategies such as diary-like motifs, excess, and collectivity she continues to explore this richly embodied world and her work continues to gain recognition within the international forum of textile art.

10

Suturing My Soul: In Pursuit
of the *Broderie de Bayeux*

Janet Catherine Berlo

A woman's place is at her embroidery.

Anglo-Saxon proverb[1]

With all due respect to Virginia Woolf who observed, "We look back through our mothers, if we are women," I suggest that we look back through our needles if we are embroiderers, quilters, seamstresses, or knitters. For my entire adult life as a feminist art historian and fiber artist, I have believed that every woman who makes art with needle and thread is entitled to claim the Bayeux Embroidery as her ancestral heritage. I write this chapter as a historian of Native American art and women's textile arts poaching on an era in which I am not an expert. Here I stitch pieces of my own life history to that of the magnificent and poetic twelfth-century object erroneously called the Bayeux Tapestry (Plate 10.1), with the work of twentieth-century French artist Louise Bourgeois as an intermediary.

The Importance of Naming: What the Bayeux
Embroidery Is and Is Not

The Bayeux Tapestry is *not* a tapestry. A tapestry is woven on a fixed loom, its designs integral to warp and weft. No tapestry could possibly be 50 centimeters tall and some 70 meters long. Rather, this work is an embroidery: wool yarn stitched upon nine conjoined lengths of hand-spun and hand-woven linen. Why have we allowed it to be called the Bayeux *Tapestry* for centuries? Of the more than one thousand entries in the object's book-length bibliography, only a handful offer its rightful name.[2] Is it, as medievalist Marilyn Caviness suggests, because today the word embroidery (*broderie*, in French) "evokes the manual work of women," a pursuit afforded less status and dignity than that of tapestry, which is "a term readily associated with the large male-dominated workshops of northern Europe in the late Middle Ages that produced images woven into the fabric?"[3]

Since its first mention in the cathedral records of Bayeux in 1476 (where it was properly characterized as an embroidery—"*broderye de ymages et escripteaulx*"),[4] it has principally been discussed in terms of its importance in celebrating the deeds of men: a two-year saga starting in 1064 with a meeting between Edward (the ailing King of England), and Harold, the Earl of Wessex. In brief: Harold, his men, and their horses embark in ships across the English Channel. Various exploits ensue in Normandy and Brittany, and Harold swears an oath to Duke William of Normandy. Harold returns to London, where King Edward dies on 6 January 1066 and Harold takes the throne that very day. Some months later, the Duke of Normandy builds ships to cross the channel, and in October of 1066 a bloody battle ensues at Hastings, at the end of which some 6000 human corpses and 600 dead horses lay on the battlefield.[5] The visual narrative, as it exists today, is incomplete, for the last section of the embroidery is missing. It has been suggested that, to bring the narrative full circle back to the British throne, it probably depicted the coronation of William the Conqueror.[6]

I have nothing to add to that historical discourse. Historian R. Howard Bloch calls the embroidery "a powerful vehicle for cultural memory at a time when even the most powerful lords were illiterate."[7] Here, I embellish it in a more free-form fashion with my thoughts on its materiality and its importance within the personal (and all too often lost) histories of women. I position it as "a powerful vehicle for cultural memory" of a different sort—a cultural memory for those of us who seek to understand the long history of the poetics of embroidery, and our places in it. At the end of this chapter, I offer some thoughts on what constitutes such a poetics.

Until recently, few who have written about the Bayeux Embroidery during the last two hundred years have characterized it as the work of women.[8] Yet knowing what we do about flax and wool in the medieval European tradition, it is entirely possible that every step, from the planting of flax seeds to the harvesting, retting, spinning, and weaving of linen, was done by women. The sheep may have been raised and the fleece washed, dyed, carded, and spun by women.[9] The eleventh century marks the beginning of the turn from a more female-centered production of cloth (family-based or in workshops in convents and aristocratic households) to the development of male-dominated guilds.[10] So the 1070s (the likely date of its creation being within ten years of the Norman Conquest in 1066) were a time of social and economic transition in the textile trades, though the custom of aristocratic women embroidering sumptuous and ambitious works continued for generations.

In terms of design and patronage, the Embroidery is customarily explained as the brainchild of important men. Most scholars agree that the Augustinian Abbey at Canterbury, England is the likely source of its design, for there is much correspondence between the embroidery's imagery and that of illuminated manuscripts made there.[11] The most popular candidate for its patron has long been Bishop Odo of Bayeux, for in the fifteenth century it hung periodically in the cathedral he consecrated there in 1077, and Odo is pictured more than once within its images.[12]

Contemporary scholarship characterizes the embroidery, variously, as the work of monks, nuns, or aristocratic women. But to most female scholars who have studied it closely, it seems self-evident that it is women's work. Carola Hicks suggests that its patron may well have been a royal woman, offering evidence that Edith Godwinson, "widow of King Edward, sister of King Harold, friend of King William, fulfils all requirements and, in addition, had particular expertise in embroidery."[13] No scholar before Hicks had thought to ask why a tale of manly exploration and bravery, if conceived by a male patron and made by monks, would have taken the unlikely form of an embroidery. Hicks points out that diverse historical sources praise Edith's intelligence, her important role in her husband's court, and her skill at embroidery and painting. Moreover, Edith "had access to a suitably trained workforce in the nunneries which were an important source of large-scale embroidery production," and "was one of the few English who retained lands and properties after the Conquest."[14] Hicks also reminds us that nunneries did not just house those with a religious vocation, but were the refuge of aristocratic widows:

> Many residents of nunneries in the years after the Conquest, whether as committed or pragmatic members, were women from great English families who had been directly involved with the events depicted in the Tapestry and who, as noblewomen, were noted for their sewing skills. Such women, trying to rebuild their shattered lives in a safe, supportive community, could easily come together to provide the specialist workforce necessary to produce the Tapestry.[15]

I have always been impressed with the magnitude of this artistic project, but over time I have become increasingly taken with its expansive vision, and with the ambition that drove its creation. I take feminist pride in the work of the deft hands of its female artists at work almost a millennium ago.

In Search of My Matrilineal Heritage in Bayeux

It is April of 2013. My best friend Aldona and I are on a train, heading west from Paris to Bayeux, in Normandy. It is a two-hour trip; it is a forty-seven-year trip. I have wanted to visit Bayeux since I was in ninth grade, in Mr. Coleman's World History class. That November of 1966, the month I turned fourteen, Mr. Coleman proposed that we undertake an art project related to one of our class themes. Already skilled at sewing both by hand and machine, I decided to replicate a section of what we then *did* call The Bayeux Tapestry. I did not need instruction. I bought burlap and embroidery floss, and drafted a sketch of the scene I would undertake: one with a great multi-colored ship, replete with horses and men. I was so flattered that Mr. Coleman wanted to keep my project that I willingly handed it over. Today, I wish I had that prime example of my adolescent ambition.

Until recently, I did not realize that it was no coincidence that I chose such a project in 1966. During the nine-hundredth anniversary of the Norman Conquest, images of the world-famous embroidery were everywhere, including the cover of the August 1966 issue of *National Geographic*.[16] While writing this essay, I ordered a copy of that magazine from Etsy. Holding it in my hands, I marvel that it is responsible for my fifty-year fascination with the longest embroidery in the world. As I page through the lengthy article and color photos of the entire span of the work of art, I am transported back to my small bedroom in Belmont, Massachusetts, where I pored over these images, choosing the one to embroider.

In Bayeux, Aldona, also an art historian, is happy to see this magnificent work of art. As an equestrienne, she is especially taken with the lively rendition of so many horses. But only for me is it what material culture scholars Rachel Maines and James Glynn call a *numinous* object. Such objects, they write, have a special "sociocultural magic" that "carries emotional weight" with an individual viewer, or a collectivity of viewers.[17] In our three days in Bayeux, I visit it three times. My mother, Jeannette Tousignant Berlo (1912–2005), was from a French-Canadian family whose first known patrilineal ancestor arrived in New France in 1640 from Normandy. As I walk the streets of Bayeux, I entertain a fantasy that perhaps he came from here. This allows me to consider the notion of a link in my DNA to this place and this embroidery, conveniently ignoring, of course, that it was almost certainly made in England. But, after all, that's what "sociocultural magic"—or wishful thinking—is all about.

The first time I enter the Musée de la Tapisserie de Bayeux, my eyes fill with tears, as if I am about to encounter someone I love whom I have not seen in decades. On this April day, I am impatient at the crowds, for I want to be alone with my beloved object. The nine-euro entrance fee includes an audio-guide in one of fourteen languages, attesting to its status as a cultural treasure of all humanity.[18] Wise to the ways of museums' crowd management skills, I conclude that the audio-guide's fast-paced narrative is designed principally to keep people *moving*. I switch mine off in between episodes and just fill my eyes with color and pattern.

I find myself keeping a leisurely pace with three British women my own age who have abandoned their audio-guides too. One is translating the Latin for her friends and then, in Liverpudlian accents, they intimately discuss these events of 900 years ago the way Americans might talk about the Great Depression of the 1930s.

"*Hic*," she says, peering closely at one scene, "announces what is happening in each scene. It means here." And she reads from the angular embroidered text above the heads of the figures: "*HIC WILLEM DUX ET EXERCITUS VENERUNT AD MONTE MICHAELIS*. Here Duke William and his army came to Mont St. Michel." I peer at the image with heightened interest, for Aldona and I are bound for Mont Saint Michel in three days. The men cross the treacherous quicksand that isolates this medieval fortress at low tide. Some are astride their mounts. Others wade through the shallows, their shields held high above their heads. One horse stumbles, his rider toppling off. The horses' bodies and the men's garments are rendered in painstakingly overlaid stitches. The colors—black, a reddish rust, biscuit, several shades of sage and celery—delineate the figures. I notice that one leg of the falling horse is black, while the rest is biscuit color, and assume a mistake. But as I look more closely, I find that in almost every case, the legs on the far side of the horses are shaded differently from the bodies and the legs on the near side, adding depth and a bit of whimsy (Figure 10.1).

The beauty of this monumental embroidery is slightly off-beat, with something of the vernacular about it. Even as an undergraduate art history student, I preferred the Romanesque to the High Gothic, the Archaic Greek to Classical perfection, and the early Renaissance of Giotto to the fully-formed Renaissance of Michelangelo. There is something so pleasingly "in process" about these early iterations, before veristic canons of representation had fully taken hold.

Mounted behind glass in a U-shaped gallery, the embroidery resides in the requisite gloom of all twenty-first-century museum textile displays. As I traverse the outside of this U, I am disappointed that there is no spot to stand and take in the entire, astonishing length of its pictorial narrative. In the years that I pored

Figure 10.1 Detail, Bayeux Embroidery: Mont St. Michel. © S. Maurice—Bayeux Museum, Bayeux, France.

over the illustrations of this work of art in books, I knew that seeing it as a series of individual frames was inaccurate. I own a small accordion-fold 1/7th size paper color reproduction of it. When unfolded around my study, it stretches for nearly 10 meters, allowing for some sense of the epic narrative.[19] When hung in the Bayeux Cathedral, above the heads of viewers, surely the original was an awe-inspiring visual narrative.

Materiality

In art history and visual studies, "materiality" has become a twenty-first-century buzzword.[20] As a scholar who has never drifted very far from the materiality of things, I am both gratified and amused by this turn of events. I teach a seminar called "Object Lessons," examining the history of material culture studies by looking closely at a series of objects, including the Bayeux Embroidery. We talk about "thing theory," and "the cultural biography of objects."[21] Of course we also handle objects. I bring in textiles from my own collection: American quilts, Maya *huipiles* from Guatemala, Kuna *molas* from Panama. What is another word for textile or fabric? *Material*, of course. So, we look at the materiality of material. I've assembled study boxes of fibers, in hopes of seducing students who seem increasingly alienated from the material world. Few of them have seen flax growing in a field, handled cotton bolls, or seen how wool is tamed in its transformation from raw fiber to roving to yarn. And they do, in fact, handle with something approaching awe the materials I pass around, as if encountering goods from an alien realm, rather than the constituent parts of clothing they wear every day. Scholars today love to analyze what it means to have an "embodied" knowledge of something, rather than simply an intellectual knowledge of it. But it seemed more logical to me to offer students a sensual approach to embodiment, using the word sensuality in its varied meanings—not simply using one's haptic sense (touch), but also reveling in the sensuousness of fine silk, merino batting, or alpaca yarn. That starting point of materials and the senses—a textile base—can lead us into the whole big "churn of history" just as readily as a text-based understanding of the Anglo-Norman encounter on the battlefields of France and England in 1066.

The factual materiality of the Bayeux tapestry has been exhaustively chronicled, with all the force that microscopes, textile specialists, and enumerations can bring to bear. Its nine lengths of hand-woven linen vary from 13.90 meters long to 2.43 meters at the fragmentary end of the textile. On this are embroidered some 626 figures, 37 buildings, 41 ships, and 202 horses.[22] The embroidery is mostly worked in two-ply, s-twist wool yarn that was dyed in the fleece, with the occasional detail embroidered in linen. The ten colors of wool are the result of three main dyes well-known to textile artists for millennia: madder, woad, and indigotin.[23] The principle stitches are stem stitch and a couching stitch that in English is now sometimes known as the "Bayeux Stitch" because of its ample use here, where it comprises the large stretches of color on the horses and ships. Unsurprisingly, textile conservators see evidence of several hands in the work.

I walk the streets of Bayeux to refresh my eyes in between visits with the textile. As I put one foot in front of the other, I am trying to side-step the shattering sorrow that engulfs me: a month earlier my husband of twenty-three years ran away from our life. His business had failed, our financial life was in ruins, he stole money from me, and—most grievously—he denied that he had ever loved me. He fled across the United States in his packed-up car, to hide out from his failures. I had written in tribute to him some twenty years earlier, "I believe that without him I could not breathe,"[24] yet I was still breathing. But the oxygen was thin, and I was often convulsed by the shallow gasps of crippling anxiety attacks. My women friends and my therapist all urged me toward a healthy, purging, righteous anger. But I was not there yet. It was all turned inward, coruscating my own body, soul, and intellect. My academic work was stalled. I cried in my office, panicked that I did not have the strength to face my students. I couldn't eat, or think. But I could pick up a needle and thread and sew. Today, as I write, I wonder if some of those twelfth-century needlewomen ensconced in abbey, castle, or manor house were fleeing their own life-shattering sorrows with each prick of their needles: Husbands, brothers, or sons dead at Hastings? Sisters lost in childbirth? Babies stillborn?

At breakfast at our inn in Bayeux, I noticed a brochure advertising lessons in Bayeux embroidery. The innkeeper telephoned to inquire on my behalf.

"She can offer you a three-hour class this very afternoon."

"Yes, yes!" I nearly shouted.

That morning, waiting impatiently for my lesson to begin, I walked the streets again, this time paying particular attention to all of the ways the embroidery had been replicated for the tourist market: towels, pot holders, playing cards, biscuit tins, jewelry, handbags, tea cozies, mugs. Such imagery had long held a talismanic meaning for me, and here it was ubiquitous. Despite the kitschy nature of most items, I felt cosseted by this flood of images.

That afternoon, I was the sole pupil of the renowned Madame Chantal James. She had made all of the replicas in the museum that demonstrate how the work was done. She owns the sole right to replicate any part of the Embroidery in the historically-accurate kits she sells, containing fine linen stamped with portions of the design, and wool yarns of the proper weight and colors. Four main stitches comprise the repertoire of the Bayeux Embroidery. The "stem stitch" (*point de tige*) is a typical outline stitch used by embroiderers everywhere; a long "satin stitch" (*point lancé*) forms the foundation for filling the large expanses delineated by the stem stitches. What Mme. James has termed the "barrette stitch" (in both French and English) is a couching stitch laid perpendicular to and over the long satin stitches to hold them down. What is most distinctive to the Bayeux Embroidery, and what makes its surface texture so rich are the tiny "point stitches" (*les picots*) fastened over the long barrette stitches, parallel to the long satin stitches. These are staggered to create a dappled surface effect. The three stitches that fill the stem-stitched outlines together form the distinctive Bayeux Stitch (*le point de Bayeux*).[25]

Though I had no intention of completing a precise replica of a section of the embroidery, I bought a piece of linen imprinted with the design of one of the Viking-style long boats with striped sail and dragon-headed prow, thinking that

I would learn some of the basics of embroidery, and then improvise my own personal saga. Under the tutelage of my ever-patient but exacting teacher, in three hours I completed approximately one square inch of embroidery: the right arm of the oarsman at the stern of the boat. It made me wonder about the embroidery on burlap I completed for Mr. Coleman in 1966. How long did it take? How fine were my stitches?

In the resolute manner that we lackadaisical Americans identify as truly French, she kept repeating to me in her limited English (as shaky as my French), "*Non,* that is not correct." I would try again. "*Mais, non.* Not correct. See, here you must make *le picot, le picot,*" and she would demonstrate again the tiny, staggered stitches that would bring the monochrome expanse of arm, or flank, or robe to life. Sunlight streamed into the large western-facing windows of the centuries-old Benedictine Abbey where she taught. I moved my chair as the sun shifted in the sky. The streaming light illuminated my embroidery hoop and—ever so slightly—thawed my frozen heart.

Cauterized and Sutured

In the months after I returned from Bayeux, I endeavored to learn how to live without my life partner of more than twenty-five years. I rearranged furniture and art, packed away photos of him and us, and bought new sheets and flatware, all in an effort to make a home that did not reflect the life that had gone up in flames. I picked up my Bayeux embroidery template, and put it down again, a dozen times. Aesthetically, I needed to process my losses in a less tightly controlled way than the methodical Bayeux stitch allowed. When I touched a sewing needle, I imagined pricking my fingers to let blood. I imagined matches too: blood and fire. Unbidden, this phrase came to me: *Everything he touched, he set on fire.* I was trying to make sense of the conflagration that was my life.

With their needles and wool yarns, the women who chronicled the Norman invasion of the autumn of 1066 did not flinch from the mayhem inflicted by men. Death, dismemberment, decapitation, an arrow in the eye socket—they stitched it all. Like invading armies everywhere, the Normans looted, pillaged, and set houses on fire (Figure 10.2). "*Hic domus incenditur*" is embroidered over the house with a flaming roof from which a woman leads a small child: *here a house is burned.*

At night during those months, in the heavy sleep induced by prescribed doses of Klonopin and Trazodone, I dreamed of domestic mayhem: fire, tears, exile,

Figure 10.2 Detail, Bayeux Embroidery: Normans setting a house on fire.
© S. Maurice—Bayeux Museum, Bayeux, France.

panic. I knew the only way to keep going forward was to channel all of this into art. I rummaged in my basement for the flat aluminum sculpture of my ex-husband's hands that he had made in design school in the 1980s. I brought it up to my quilt studio and began to trace their outlines on cloth. I sandwiched thin cotton quilt batting between layers of fabric, marked the shapes of his hands in pencil, cut them out, and stitched haphazardly across and around them with a machined zig-zag stitch. I bought candles, long wooden matches, and the first pack of cigarettes I had purchased since I was fifteen. That summer of 2013, I burned holes in the palms of the cloth hands. I set the fingers on fire, and doused them with water.

All the anger I had internalized as crippling anxiety attacks, I let loose on those cloth replicas of his capable, artistic, masculine hands. Some months later, on large pieces of linen, I embroidered, in the spidery style of the Bayeux Embroidery, *Everything he touched, he set on fire.* Then for good measure, I did it in Latin, too. *Quidquid attigit, succendit?* Well, close enough. I began to embroider some long boats—larger and messier than those on the Bayeux embroidery—and planned to fill them not with warriors and horses, but with passages from old, handwritten love letters digitally printed on cloth. I would scorch them too, sending those love letters out for a burial at sea.

During this time, I came across one of Louise Bourgeois's late textile works. On a man's blue and white handkerchief, she had embroidered in capital letters:

I HAVE BEEN
TO HELL AND
BACK.

AND LET ME
TELL YOU,
IT WAS
WONDERFUL.[26]

I laughed out loud—not a sound I had uttered much in the past year. I was still in the HELL part. My own boat had not yet reoriented its course toward WONDERFUL. I pursued this astonishingly prolific artist, seeking out, in particular, her work involving cloth.

Louise Bourgeois (1911–2010) was born to a family of Aubusson tapestry restorers in France. Her life as an artist spanned nearly nine decades, starting from her precociously talented childhood when, at age eight, she expertly drew imagery on the warp threads for the restorers to weave with wool fibers. Her mother was expert at dyestuffs, as was her mother before her. I think of the colors of the wools in the Bayeux Embroidery when I read Bourgeois' recollection of her mother's work:

All she lived for was the dyeing of the wool and the repair. My mother was a scientist by nature, and decided that she would repair only the old tapestries made before 1830. Before that date, the tapestries were woven on the warp of wool, but after that they were woven on a warp of cotton . . . The wool, when it comes from the animal, smells a mile away. First the grease had to be removed through alkaline baths. Then the spinner prepared the wool by hand, twisting it, lifting the wool from the pile, twisting it with her fingers into a spiral-shaped spindle. There would still be grease in the wool, so the thread, now looped into skeins about two feet long, was bathed in vats of ammonia outside near the river. Then it would be rinsed in the river.[27]

Bourgeois goes on to describe the soaking of the skeins in progressively darker dye baths. Her mother found that chemical dyes would fade, so she used only natural dyes. Nearly nine hundred years after the making of the Bayeux Embroidery, European women were still engaged in the same processes of spinning and dyeing.

Though her entire adult life was spent in the contemporary art world in New York, Bourgeois did not achieve international fame until her Museum of Modern

Art retrospective in 1982, when she was seventy-one.[28] She made art until the week before her death in 2010. Her installation series *Cells* concerns pain and isolation, both physical and psychological. In *Cell I* (1991), the walls of a tiny room are demarcated by a series of large, worn wooden doors. Barred from entry, the viewer can merely peer through glass windowpanes (Plate 10.2). Within the room are lamps, a chair, and small tables strewn with objects, but the main feature is an iron bedstead. There is no mattress, but its bed linens are formed of folded, worn French mail sacks, embroidered in red with phrases from the artist's diaries: "I need my memories. They are my documents," and "Art is the guarantee of sanity."[29] I wanted to go in and lay down on that bed. I wanted to transform my own guest room to such a cell, hung with linens embroidered with the words of my grief.

Not much attention has been paid to Bourgeois's embroideries. She is best known for her work in stone, latex, and cast bronze, especially her enormous cast-bronze spiders that grace museums all over the world.[30] To her, the spider harks back to the female, the mother, and to the Classical spinner of thread, Arachne. What male artist would say of the act of drawing, "It is a secretion, like a thread in a spider's web … it is a knitting, a spiral, a spider web?"[31] In this observation Bourgeois brings all the arts back to the primordial spinner. I have no interest in drawing. For me, it is all about the needles: sewing needles, felting needles, quilting needles, knitting needles. What has been pulled apart must be sutured together.

"A Fascination with the Needle": Toward a Poetics of Embroidery

When I was growing up, all the women in my house were using needles. I've always had a fascination with the needle, the magic power of the needle. The needle is used to repair the damage. It's a claim to forgiveness. It is never aggressive; it's not a pin.

Louise Bourgeois[32]

In recent decades, scholars in the humanities have written persuasively about the poetics of space and of painting.[33] But what of the poetics of embroidery? How can we talk about embroidery in a way that enlarges our understanding of it as an art form and as an embodied practice that sheds light on the lives of women? Poetics, as it has been amplified from its more narrow literary meaning, aims to illuminate phenomenological practices—in terms of embroidery, that is to say, our subjective experiences as practitioners, viewers, and users of this art.

Literature on craft practices in general are helpful here. Jeweler Bruce Metcalf's 1993 manifesto, "Replacing the Myth of Modernism," is a paean to the handmade object. He argues that truly valuing craft requires "a metaphysical revision: the return of labor to equal status with thought."[34] This is an important insight that does not get nearly enough traction. The work of our hands *is* our thought made manifest, as it was for the women who labored over the Bayeux Embroidery. So, what are some aspects of the poetics of embroidery?

Tactility. All artists love the sensory aspects of their materials: the tang of linseed oil, the creamy viscosity of paint poured on a surface, the smell of wood as the circular saw bites into it. But textiles rank first among the works we long to touch. Museum exhibits of quilts, for example, sport many more signs exhorting, "do not touch" than do exhibits of works in other media. And who can be in the presence of Sheila Hicks's monumental *The Principal Wife* (1968) and not want to lean into its coils in which the compliant strands of beige linen, like so many horses' tails, are held captive by the precise wrappings of lustrous silk and acrylic yarn.[35]

The week after my husband fled, I took refuge in the studio of Rochester textile artist Jeanne Raffer Beck, volunteering to help her sort and package materials for an enormous studio sale as she radically changed direction in her work. A staggering heap of pieces of cotton, damask, silk, and linen filled the center of her large studio. In it were fragments of embroideries, experiments in silk-screen printing, yardage never used, and cotton drop cloths stained in intriguing ways. My task was to package grab-bags that would hold $10 assortments of enticing raw materials. But first I needed to fall backward into that mountain of partly-worked cloth, while Jeanne took my picture. Briefly, I was swaddled in joy, safety, and artistic possibility. I wanted to rest within the embrace of that cloth mountain for weeks, perhaps until my wounds stabilized within its bandages. In its therapeutic properties, this was far beyond what my two sisters and I, all quilters, call "fondling fabric," as in "I'm feeling blue; I need to spend a day in the studio fondling fabric."

Performativity. Embroiderers often perform autobiographical acts. The girlhood embroiderers of eighteenth- and nineteenth-century North America left a legacy of artistic accomplishments made under the supervision of schoolmistresses in female academies. These include samplers with names, ages, and other autobiographical details worked in thread, as well as maps, and mourning embroideries for beloved family members.[36] At the beginning of the twentieth century, as part of the American Colonial Revival, Mary Saltonstall Parker (1856–1920) designed and embroidered more than sixteen samplers that expressed both personal and cultural autobiography. For example, using the nautical imagery of the Bayeux Embroidery, she commemorated the military enlistment of her two sons in the First World War, as well as the completion of her sampler in November 1918, "in the Dawn of Peace," as words she embroidered on it proclaimed.[37]

Medieval French women of the aristocracy often sang as they embroidered. Termed *chanson de toile*, these songs depict an identity for these women that was bound up in love and work. While these songs are best known from the thirteenth century, perhaps it is not a stretch to imagine the makers of the Bayeux Embroidery singing as they worked. Stanzas such as, "If I knew of a courtly knight who was praised and valued for his skill in combat, I would love him with all my heart," or "How sweet the name of love is. I never thought I would feel pain from it,"[38] let us imagine their hopes, hurts, and aspirations.

But, beyond this, performativity manifests itself differently in large-scale works of textile art. By inhabiting a grand space, the Bayeux Embroidery, or Sheila Hicks's *The Silk Rainforest* (1975, 2.5 meters high by almost 7 meters long) demand to be reckoned with. They reject the invisibility, the meekness of much of women's textile arts in the western world. When women take embroidery and other textile arts beyond their accustomed uses—out of the private, domestic, female sphere and make them large (Hicks), unruly (Bourgeois), or historically ambitious (the Bayeux embroiderers) it is a performative act. It performs gender in an unaccustomed way, demanding acknowledgement on a scale that tiny textiles do not. In Judith Butler's words, a performance can "tacitly restructure how we sense the world."[39] For me as a young adolescent, the Bayeux Embroidery did this, and for me as an adult, Louise Bourgeois's *Cells* did this.

Mindful deliberation: the slow stitch. No doubt twelfth-century women thought their world was changing at a fast pace: male professional guilds replacing female handiworkers, a new cosmopolitan order after the Norman Conquest, stone cathedrals rising to ever-new heights. In recent decades, various "slow" movements have emerged, in response to the depredations of industrial agriculture and the over-networked life.[40] Slowing down seems not only desirable but imperative. Curiously, I search the thesaurus in vain for a synonym for slow that is not pejorative. Most suggest sloth: procrastination, indolence, flagging. How about adjectives drawn from Buddhist spiritual practice: mindful, deliberate? Of course, these involve sitting still, just as embroidery does. It can be difficult to be alone with ourselves, with the labor of our hands. One can brood on the *crises de coeur* that brought us to the needle. The mind can work and rework every small stitch of pain, every thread of life left in a knotted mess, every blood-drawing prick of the heart. The idea of the slow stitch has resonated in many needleworkers' hearts. Claire Wellesley-Smith's *Slow Stitch: Mindful and Contemplative Textile Arts* has gone through multiple printings since its publication in 2015.[41]

Sensuality and embodiment. Throughout my twenties and thirties, I kept above my desk a quote by the great American feminist poet Adrienne Rich (1929–2012): "I am asking whether women cannot begin, at last, to think through the body, to connect what has been so cruelly disorganized—our great mental capacities, hardly used; our highly developed tactile sense; our genius for close observation; our complicated, pain-enduring, multi-pleasured physicality."[42] She published this in a book about motherhood, in 1976, when I was in my second year of graduate school, and much in need of sustenance by wise women. I was never interested in becoming a mother. I sought my fulfilment in both scholarly and creative writing and in making art. My "tactile sense," my "multi-pleasured physicality"—I use these in pursuit of pleasure, nourishment, and healing. As I said, *we think through our needles*. As Bourgeois said, *the needle is used to repair the damage. It's a claim to forgiveness.*

Coda: "Heal Your Own Heart"

In the summer of 2016, I put this nearly-completed essay aside to spend a month in southwest France with my new man-friend. When I discovered that the Guggenheim Museum in Bilbao, Spain—only a few hours away by car—was exhibiting more than thirty of Louise Bourgeois's *Cells*, I asked if he would drive me there. I have teared up in front of works of art many times. But only when confronted by so many of Bourgeois's potent and evocative *Cells* have I experienced a full-blown attack of "Stendhal Syndrome," named for the French novelist's 1817 experience in front of Giotto's Florentine frescoes: "I was in a state of ecstasy," he wrote. "I had palpitations of the heart."[43]

As for me, I actually sobbed out loud. Hot flashes overtook my body, though I am a decade past that phenomenon. I felt an overwhelming sense of identification with Bourgeois's elusive yet potent constructions, made from old garments, cast-off furniture, fragments of tapestries, and embroideries of muttered utterances. An even greater gravitational pull than I felt in the presence of my beloved Bayeux Embroidery drew me into their orbit.

I vowed that very day to embark upon my own autobiographical installation as soon as I returned home. Two years later, it is still in progress. Much black paint and much red yarn, some of it begged from friends and colleagues who knit and weave. Black walnut shells that have been hollowed out by squirrels, and yarn-wrapped animal bones. Black spools of different sizes that I built (with the help of the dexterous, brilliant, and art-loving man who drove me to Bilbao) and wound with red yarns of differing thicknesses. At the center of the installation is an oak piano bench I have had for many years and always meant to refinish. I upholstered the lid with black wool, with the phrase "heal your own heart" embroidered in white around an oversized sculptural red wool anatomically-correct heart stuffed with wool and shredded love letters.

Heal Your Own Heart: Homage to Louise Bourgeois is now part of my living room. I live here alone, happily so. Willfully so. Sometimes my dining table holds sewing projects for weeks at a time. I can pick up a random bit of embroidery from the coffee table, and stitch while I sip a glass of Merlot. *Heal your own heart*: all it takes is a needle and thread, and infinite, infinite patience.

Notes

Introduction: Stitching the Self

1   See, for instance, Christopher Breward, "Sewing Soldiers," in *Quilts 1700–2010: Hidden Histories, Untold Stories*, ed. Sue Prichard, 84–87 (London: V&A Publishing, 2010); Joseph McBrinn, "'The work of masculine fingers': The Disabled Soldiers' Embroidery Industry, 1918–1955," *Journal of Design History* 31, no. 1 (2016): 1–23; T. Röske, "Agnes Richter's Jacket," *Epidemiology and Psychiatric Sciences* 23, no. 3 (2014): 227–29; Sabine Wieber's essay in this volume; and Kirsty Robertson, "Threads of Hope: The *Living Healing Quilt Project*," *English Studies in Canada* 35, no. 1 (2009): 85–107.

2   Jenni Parker, "Mental Health and Stitching," Fine Cell Work, 18 May 2018, accessed 25 July 2018, https://finecellwork.co.uk/blogs/blog-events/mental-health-and-stitching.

3   "Tony's Story," Fine Cell Work, 5 December 2017, accessed 25 July 2018, https://finecellwork.co.uk/blogs/blog-events/tonys-story.

4   Heather Pristash, Inez Schaechterle, and Sue Carter Wood, "The Needle as the Pen: Intentionality, Needlework, and the Production of Alternate Discourses of Power," in *Women and the Material Culture of Needlework and Textiles, 1750–1950*, ed. Maureen Daly Goggin and Beth Fowkes Tobin, 13–29 (Farnham, UK: Ashgate, 2009), 27.

5   Michael Yonan, "Toward a Fusion of Art History and Material Culture Studies," *West 86th* 18, no. 2 (2011): 232–48.

6   Yonan, 235.

7   Yonan, 235.

8   Julia Bryan-Wilson, *Fray: Art + Textile Politics* (Chicago: University of Chicago Press, 2017), 32–33.

9   Maureen Daly Goggin, "Introduction: Threading Women," in *Women and the Material Culture of Needlework and Textiles, 1750–1950*, ed. Maureen Daly Goggin and Beth Fowkes Tobin, 1–10 (Farnham, UK: Ashgate, 2009), 3.

10 Rozsika Parker and Griselda Pollock, *Old Mistresses: Women, Art and Ideology* (London: I. B. Tauris, 2013 [1981]), 70.

11 Alice Barnaby, "Dresses and Drapery: Female Self-fashioning in Muslin, 1800–1850," in *Crafting the Woman Professional in the Long Nineteenth Century: Artistry and Industry in Britain*, ed. Kyriaki Hadjiafxendi and Patricia Zakreski, 89–104 (Farnham, UK: Ashgate, 2013), 95.

12 The literature here is vast, and the following presents only a small selection: Goggin and Tobin, eds, *Women and the Material Culture of Needlework and Textiles*; T'ai Smith, *Bauhaus Weaving Theory: From Feminine Craft to Mode of Design* (Minneapolis: University of Minnesota Press, 2014); Janice Helland, "Ishbel Aberdeen's 'Irish' Dresses: Embroidery, Display and Meaning, 1886–1909," *Journal of Design History* 26, no. 2 (2012): 152–67; Sabine Wieber, "The Warp and the Weft: Tradition and Innovation in Skaerbaek Tapestries, 1896–1903," *Journal of Design History* 28, no. 4 (2015): 331–47.

13 There are notable exceptions, however, including the work of Christopher Breward and Peter McNeil. See, for instance, Christopher Breward, *The Hidden Consumer: Masculinities, Fashion and City Life, 1860–1914* (Manchester: Manchester University Press, 1999); Christopher Breward, *The Suit: Form, Function, and Style* (London: Reaktion, 2016); Peter McNeil, *Pretty Gentlemen: Macaroni Men and the Eighteenth-century Fashion World* (New Haven, CT: Yale University Press, 2018).

14 McBrinn, "'The work of masculine fingers'"; Joseph McBrinn, "Needlepoint for Men: Craft and Masculinity in Postwar America," *Journal of Modern Craft* 8, no. 3 (2015): 301–31; Joseph McBrinn, "Queer Hobbies: Ernest Thesiger and Interwar Embroidery," *Textile* 15, no. 3 (2017): 292–323.

15 See, for instance, Michelle Maskiell, "Consuming Kashmir: Shawls and Empires, 1500–2000," *Journal of World History* 13, no. 1 (2002): 27–65; and Jean Comaroff, "The Empire's Old Clothes: Fashioning the Colonial Subject," in *Cross-Cultural Consumption: Global Markets, Local Realities*, ed. David Howes, 19–38 (London: Routledge, 1996).

16 Kyriaki Hadjiafxendi and Patricia Zakreski, "Introduction: Artistry and Industry— The Process of Female Professionalisation," in *Crafting the Woman Professional in the Long Nineteenth Century: Artistry and Industry in Britain*, ed. Kyriaki Hadjiafxendi and Patricia Zakreski, 1–22 (Farnham, UK: Ashgate, 2013), 2.

17 Kristina Huneault, "Professionalism as Critical Concept and Historical Process for Women and Art in Canada," in *Rethinking Professionalism: Women and Art in Canada, 1850–1970*, ed. Kristina Huneault and Janice Anderson, 3–52 (Montreal & Kingston: McGill-Queen's University Press, 2012), 9.

18 Stephen Knott, *Amateur Craft: History and Theory* (London: Bloomsbury Academic, 2015).

19 Knott, xiii.

20 Huneault, 14.

21 Huneault, 8.

22 Huneault, 7.

23 Huneault, 7.

24 Julia Bryan-Wilson makes a similar suggestion in *Fray*; she writes, "Rather than adopt a binary scheme in which amateurism is defined, oppositional, against

professionalism, I understand these as ever-mobile terms in a broader, flexible matrix that admits a range of individual and collective production by all kinds of self-proclaimed textile makers. This book structurally asserts how, in the case of textiles, fine art and amateur practices are mutually coconstitutive, constantly informing each other and viewed radically differently depending on context." Bryan-Wilson, 5.

25 For a consideration of the constraints of professionalism as a category through which to analyze artistic achievement in relation to Indigenous women's production, see Sherry Farrell Racette, "'I Want to Call Their Names in Resistance': Writing Aboriginal Women into Canadian Art History, 1880–1970," in *Rethinking Professionalism: Women and Art in Canada, 1850–1970*, ed. Kristina Huneault and Janice Anderson, 285–326 (Montreal & Kingston: McGill-Queen's University Press, 2012).

26 Rozsika Parker, *The Subversive Stitch: Embroidery and the Making of the Feminine* (London: I. B. Tauris, 2010 [1984]); Annette B. Weiner and Jane Schneider, eds, *Cloth and Human Experience* (Washington, D.C.: Smithsonian, 1988).

27 Lisa Tickner, *The Spectacle of Women: Imagery of the Suffrage Campaign, 1907–14* (Chicago: University of Chicago Press, 1988).

28 Laurel Thatcher Ulrich, *The Age of Homespun: Objects and Stories in the Creation of an American Myth* (New York: Vintage Books, 2002 [2001]).

29 For a thoughtful list of scholarship in this area, see Aram Han Sifuentes, Lisa Vinebaum, and Namita Gupta Wiggers, *Unsettling Coloniality: A Critical and Radical Fiber/Textile Bibliography* available through the Critical Craft Forum, http://www.criticalcraftforum.com/unsettling-coloniality-a-critical-and-radical-fibertextile-bibliography/. As the authors explain, the aim of this project is to identify resources that contribute to conversations "addressing decolonization, unsettling coloniality, and identifying and rupturing structures of white power and privilege in society, the art world, and in the field of fiber and textiles."

30 Beverly Lemire, *Cotton* (Oxford: Berg, 2011), 87.

31 Beverly Lemire, "Domesticating the Exotic: Floral Culture and the East India Calico Trade with England, 1600–1800," *Textile: The Journal of Cloth and Culture* 1, no. 1 (2003): 65–85. Similar analyses of the domestication of exotic textiles and design motifs can be found in Susan S. Bean, "Bandanna: On the Indian Origins of an All-American Textile," *Textiles in Early New England: Design, Production, and Consumption*, 168–83 (Boston: Boston University, 1997); and Maskiell, "Consuming Kashmir."

32 Amelia Peck, "Trade Textiles at the Metropolitan Museum: A History," in *Interwoven Globe: The Worldwide Textile Trade, 1500–1800*, ed. Amelia Peck, 2–11 (New York: Metropolitan Museum of Art, 2013), 3.

33 Jessica Hemmings, "Introduction," in *Cultural Threads: Transnational Textiles Today*, ed. Jessica Hemmings, 8–25 (London: Bloomsbury, 2015), 12. The term "material vector" comes from Maskiell, "Consuming Kashmir."

34 Christine Checinska, "Crafting Difference: Art, Cloth and the African Diasporas," in *Cultural Threads: Transnational Textiles Today*, ed. Jessica Hemmings, 144–67 (London: Bloomsbury, 2015), 148.

35 Checinska, 148.

36 For a consideration of how strategies of discourse and display were mobilized to reposition the ways in which the American public viewed and interpreted quilts, see Karin Elizabeth Peterson, "Discourse and Display: The Modern Eye, Entrepreneurship, and the Cultural Transformation of the Patchwork Quilt," *Sociological Perspectives* 46, no. 4 (2003): 461–90.

37 Jonathan Holstein, *Abstract Design in American Quilts* (New York: Whitney Museum of American Art, 1971), 10.

38 See, for instance, Janet Catherine Berlo and Patricia Cox Crews, *Wild by Design: Two Hundred Years of Innovation and Artistry in American Quilts* (Seattle: University of Washington Press in association with the International Quilt Study Center at the University of Nebraska-Lincoln, 2003).

39 See, for instance, John Beardsley, et al., *The Quilts of Gee's Bend* (Atlanta, GA: Tinwood, 2002); Gladys-Marie Fry, *Stitched from the Soul: Slave Quilts from the Antebellum South* (Chapel Hill: University of North Carolina Press, 2002 [1989]); and Kyra E. Hicks, *This I Accomplish: Harriet Powers' Bible Quilt and Other Pieces* (Arlington, VA: Black Threads Press, 2009).

40 Elissa Auther, *String, Felt, Thread: The Hierarchy of Art and Craft in American Art* (Minneapolis: University of Minnesota Press, 2010).

41 For a history of craftivist practice, see Kirsty Robertson, "Rebellious Doilies and Subversive Stitches: Writing a Craftivist History," in *Extra/Ordinary: Craft and Contemporary Art*, ed. Maria Elana Buszek, 184–203 (Durham, NC: Duke University Press, 2011).

42 Jules Prown, "Style as Evidence," *Winterthur Portfolio* 15, no. 3 (1980): 198.

43 Arjun Appadurai, "Introduction: Commodities and the Politics of Value," in *The Social Life of Things: Commodities in Cultural Perspective*, ed. Arjun Appadurai, 3–63 (Cambridge: Cambridge University Press, 1981).

44 Gillian Rose, *Visual Methodologies: An Introduction to the Interpretation of Visual Materials*, 2nd edn (Los Angeles: Sage, 2007), 223.

45 Beth Fowkes Tobin and Maureen Daly Goggin, "Introduction: Materializing Women," in *Women and Things, 1750-1950: Gendered Material Strategies*, ed. Maureen Daly Goggin and Beth Fowkes Tobin, 1–14 (Farnham, UK: Ashgate, 2009), 2. The other volumes in this series are Goggin and Tobin, eds, *Women and the Material Culture of Needlework and Textiles, 1750–1950*, cited above; Maureen Daly Goggin and Beth Fowkes Tobin, eds, *Material Women, 1750–1950: Consuming Desires and Collecting Practices* (Farnham, UK: Ashgate, 2009); and Maureen Daly Goggin and Beth Fowkes Tobin, eds, *Women and the Material Culture of Death* (Farnham, UK: Ashgate, 2013).

46 Hadjiafxendi and Zakreski, eds, *Crafting the Woman Professional*.

47 Janice Helland, Beverly Lemire, and Alena Buis, eds, *Craft, Community and the Material Culture of Place and Politics, 19th–20th Century* (Farnham, UK: Ashgate, 2014). See, in particular, Anne de Stecher's "Souvenir Art, Collectable Craft, Cultural Heritage: The Wendat (Huron) of Wendake, Quebec," and Claire Wintle's "Negotiating the Colonial Encounter: Making Objects for Export in the Andaman Islands, 1858–1920" in this volume.

48 Pristash, Schaechterle, and Wood, 14–15.

49 Beverly Gordon identifies a number of these words and phrases in *Textiles: The Whole Story* (New York: Thames & Hudson, 2011), 22.

50 Victoria Mitchell, "Textiles, Text and Techne," in *The Textile Reader*, ed. Jessica Hemmings, 5–13 (London: Berg, 2012), 7.

51 Jasleen Dhamija, "Textile: The Non-verbal Language," in *Reinventing Textiles*, vol. 3, *Postcolonialism and Creativity*, ed. Paul Sharrad and Anne Collett, 51–54 (Bristol: Telos, 2004), 51.

52 Elaine Showalter, "Piecing and Writing," in *Textiles: Critical and Primary Sources*, vol. 4, *Identity*, ed. Catherine Harper, 203–19 (London: Berg, 2012).

53 Janet Catherine Berlo, "Beyond *Bricolage*: Woman and Aesthetic Strategies in Latin American Textiles," in *Textile Traditions of Mesoamerica and the Andes: An Anthology*, ed. Margot Blum Schevill, Janet Catherine Berlo, and Edward B. Dwyer, 437–67 (New York: Garland, 1991), 447.

54 John Styles, "Objects of Emotion: The London Foundling Hospital Tokens, 1741–60," in *Writing Material Culture History*, ed. Anne Gerritsen and Giorgio Riello, 165–71 (London: Bloomsbury, 2015), 166.

55 Pristash, Schaechterle, and Wood, 16.

56 Pristash, Schaechterle, and Wood, 14.

57 Hadjiafxendi and Zakreski, 18.

58 Like Zimmermann, Phillips attempted to transform knitting practice in America through educational publication. Her *Creative Knitting: A New Art Form* (first issued 1971) outlined an array of stitches and techniques with the hope of encouraging knitters to turn inspiration into reality, and to employ "their talents in a more creative way." Mary Walker Phillips, *Creative Knitting: A New Art Form*, ed. Patricia Abrahamian, new and expanded edn (Mineola, NY: Dover, 2013), 12.

59 Pristash, Schaechterle, and Wood, 13.

60 Tickner, 66.

61 Judy Attfield, "Change: The Ephemeral Materiality of Identity," in *Textiles: Critical and Primary Sources*, vol. 4, *Identity*, ed. Catherine Harper, 180–202 (London: Berg, 2012), 181.

62 Cheryl Buckley and Hilary Fawcett, *Fashioning the Feminine: Representation and Women's Fashion from the Fin de Siècle to the Present* (London: Tauris, 2002), 7.

Chapter 1 The Identity of an Embroidering Woman: The Needle Arts in Brussels, Belgium, 1850–1914

Acknowledgments

I would like to express my gratitude to my supervisor Prof. Dr. Katlijne Van der Stighelen (KU Leuven), to the editors Johanna Amos and Lisa Binkley, and to the anonymous reviewers for their advice and suggestions. Primary results of this book chapter were presented during the UAAC conference session "Stitching the Self: Exploring the Power of the Needle" at NSCAD University in Halifax, Canada held 5–7 November 2015. A YouReCa travel grant given by the KU Leuven Doctoral School for the Humanities and Social Sciences enabled me to attend this conference.

1   Wendy Wiertz, *Vrouwen met stijl. Vier penseelprinsessen in Hingene* (Antwerp: Kasteel d'Ursel, with Provinciebestuur Antwerpen, 2013), Exhibition catalogue, 84–115.

2   Anne Higonnet, "Vrouwen in de kunst: verschijningsvormen, ontspanning en beroep," in *Geschiedenis van de vrouw*, vol. 4, *De negentiende eeuw*, ed. Georges Duby and Michelle Perrot, 225–38 (Paris: Plon, 1991), 313.

3   Rozsika Parker and Griselda Pollock, *Old Mistresses: Women, Art and Ideology* (New York: Pantheon, 1981), 50–51, 58–70, 80–81; Rozsika Parker, *The Subversive Stitch: Embroidery and the Making of the Feminine*, rev. edn (London: I.B. Tauris, 2010).

4   "Does one have to conclude that the feminine industry (I do of course speak here of the privileged women who are not obliged to work) is nearly depleted? Certainly not." Alma, "Pénélopes modernes," *Bruxelles Féminin*, 1 November 1904, 11–12, 11. All translations are the author's own.

5   "The number of young women and young girls in this place, who devote their free time to execute delicate, artistic and practical fancywork, rises each day. This is a very intelligent and certainly a much more interesting way to spend one's free time [. . .] than those unfruitful trials of grand art in which some snobs take delight." Alma, 11.

6   "13 mars 1886: Nous prenons des leçons de dentelle. Henriette et Lololle en font déjà de fort jolies." ["13th March 1886: We are taking lessons in making bobbin lace. Henriette and Lololle already make beautiful pieces."]. Typescript *Jeanne de Villermont, Memorandum*, 1867–1926, private archives, Boussu-en-Fagne; Wendy Wiertz, "Une 'femme complète.' La Comtesse Marie de Villermont (1848–1925)," *Le Parchemin* 430 (2017): 289–308.

7   "My mother whose fairylike fingers were indefatigable, loved nothing more than passing long hours of the day embroidering or sewing for the poor on the castle's terrace." Typescript *Marie de Villermont, Mes souvenirs, c.* 1925, 62, private archive, Boussu-en-Fagne.

8   Ann Bermingham, *Learning to Draw: Studies in the Cultural History of a Polite and Useful Art* (New Haven, CT: Yale University Press, 2000), x–xi; Lanto Synge, *Art of Embroidery: History of Style and Technique* (Woodbridge, UK: Antique Collectors' Club, with The Royal School of Needlework, 2001), 71–74; Christophe Loir, *L'émergence des beaux-arts en Belgique: institutions, artistes, public et patrimoine (1773–1835)*, Études sur le XVIIIe siècle 10 (Brussels: Éditions de l'Université de Bruxelles, 2004), 108.

9   Éliane Gubin, "Politics and Anticlericalism: Belgium," in *Girls' Secondary Education in the Western World: From the 18th to the 20th Century*, eds. James C. Albisetti, Joyce Goodman, and Rebecca Rogers, 121–32 (Basingstoke, UK: Palgrave Macmillan, 2010), 122.

10   Valérie Piette, "Un réseau privé d'éducation des filles. Institutrices et pensionnats à Bruxelles (1830–1860)," *Sextant* 13–14 (2000): 149–77, 150, 165, 171, 173; Rebecca Rogers, *From the Salon to the Schoolroom: Educating Bourgeois Girls in Nineteenth-century France* (University Park, PA: Pennsylvania State University Press, 2005), 19–35; James C. Albisetti, Joyce Goodman, and Rebecca Rogers, "A Historical Introduction," in *Girls' Secondary Education in the Western World: From the 18th to the 20th Century*, eds. James C. Albisetti, Joyce Goodman, and Rebecca Rogers, 1–9 (Basingstoke: Palgrave Macmillan, 2010), 3–5; Gubin, 121–32.

11   "L'École professionnelle Bischoffsheim," *Bruxelles Féminin*, 1 December 1903, 8–9; Phyllis Stock, *Better than Rubies: A History of Women's Education* (New York: Capricorn Books, 1978), 158; Marianne de Vreese, "L'association pour l'enseignement professionnel des femmes et les débuts de l'école Bischoffsheim à Bruxelles, 1864–1868," *Revue belge d'Histoire contemporaine/ Belgisch Tijdschrift voor Nieuwste Geschiedenis* 22, no. 3–4 (1991): 630–40; Françoise Mayeur, "L'éducation des filles: Le modèle laïque," in *Histoire des femmes en Occident*, vol. 4, *Le XIXe siècle*, eds. Georges Duby and Michelle Perrot (Paris: Plon, 1991), 238; Gubin, 126.

12   Gubin, 126.

13   "L'École professionnelle Bischoffsheim," 8–9; de Vreese, 630–46; Mayeur, 238; Gubin, 126.

14   "Auguste Orts," in *Biographie Nationale* (Brussels: Académie Royale, 1901), 16:334.

15   James F. McMillan, *France and the Women 1789–1914: Gender, Society and Politics* (London and New York: Routledge, 2000), 4–6.

16   The painter Louis De Taeye (1822–1891) wrote in 1882 *Traité général de l'enseignement des arts du dessin* inserted in *Études sur les arts plastiques en Belgique*. Louis De Taeye and Edmond-Louis De Taeye, *Études sur les arts plastiques en Belgique* (Brussels: Bruylant Christophe & Cie, 1891), 293; Pieter D'Hondt, *L'Académie royale des Beaux-Arts et École des Arts décoratifs de Bruxelles. Notice historique publiée à l'occasion du Centenaire de la réouverture de cette institution*

artistique (1800–1900) (Brussels: J. Lebègue & Cie, 1900), 140; Georges Mayer, "Histoire de l'Académie de Bruxelles et évolution de son enseignement," in *Académie Royale des Beaux-Arts de Bruxelles. 275 ans d'enseignement/ 275 jaar onderwijs aan de Koninklijke Academie voor Schone Kunsten van Brussel*, 21–40 (Brussels: Gemeentekrediet, 1987), catalogue of an exhibition at the Royal Museums of Fine Arts of Belgium, Brussels, 34–35; Sabine Van Cauwenberge and Leen de Jong, "Vrouwelijke kunstenaars in België van 1800–1950," in *Elck zijn waerom. Vrouwelijke kunstenaars in België en Nederland 1500–1950*, eds. Katlijne Van der Stighelen and Mirjam Westen, 68–87 (Ghent: Ludion, 1999), catalogue of an exhibition at the Royal Museum of Fine Arts, Antwerp and the Museum for Modern Art, Arnhem, 73; Alexia Creusen, *Femmes artistes en Belgique. XIXe et début XXe siècle* (Paris: L'Harmattan, 2007), 53; Daniela Nicolosa Prina, "L'Unité des arts avant l'art nouveau. La réforme de l'enseignement artistique et industriel en Belgique pendant la deuxième moitié du XIXème siècle" (PhD diss., Politecnico di Torino, Turin and Katholieke Universiteit Leuven, Leuven, 2009); Niels Matheve, "'Kunst is geld.' Het politiek beleid ten aanzien van het Belgische kunstonderwijs in de negentiende eeuw," *De Negentiende Eeuw* 37, no. 2 (2013): 97–115, 100, 109–10.

17 Pol De Mont, "Hedendaagse Gebruikskunst. I Mevrouw De Rudder," *Kunst & Leven* 1, no. 5 (1902): 1–7, 1.

18 Sander Pierron, "Hélène De Rudder," *Notre Pays. Revue panoramique Belge*, 4 January 1920, 343; Pierre Baudson, "De Rudder, Isidore (Bruxelles 1855–Uccle/ Bruxelles 1943)," in *Académie Royale des Beaux-Arts de Bruxelles. 275 ans d'enseignement/ 275 jaar onderwijs aan de Koninklijke Academie voor Schone Kunsten van Brussel* (Brussels: Crédit Communal/ Gemeentekrediet, 1987), catalogue of an exhibition at the Royal Museums of Fine Arts of Belgium, Brussels, 319–20; Paul Chantraine, "Précisions sur la vie et l'œuvre brodé d'Hélène De Rudder (1869–1962)" (MA diss., Université Catholique de Louvain, Louvain-la-Neuve, 1989), 34–35; Patricia Wardle, "War and Peace: Lace Designs by the Belgian Sculptor Isidore de Rudder (1855–1943)," *Bulletin van het Rijksmuseum* 37, no. 2 (1989): 73–90, 73–75; De Vreese, 645; Paul Piron, *De Belgische beeldende kunstenaars uit de 19de en 20ste eeuw* (Brussels: Art in Belgium, 1998), 1:422; Wim Pas and Greet Pas, "De Rudder, Isidore Liévin," in *Dictionnaire biographique. Arts plastiques en Belgique. Peintres, sculpteurs, graveurs. 1800–2002* (Antwerp: De Gulden Roos Arto, 2002), 374–75; Vicky Hobbels, "De kunst van het borduren tijdens de Art Nouveau. Hélène en Isidore De Rudder: een artistieke samenwerking" (MA diss., Ghent University, Ghent, 2004), 88–89; Alexia Creusen, "Du Ménil Hélène (1869–1962), épouse De Rudder. Brodeuse," in *Dictionnaire des femmes belges. XIXe et XXe siècles*, eds. Éliane Gubin, Catherine Jacques, Valérie Piette, et al. (Brussels: Éditions Racine, 2006), 220–21; Paul Piron, "De Rudder-Du Menil, Hélène (Ieper, 1869–Nice/ Frankrijk, 1962)," in *De Belgische beeldende kunstenaars van de 19de tot de 21e eeuw* (Ghent: Ludion, 2016), 1:733–34.

19 "Isn't he the one who has drawn all of her cartoon projects?" "It's he who drew all cartoon projects imagined by the embroideress and helped her to realize her artist's dreams." Pierron, 343.

20 [François] Thiébault-Sisson, "L'art décoratif en Belgique," *Art et Décoration* 1 (1897): 3–23, 22–23; Chantraine, 161–65; Barbara Caspers, "Les liens de parenté dans la construction des carrières des femmes artistes en Belgique," in *Femmes artistes. Les peintresses en Belgique (1880–1914)*, ed. Denis Laoureux, 31–45 (Milan: Silvana Editoriale, 2016), catalogue of an exhibition at Musée Félicien Rops, Namur, 44.

21 Piron, *De Belgische beeldende kunstenaars van de 19de tot de 21e eeuw*, 1:734.

22 "En effet, si Mme De Rudder brode, si un atelier assez nombreux de brodeuses travaille, désormais, chez elle et sous sa direction." "Indeed, when Mrs. De Rudder embroiders, when a studio with numerous embroiderers works, even then, at her place and under her supervision." Marguerite Van de Wiele, "Les Femmes Artistes. M. et Mme Isidore De Rudder," *Bruxelles Féminin*, 15 November 1903, 6–7; Cécile Dulière, "Naald en draad," in *Art Nouveau Belgïe: Europalia 80 Belgïe 150*, 141–44 (Brussels: Europalia Brussels, 1980), catalogue of an exhibition at Paleis voor Schone Kunsten, Brussels, 142; Creusen, "Du Ménil Hélène," 220–21; Creusen, *Femmes artistes*, 130; Alexia Creusen, "Femme et artiste dans la Belgique du XIXe siècle," in *Femmes artistes. Les peintresses en Belgique (1880–1914)*, ed. Denis Laoureux, 17–30 (Milan: Silvana Editoriale, 2016), catalogue of an exhibition at Musée Félicien Rops, Namur, 29.

23 *Thiébault-Sisson*, 22; Pierron, 347; Dulière, 142–43.

24 *Salon triennal des Beaux-Arts 1903. Catalogue* (Brussels: Imprimerie Fred. Tilbury, 1903), cat. nr. 1656–1659, Pl. LVI; "Peut-être, grâce à l'initiative de cette femme de goût, notre époque verra-t-elle se réaliser une renaissance de cet art subtil des brodeurs, dont on a trop méconnu le charme et la saveur." ["Maybe, thanks to the initiative of this woman with taste, our time will see the realization of a renaissance of this subtle embroiderers' art, which one has for too long denied the charm and appeal."] "La sculpture et l'art appliqué au Salon triennial," *Bruxelles Féminin*, 15 October 1903, 5–7, 7.

25 De Mont, 2–4; Pierron, 347.

26 Mary Smith Lockwood and Elizabeth Glaister, *Art Embroidery: A Treatise on the Revived Practice of Decorative Needlework* (London: Marcus Ward, 1878); Abraham Marie Hammacher, "Belgïe, Europa, Amerika," in *Art Nouveau Belgïe: Europalia 80 Belgïe 150*, 23–30 (Brussels: Europalia Brussels, 1980), catalogue of an exhibition at Paleis voor Schone Kunsten, Brussels, 23, 25, 28, 30; Dulière, 141–44; Françoise Aubry, "Art nouveau in Belgïe. Van het genot van ornamentiek tot de deugd van soberheid," in *Art Nouveau & design. Sierkunst van 1830 tot Expo 58*, ed. Claire Leblanc, 82–103 (Tielt: Lannoo, 2005); Petra Ten-Doesschate Chu, *Nineteenth-Century European Art*, 3rd edn (Boston: Prentice Hall, 2012), 350–56.

27 Chantraine, 38–39; Wardle, 78–90; Karen Thompson and Doris Bowman, "Belgian War Lace," *Women in World War I*, The National Museum of American History, accessed 21 June 2017, http://americanhistory.si.edu/collections/object-groups/women-in-wwi/belgian-war-lace.

28 "beautiful ladies hat, made by Miss Devleeschoudere, milliner in demand by the actresses of the *Théâtre du Parc*." "Mondanités," *L'Éventail*, 28 February 1892.

29 F. K. Prochaska, *Women and Philanthropy in Nineteenth-century England* (Oxford: Oxford University Press, 1980), 45–72; Bonnie G. Smith, *Ladies of the Leisure Class: The Bourgeoises of Northern France in the Nineteenth Century* (Princeton, NJ: Princeton University Press, 1981); Annelies Hemelsoet, "Liefdadigheid als roeping van de dame: Het sociaal engagement van de adellijke vrouw in het 19de-eeuwse Gent (1845–1880)," *Handelingen der maatschappij voor geschiedenis en oudheidkunde te Gent*, n. s., 56 (2000): 251–82; Leen Van Molle, "Comparing Religious Perspectives on Social Reform," in *Charity and Social Welfare*, ed. Leen Van Molle, 7–33 (Leuven: Leuven University Press, 2017).

30 The seven international exhibitions of which most are recognized as world exhibitions were mounted in the following years and cities: 1885 Antwerp, 1894 Antwerp, 1897 Brussels, 1905 Liège, 1909 Liège, 1910 Brussels, and 1913 Ghent.

31 Maarten Mahieu, "De Belgische wereldtentoonstelling voor de Eerste Wereldoorlog als spiegel van en actor in de sociale kwestie" (MA diss., Ghent University, Ghent, 2004), 168–75.

32 "A number of women have exhibited superb reposed leather, decorative embroideries, church ornaments, flags, tapestries, artistic furniture. The grand prix has been awarded to Miss Suzanne Weiller for her superb screen, an outstanding work." Elise Chesneau, "Sixième croquis d'exposition," *Revue nationale*, 1 October 1905, 10–11, 11.

33 "Finally, the point of the current Salon, which really is this year attractive and innovative: a section of applied arts." "La sculpture et l'art appliqué au Salon triennial," 5.

34 *Salon triennal des Beaux-Arts 1903*; *Exposition générale des Beaux-Arts. Bruxelles 1907* (Brussels: A. Lesigne, 1907); *Exposition universelle et internationale de Bruxelles 1910. Beaux-Arts. Catalogue général* (Brussels: A. Lesigne, 1910); *Exposition générale des Beaux-Arts (Salon Triennal-Bruxelles 1914)* (Brussels: L'Imprimerie (Anc Établ Ve Monnom) Société Anonyme, 1914).

35 *Salon triennal des Beaux-Arts 1903*.

36 *Exposition générale des Beaux-Arts. Bruxelles 1907*.

37 Piron, *De Belgische beeldende kunstenaars van de 19de tot de 21e eeuw*, 1:209.

38 Piron, *De Belgische beeldende kunstenaars van de 19de tot de 21e eeuw*, 2:851.

39 *L'Indépendance Belge*, 26 July 1898.

40 Siska Beele, "Clara Voortman-Dobbelaere," in *Elck zijn waerom. Vrouwelijke kunstenaars in België en Nederland 1500–1950*, eds. Katlijne Van der Stighelen and Mirjam Westen (Ghent: Ludion, 1999), a catalogue for an exhibition at the Royal Museum of Fine Arts, Antwerp and the Museum for Modern Art, Arnhem, 268; Caroline D'Hondt, "Clara Voortman-Dobbelaere (Gent, 1853–Menton, 1926). Een burgerlijk leven in artistieke kringen vereeuwigd via houtskool- en pasteltekeningen, olieverfschilderijen en sierkunsten" (MA diss., University of Ghent, Ghent, 2012).

41 Henriette Bosché predominantly appeared in the press during the Interbellum: *La Nation Belge* (12 April 1924; 21 June 1926); *La Meuse* (13 April 1924; 26 May 1936); *L'Indépendance Belge* (9 April 1924; 30 June 1934); *L'Avenir du Luxembourg* (21 June 1926). Irène D'Olszowska's name only appeared once in *La Nation Belge* (8 April 1934), and Clara Voortman was named in several papers: *Vaderland* (15 December 1911; 16 December 1911; 17 December 1911; 20 December 1911; 25 December 1911; 28 December 1911; 24 May 1912); *L'Indépendance Belge* (2 October 1907; 13 January 1908; 17 January 1908; 22 December 1912); *Journal de Bruxelles* (25 October 1900; 5 June 1901; 24 January 1908); *Het Laatste Nieuws* (13 January 1908; 13 March 1912); *Gazette de Charleroi* (28 December 1912).

Chapter 2 "Experiments in silk and gold work afterwards to bloom": The Embroidering of Jane Burden Morris

Acknowledgments

I thank the Social Sciences and Humanities Research Council, the Bader Fellowship program, and the Queen's University Fund for Scholarly Research and Creative Work and Professional Development (Adjuncts) for funding the research upon which this chapter is based.

1 Jane Morris, in Add. MS 45341, British Library.

2 Historically the execution of this work was attributed to Jane Morris; however, more recently the embroidery has been credited to Jane's sister, Elizabeth Burden. See A. R. Dufty, *Morris Embroideries: The Prototypes* (London: Society of Antiquaries, 1985), 29; Tessa Wild, *William Morris and His Palace of Art* (London: Philip Wilson, 2018), 90–91. Image by kind permission of the Society of Antiquaries of London.

3 General Register Office, Holywell, Oxford, 1851 Census for England and Wales.

4 Leena A. Rana, "Stories behind the Stitches: Schoolgirl Samplers of the Eighteenth and Nineteenth Centuries," *Textile* 12, no. 2 (2014): 158–79, 160.

5 J. W. Mackail, *The Life of William Morris* (London: Longman, 1899), 1:142–43.

6 For a fascinating discussion of the nineteenth-century significance of Berlin woolwork see Talia Schaffer, "Berlin Wool," *Victorian Review* 34, no. 1 (2008): 38–43.

7 Harley MS 4380, f. 1 and f. 10v, British Library. Several other patterns from this manuscript appear in Morris's early work. See, for instance, Alison Smith, "*Qui bien aime tard oublie,* early 1860s," in *Pre-Raphaelites: Victorian Avant-garde,* by Tim Barringer, Jason Rosenfeld, and Alison Smith (London: Tate, 2012), 183.

8 Wendy Parkins, *Jane Morris: The Burden of History* (Edinburgh: Edinburgh University Press, 2013), 150.

9 Morris, in BL Add. MS 45341.

10 Parkins, *Jane Morris,* 150.

11 Linda Parry, "Textiles," in *William Morris,* ed. Linda Parry (New York: Abrams, 1996), 226. The Morrises' daughters, Jenny and May, were born in 1861 and 1862, respectively.

12 Morris, in BL Add. MS 45341.

13 See, for instance, Georgiana Burne-Jones, *Memorials of Edward Burne-Jones* (London: Macmillan, 1909–12), 1:218: "[William] Morris was a pleased man when he found that his wife could embroider any design that he made, and did not allow her talent to remain idle."

14 Only Ariadne (planned) and Lucretia (completed) overlap.

15 In a letter to his daughter, Morris writes, "I am glad you have been to Hardwick; it is in a very genuine state still I believe: I think it must be 20 years ago since I went there." See William Morris to Jenny Morris, [13 June 1877], in *The Collected Letters of William Morris,* ed. Norman Kelvin (Princeton, NJ: Princeton University Press, 1984–96), 1:377. See also, Ray Watkinson, "Morris's Beginnings in Embroidery," *Journal of William Morris Studies* 8, no. 1 (1988): 25–28.

16 Morris, in BL Add. MS 45341.

17 These figures, Hippolyte, Helen, and Lucretia, now comprise a screen in the collection of Castle Howard. St Catherine was attached to a plain background, which, according to visual evidence, was at one point used as a portiere by the Burne-Joneses. It is now in the collection of the Society of Antiquaries, Kelmscott Manor.

18 Wendy Parkins, "Feeling at Home: Gender and Creative Agency at Red House," *Journal of Victorian Culture* 15, no. 1 (2010): 61–81, 74.

19 See, for instance, Sheila Kirk, *Philip Webb: Pioneer of Arts and Crafts Architecture* (Chichester, UK: Wiley-Academy, 2005); Parry, *William Morris;* Diane Waggoner, ed., *"The Beauty of Life": William Morris and the Art of Design* (New York: Thames & Hudson, 2003).

20 Jan Marsh, "The Female Side of the Firm," *Crafts* 140 (1996): 42–45, 43.

21 Violet Hunt, "Kelmscott to Kelmscott," *Journal of William Morris Studies* 2, no. 3 (1968): 6–17, 9.

22 Anthea Callen, *Angel in the Studio: Women Artists in the Arts and Crafts Movement, 1870–1914* (London: Astragal, 1979), 219.

23 Morris, Marshall, Faulkner & Co., Minute book commencing 10 December 1862, DD/235/1, Hammersmith and Fulham Archive, London.

24 Parry, "Textiles," 226. A review in the *Clerical Journal* does specify "hangings of serge." See Dufty, 10.

25 Dufty, 11.

26 "The Medieval Court, International Exhibition," *The Building News and Architectural Review: A Weekly Illustrated Record of the Progress of Architecture, Sculpture, Painting, Engineering, Metropolitan Improvements, Sanitary Reform, &c.*, 8 August 1862, 99. See Joanna Banham and Jennifer Harris, eds, *William Morris and the Middle Ages* (Manchester: Manchester University Press, 1984) for further accounts of the exhibition's reception.

27 Jan Marsh, *Jane and May Morris: A Biographical Story, 1839–1938* (n.p.: Jan Marsh, 2000), 168.

28 For instance, in a letter from December 1877, William Morris bemoans the difficulties of tracking payments and materials in his wife's absence. See William Morris to Jane Morris, 14 December 1877, in *The Collected Letters of William Morris*, ed. Norman Kelvin, 1:419–20.

29 The V&A lists this work as that of Jane and May Morris; however, in the 1914 catalogue for the arts and crafts exhibition in Paris, for which May coordinated many items, the work is credited to Jane only. See Board of Trade, *Arts décoratifs de Grande-Bretagne et d'Irlande: exposition, Palais du Louvre, Pavillon de Marsan, Avril-Octobre 1914* ([London]: H. M. Stationery Office, [1914]).

30 May Morris, quoted in Annette Carruthers, *The Arts and Crafts Movement in Scotland: A History* (New Haven, CT: Yale University Press, 2013), 211–12.

31 Board of Trade, *Ghent International Exhibition 1913: Catalogue of the British Arts and Crafts Section* (London: Board of Trade Exhibitions Branch, [1913]); Board of Trade, *Arts décoratifs de Grande-Bretagne*.

32 According to museum records, the Morris & Co. example may also have been intended for Rounton Grange.

33 M. S. Lockwood and E. Glaister, *Art Embroidery: A Treatise on the Revived Practice of Decorative Needlework* (London: Marcus Ward, 1878), 8–9.

34 Kyriaki Hadjiafxendi and Patricia Zakreski, "Introduction: Artistry and Industry—The Process of Female Professionalisation," in *Crafting the Woman Professional in the Long Nineteenth Century: Artistry and Industry in Britain*, ed. Kyriaki Hadjiafxendi and Patricia Zakreski, 1–22 (Farnham, UK: Ashgate, 2013), 19.

35 These include *La Pia de'Tolomei* (1868; Spencer Museum of Art), *The Blue Silk Dress (Mrs. William Morris)* (1868; Kelmscott Manor/Society of Antiquaries), *Mariana* (1870; Aberdeen Art Gallery & Museums), *Veronica Veronese* (1872; Delaware Art

Museum), *Marigolds* (1873; Nottingham Castle Museum and Art Gallery), and *La Donna della Finestra* (1879; Fogg Museum).

36 This gown also features in *Mariana*.

37 Dante Gabriel Rossetti to Jane Morris, 5 May 1868, in *Dante Gabriel Rossetti and Jane Morris: Their Correspondence*, ed. John Bryson and Janet Camp Troxell (Oxford: Clarendon Press, 1976), 2.

38 Dante Gabriel Rossetti to Jane Morris, 5 May 1868, in *Dante Gabriel Rossetti and Jane Morris: Their Correspondence*, ed. John Bryson and Janet Camp Troxell, 2.

39 Dante Gabriel Rossetti to Henry Treffry Dunn, 29 May 1873, in *The Correspondence of Dante Gabriel Rossetti*, ed. William E. Fredeman (Woodbridge, UK: Boydell and Brewer, 2002–10), 6:158.

40 Dante Gabriel Rossetti to Theodore Watts-Dunton, 11 March 1874, in *The Correspondence of Dante Gabriel Rossetti*, ed. William E. Fredeman, 6:424.

41 Dante Gabriel Rossetti to Jane Morris, 29 February 1880, in *Dante Gabriel Rossetti and Jane Morris: Their Correspondence*, ed. John Bryson and Janet Camp Troxell, 143.

42 Rossetti's letters suggest Morris wore the garment to at least one party early in 1870. See Dante Gabriel Rossetti to Jane Morris, 7 March 1870, in *The Correspondence of Dante Gabriel Rossetti*, ed. William E. Fredeman, 4:393.

43 Emma Lazarus to Helena deKay Gilder, 4 July 1883, in *Emma Lazarus in Her World: Life and Letters*, by Bette Roth Young (Philadelphia: Jewish Publication Society, 1995), 111.

44 This style is also sometimes described as aesthetic or Pre-Raphaelite dress.

45 "Aesthetic Dress," *Queen* (1881): 344.

46 Jeanette Marshall, 1883, quoted in Zuzanna Shonfield, *The Precariously Privileged: A Professional Family in Victorian London* (Oxford: Oxford University Press, 1987), 117.

47 Vernon Lee to [her mother], 5 July 1881, in *Vernon Lee's Letters*, ed. Irene Cooper Willis (London: privately printed, 1937), 70.

48 May Morris, *The Introductions to "The Collected Works of William Morris"* (New York: Oriole, 1973), 1:143. This is the blue silk gown of Rossetti's portrait of Morris.

49 Caroline Dakers, *The Holland Park Circle: Artists and Victorian Society* (New Haven, CT: Yale University Press, 1999), 28.

50 Anon., quoted in Dakers, 28.

51 For a further discussion of this garment in the context of artistic dress practices, see Robyne Erica Calvert, "Fashioning the Artist: Dress in Victorian Britain, 1848–1900" (PhD diss., University of Glasgow, 2012), 62–63.

52 Vernon Lee to [her mother], 5 July 1881, in *Vernon Lee's Letters*, ed. Irene Cooper Willis, 70.

53 William Morris himself is known to have worn a rural laborer's smock on occasion, and the V&A possesses a hand-embroidered indigo smock (*c.* 1875; T.216–1979) made by Georgiana Burne-Jones for the socialist-designer.

54 Burne-Jones, *Memorials*, 1:210.

55 For a discussion of Elizabeth Burden's accomplishments in embroidery, see Lynn Hulse, "Elizabeth Burden and the Royal School of Needlework," *Journal of William Morris Studies* 21, no. 1 (2014): 22–34.

56 Jane Morris to Theodore Watts-Dunton, [late October/early November 1887], in *The Collected Letters of Jane Morris*, ed. Frank C. Sharp and Jan Marsh (Woodbridge, UK: Boydell, 2012), 159.

57 Swinburne lived with Watts-Dunton at The Pines, Putney from 1879 until his death in 1909.

58 Morris regularly experienced back pain and headaches, though no definitive cause has been determined. The Morrises' eldest daughter, Jenny, was diagnosed with epilepsy as a teenager, and although the family had assistance, they kept Jenny at home as much as possible, even as her condition worsened.

59 Philip Webb to Jane Morris, [January 1869], in *The Letters of Philip Webb*, ed. John Aplin (London: Routledge, 2016), 1:24.

60 Jane Morris to Philip Webb, 25 July [1871], in *The Collected Letters of Jane Morris*, ed. Frank C. Sharp and Jan Marsh, 47.

61 Image by kind permission of the Society of Antiquaries of London.

Chapter 3 Becoming the Boss of Your Knitting: Elizabeth Zimmermann and the Emergence of Critical Knitting

1 Two texts were foundational to my analysis in this work: Sandra Alfoldy, *Crafting Identity: The Development of Professional Fine Craft in Canada* (Montreal & Kingston: McGill-Queen's University Press, 2005); and Dorothy Holland and Jean Lave, *History in Person: Enduring Struggles, Contentious Practice, Intimate Identities* (Santa Fe: School of American Research Press, 2001).

2 The US publication of *Vogue Knitting Book* is somewhat confusing as multiple *Vogue Knitting* periodicals drifted in and out of publication across the UK, Canada, and the United States. My work is based on Conde Nast's New York publication, OCLC # 15098883.

3 This analysis is based on the author's personal collection of *Vogue Knitting Book* (Conde Nast, New York, 1950–1969), *The Workbasket* (Modern Handcraft, Kansas City, 1950–1970), and twelve *Women's Day* specialty knitting publications (Fawcett Publications, Greenwich, CT, 1950–1973). None of these periodicals were available in public collections.

4 Betty Cornell, *Betty Cornell's Teen-Age Knitting Book* (New York: Prentice Hall, 1953).

5   Ida Riley Duncan, *Knit to Fit: A Comprehensive Guide to Hand and Machine Knitting* (New York: Liveright Publishing 1966), 94.

6   Ibid., 3.

7   Elizabeth Zimmermann, initial version of *Knitter's Almanac*, entry dated 27–28 January 1971, unpublished typescript, Schoolhouse Press Archives, Pittsville, WI, 29.

8   Ibid., 31.

9   Ibid.

10 Ibid., 31–32.

11 Ibid., 174.

12 Elizabeth Zimmermann, "Norwegian Sweaters: The Easy Way," *Woman's Day*, January 1955, 42–43, 119–20, directions 110–11.

13 Steeking is a technique for cutting hand-knit fabric, thus allowing for armholes and cardigan fronts in circular knitting.

14 Ibid., 120.

15 The WDC's multiple constitutional changes around membership (1955–1966) reveal a fascinating struggle within the organization to finally define the various states of practice between amateur and professional craftsmanship. See Wisconsin Designer Craftsman Collection, Milwaukee Art Museum Archives and Library, Milwaukee, WI.

16 Sandra Alfoldy, *Crafting Identity: The Development of Professional Fine Craft in Canada* (Montreal & Kingston: McGill-Queen's University Press, 2005).

17 Margaret Fish, "Unusual Gifts Available in Two Exhibits of Craft," *Milwaukee Sentinel*, 16 November 1958, Schoolhouse Press Archives, Pittsville, WI.

18 These original *Newsletters* were published in Meg Swanson, ed., *The Opinionated Knitter: Elizabeth Zimmermann's Newsletters 1958–1968* (Marshfield, WI: Schoolhouse Press, 2005).

19 Zimmermann used this term repeatedly. *Knitter's Almanac* was dedicated "to the Unsure Knitter, to the Blind Follower, and to all those who do not yet know that they can design their own knitting." See Elizabeth Zimmermann, *Knitter's Almanac* (New York: Charles Scribner's Sons, 1974).

20 Helen Snyder to Elizabeth Zimmermann, n.d. [*c.* 1979], Schoolhouse Press Archive, Pittsville, WI.

21 Susan Whiton to Elizabeth Zimmermann, n.d., Schoolhouse Press Archive, Pittsville, WI.

22 Linda Ligon, "Elizabeth Zimmermann: The Godmother of Knitting," *Interweave Knits*, Spring 2000, reprinted in Susan Strawn, *Knitting America* (Minneapolis, MN: Voyageur Press, 2007), 193.

23 Ruth Henry to Elizabeth Zimmermann, 8 March 1968, Schoolhouse Press Archives, Pittsville, WI.

24 Linda Dyett, untitled clipping hand identified as *The Village Voice*, April 1985, Schoolhouse Press Archives, Pittsville, WI.

25 Dorothy Camper to Elizabeth Zimmermann, n.d., Schoolhouse Press Archives, Pittsville, WI.

26 Norma Ellman, "Letters from Readers: Bench Notes," *Knitter's*, Fall 1989, 3.

27 Barbara Rondeau, Leisure Arts, "Letters," *Knitter's*, Summer 1989, 3.

28 "Letters: Chris Hyland," *Knitter's*, Winter 1989, 4–5.

29 Mary Klawitter to Elizabeth Zimmermann, n.d., Schoolhouse Press Archives, Pittsville, WI.

30 www.ravelry.com

31 Susan Blackwell Ramsey, *CoEvolution Quarterly*, undated, Schoolhouse Press Archives, Pittsville, WI; Susan Raven, "Week Two Born Again Knitting: Ribbing You Along," *Sunday Times Magazine* (London), 9 December 1984.

32 Elizabeth Zimmermann, typescript note dated January 1989, Schoolhouse Press Archives, Pittsville, WI.

33 Douglas Martin, "E. Zimmermann is Dead at 89; Revolutionized Art of Knitting," *New York Times*, 12 December 1999.

34 Elizabeth Zimmermann, initial version of *Knitter's Almanac*, entry dated "Tuesday, May 18," unpublished typescript at Schoolhouse Press Archives, Pittsville, WI, 173.

35 User Statistics, Ravelry, https://www.ravelry.com/statistics/users (accessed 29 August 2018).

36 Ibid.

37 Stephen West, "Baby, You're a Knitter," Westknits Mystery Knit-A-long Invitation, published 3 November 2015. https://www.youtube.com/watch?v=jwmfP0PNOLg.

Chapter 4 "Knitting is the saving of life; Adrian has taken it up too": Needlework, Gender, and the Bloomsbury Group

1   *The Hours*, directed by Stephen Daldry (Paramount Pictures, Miramax, 2002). The exchange does not appear in the Woolfs' original conversation that takes place in Richmond train station in Michael Cunningham's novel but is a dramatization that first appears in David Hare's screenplay for the film. See Michael Cunningham, *The Hours: A Novel* (New York: Farrar, Straus & Giroux, 1998), 170–72; and David Hare, *The Hours: Screenplay* (London: Faber and Faber, 2003), 93.

2   Hermione Lee, author of the first authorized biography since Woolf's nephew Quentin Bell's two-volume publication (1972), has further highlighted some of the complex issues surrounding the depiction of fact in fiction and has questioned some of the curious choices of the filmmakers (such as the bizarre prosthetic nose

Nicole Kidman wore in her award-winning depiction of Woolf). See Hermione Lee, *Virginia Woolf's Nose: Essays on Biography* (Princeton and London: Princeton University Press, 2005), 37–62; and Hermione Lee, *Virginia Woolf* (London: Chatto & Windus, 1996).

3   *Carrington*, directed by Christopher Hampton (Polygram/Dora Productions, 1995). Hampton wrote both the screenplay, based on Michael Holroyd's biography of Lytton Strachey (1967–68), and directed the film; see Christopher Hampton, *Carrington* (London: Faber and Faber, 1995), 6. The scene appears to be an amalgam of two trips to Asheham by Strachey, the first in early September 1913, at the invitation of Clive and Vanessa Bell. On this occasion Strachey sat for portraits by Roger Fry, Duncan Grant, and Vanessa Bell. Virginia and Leonard Woolf were not present, as she had been hospitalized after her breakdown. The second visit was in the autumn of 1915, again at the invitation of the Bells. This is the trip that Hampton is probably trying to dramatize, as it was here that Strachey met Carrington, an event Holroyd describes as "seismic," and thus warrants emphasis in the film's linear narrative. See Michael Holroyd, *Lytton Strachey: A Critical Biography*, vol. 2, *The Years of Achievement (1910–1932)* (London: Heinemann, 1968), 96–98, 182–84 [182].

4   The Bloomsbury group was a network of friends and lovers who initially lived, worked, and socialized in this small area of central London in the early-twentieth century, and who generated new ways of thinking about everything from aesthetics and morality, to gender, domesticity, and modernity. For the history of the Bloomsbury group, and origination of the term, see Quentin Bell, *Bloomsbury* (London: Weidenfeld and Nicolson, 1968); Leon Edel, *Bloomsbury: A House of Lions* (London: Hogarth Press, 1979); and S. P. Rosenbaum, *A Bloomsbury Group Reader* (Oxford: Blackwell, 1993). The key texts that pay particular attention to the group's central artistic concerns are Richard Shone, *Bloomsbury Portraits: Vanessa Bell, Duncan Grant and Their Circle* (London: Phaidon, 1976); Richard Shone, *The Art of Bloomsbury: Roger Fry, Vanessa Bell and Duncan Grant* (London: Tate Gallery Publishing, 1999); and Christopher Reed, *Bloomsbury Rooms: Modernism, Subculture, and Domesticity* (New Haven and London: Yale University Press, 2004).

5   Elizabeth Goodwin Perry, "Textile as Material, Method and Meaning, in Virginia Woolf's Fiction" (PhD diss., University of Pittsburgh, 1990), 8.

6   Virginia Woolf, "Sketches of the Past," and "Old Bloomsbury," in *Virginia Woolf: Moments of Being: Unpublished Autobiographical Writings*, ed. Jeanne Schulkind (London: Triad/Granada, 1978), 97 and 200.

7   Joan Russell Noble, ed., *Recollections of Virginia Woolf by Her Contemporaries* (London: Peter Owen, 1972), 157 and 152.

8   Noble, ed., *Recollections of Virginia Woolf*, 56–57.

9   Diary entry, 31 March 1940, in *The Diary of Virginia Woolf*, vol. 5, *1936–1941*, ed. Anne Olivier Bell and Andrew McNeillie (London: The Hogarth Press, 1984), 277.

10 See Shone, *Bloomsbury Portraits*, 93.

11 Sir George Savage, *Insanity and Allied Neuroses: Practical and Clinical* (London: Cassell, 1896 [1884]), 235.

12 Letter from Virginia Stephen to Leonard Woolf, 5 March 1912, in *The Letters of Virginia Woolf*, vol. 1, *The Flight of the Mind, 1888–1912*, ed. Nigel Nicolson and Joanne Trautmann (London: The Hogarth Press, 1975), 318.

13 Virginia Woolf, "Old Bloomsbury," 198.

14 Letter from Woolf to Violet Dickinson, quoted in Jean MacGibbon, *There's the Lighthouse: A Biography of Adrian Stephen* (London: James & James, 1997), 38.

15 For this context see Graham Richards, "Britain on the Couch: The Popularization of Psychoanalysis in Britain, 1918–1940," *Science in Context* 13, no. 2 (Summer 2000): 183–230; and Perry Meisel and Walter Kendrick, eds, *Bloomsbury/Freud: The Letters of James and Alix Strachey, 1924–1925* (New York: Basic Books, 1985).

16 Joan Riviere, "Womanliness as a Masquerade," *The International Journal of Psychoanalysis* 10 (1929): 303–13. Riviere's idea of "masquerade" has been hugely influential on later psychoanalytical explorations of gender and sexual identity as both "imaginary" and "symbolic"; for instance, see Jacques-Alain Miller, ed., *The Seminar of Jacques Lacan*, Book XI, *The Four Fundamental Concepts of Psychoanalysis*, trans. Alan Sheridan (New York and London: W.W. Norton, 1978 [1973]), 193. More recently feminists and queer theorists have cited Riviere's ideas as pioneering in understanding gender and sexual identity in terms of "performativity." See Judith Butler, "Lacan, Riviere, and the Strategies of Masquerade," in *Gender Trouble: Feminism and the Subversion of Identity*, 43–57 (New York: Routledge, 1990).

17 Lytton Strachey to Clive Bell, 22 October 1914, in *The Letters of Lytton Strachey*, ed. Paul Levy (London: Viking, 2005), 240–41. And see Holroyd, *Lytton Strachey*, 2:135.

18 Lytton Strachey to J. M. Keynes, 24 September 1914, quoted in Robert Skidelsky, *John Maynard Keynes*, vol. 1, *Hopes Betrayed, 1883–1920* (London: Macmillan, 1983), 296; and see Julie Anne Taddeo, *Lytton Strachey and the Search for Modern Sexual Identity: The Last Eminent Victorian* (New York: Harrington Park Press, 2002), 168 [note 111].

19 See Hermione Lee, *The Novels of Virginia Woolf* (London: Methuen, 1977); Perry Meisel, *The Absent Father: Virginia Woolf and Walter Pater* (New Haven and London: Yale University Press, 1980); Gayatri Chakravorty Spivak, "Unmaking and Making in *To the Lighthouse*," in *Other Worlds: Essays in Cultural Politics*, 30–45 (New York: Methuen, 1987); Jane Marcus, *Virginia Woolf and the Languages of Patriarchy* (Bloomington & Indianapolis: Indiana State University Press, 1987); Sayaka Okumura, "Women Knitting: Domestic Activity, Writing, and Distance in

Virginia Woolf's Fiction," *English Studies* 82, no. 2 (2008): 166–81; and Perry, "Textile as Material, Method and Meaning."

20 Virginia Woolf to Lady Robert Cecil, 29 September 1915, in *The Letters of Virginia Woolf*, vol. 2, *The Question of Things Happening, 1912–1922*, ed. Nigel Nicolson and Joanne Trautmann (London: The Hogarth Press, 1976), 64.

21 Perry, "Textile as Material, Method and Meaning," 63; and see Meisel, *The Absent Father*, 176–78.

22 Diary entry, 19 August 1920, in *The Diary of Virginia Woolf*, vol. 2, *1920–1924*, ed. Anne Olivier Bell and Andrew McNeillie (London: The Hogarth Press, 1978), 59; and diary entry, 19 August 1920, ibid, 59; and Virginia Woolf to Angelica Bell, 26 October 1940, in *The Letters of Virginia Woolf*, vol. 6, *Leave the Letters Till We're Dead, 1936–1941*, ed. Nigel Nicolson and Joanne Trautmann (London: The Hogarth Press, 1980), 442.

23 Virginia Woolf to Vanessa Bell, 17 September 1925, in *The Letters of Virginia Woolf*, vol. 3, *A Change of Perspective, 1923–1928*, ed. Nigel Nicolson and Joanne Trautmann (London: The Hogarth Press, 1977), 210.

24 Virginia Woolf to Vanessa Bell, 2 September 1925, ibid, 3:202.

25 Vita Sackville-West to Harold Nicolson, 13 June [1926], in *Vita and Harold: The Letters of Vita Sackville-West and Harold Nicolson, 1910–1962*, ed. Nigel Nicolson (London: Weidenfeld & Nicolson, 1992), 146.

26 Virginia Woolf to Vanessa Bell, end of August 1927, in *The Letters of Virginia Woolf*, ed. Nicolson and Trautmann, 3:414–15.

27 Virginia Woolf to Angelica Bell, 21 December 1940, in *The Letters of Virginia Woolf*, ed. Nicolson and Trautmann, 6:452.

28 Helen Sword, "Leda and the Modernists," *PMLA* 107, no. 2 (1992): 305–18, 306; Virginia Woolf to Angelica Bell, 27 August 1940, in *The Letters of Virginia Woolf*, ed. Nicolson and Trautmann, 6:423. Leda was the subject of paintings by Duncan Grant and poems by D. H. Lawrence and W. B. Yeats, which Woolf would have known.

29 See Elizabeth P. Richardson, *A Bloomsbury Iconography* (Winchester: St. Paul's Bibliographies, 1989), 184 [G7]. Richardson attributes her source to *Monk's House, East Sussex* (London: The National Trust, 1982), 4.

30 Frances Spalding, *Vanessa Bell* (London: Weidenfeld & Nicolson, 1983), 167.

31 Alexandra Gerstein, ed., *Beyond Bloomsbury: Designs of the Omega Workshops 1913–1919* (London: The Courtauld Galleries in association with Fontanka, 2009), 149.

32 Paul Nash, "Modern English Textiles," *Artwork* 2, no. 6 (1926): 80–87, 83.

33 Frances Spalding, *Duncan Grant* (London: Chatto & Windus, 1997), 133; and Spalding, *Vanessa Bell*, 151.

34 This method became known as "Couéism." Emile Coué came to London in 1921–1922 and Ethel Grant may have attended one of his public speaking events or

known his work through his writings. See Robert Graves and Alan Hodge, *The Long Week-End: A Social History of Great Britain, 1918–1939* (London: W.W. Norton, 1940), 188–89.

35 Dean R. Rapp, "'Better and Better–': Couéism as a Psychological Craze of the Twenties in Britain," *Studies in Popular Culture* 10, no. 2 (1987): 17–36, 17–18.

36 See R. T. Williamson, "Remarks on the Treatment of Neurasthenia and Psychasthenia Following Shell Shock," *British Medical Journal* 2, no. 2970 (1 December 1917): 713–15.

37 See, for example, Violet Cooper, "Embroidery and the Mental Patient," *Journal of the Association of Occupational Therapists* 3, no. 1 (February 1940): 5–7.

38 For the treatment of Morrell's nervous breakdown and depressions see Sandra Jobson Darroch, *Ottoline: The Life of Lady Ottoline Morrell* (London: Faber, 1974), 38 and 133; Miranda Seymour, *Ottoline Morrell: Life on the Grand Scale* (London: Hodder & Stoughton, 1992), 41 and 158.

39 A. E. L., "The World of Women," *The Illustrated London News*, issue 4435, 19 April 1924, 710. Morrell's panel after a design by Lamb is now untraced.

40 For this organization, see my "'The work of masculine fingers': The Disabled Soldiers' Embroidery Industry, 1918–1955," *Journal of Design History* 31, no. 1 (February 2018): 1–23.

41 For this context, see my "'Nothing is more terrifying to me than to see Ernest Thesiger sitting under the lamplight doing this embroidery': Ernest Thesiger (1879–1961), 'Expert Embroiderer,'" *TEXT: Journal for the Study of Textile Art, Design and History* 43 (2015/16): 20–26; and "Queer Hobbies: Ernest Thesiger and Interwar Embroidery," *Textile: Cloth and Culture* 15, no. 3 (September 2017): 292–322.

42 Taddeo, *Lytton Strachey and the Search for Modern Sexual Identity*, 105.

43 Virginia Woolf confessed to her sister her dislike of "a chair covered in bright yellow check, bought at the Omega," and shopping for an "18th century embroidery" to cover it from the fashionable Burnets and Souhami's; Virginia Woolf to Vanessa Bell, 15 July 1918, in *The Letters of Virginia Woolf*, ed. Nicolson and Trautmann, 2:259. Carrington recorded that "Lytton bought on my advice a most lovely bedspread, Queen Anne embroidery with a big sun flower in the middle, very pale colours, with flowers embroidered all over it. It is a vision of delight." See Carrington to Gerald Brennan, 18 December 1921, in *Carrington: Letters and Extracts from Her Diaries*, ed. David Garnett (London: Jonathan Cape, 1970), 200.

44 "Art Exhibition: Mr. Duncan Grant," *The Times*, 22 April 1927, 10.

45 Illustrated in Tony Bradshaw, *The Bloomsbury Artists: Prints and Book Design—a Catalogue* (Aldershot, UK: Scholar Press, 1999), 79 [no. 149].

46 Judith Collins, *The Omega Workshops* (London: Secker & Warburg, 1983), 106. And see A. Ruth Fry, *A Quaker Adventure: The Story of Nine Years' Relief and*

Reconstruction (London: Nesbit, 1926), 262–63, 287–88; Enid Huws Jones, *Margery Fry: The Essential Amateur* (London: Oxford University Press, 1966), 94–100; Roger Fry, "The Friends' Work for War Victims in France," *Charleston* 12 (Autumn/Winter 1995): 22–24; and Lynn Szygenda, "Roger Fry and the Friends' War Victims Relief Expedition," *Embroidery* 55 (November/December 2004): 45.

47 Melinda Cross notes that they used various mesh sizes and a "majority of the original designs were produced on hessian or sacking" in "cross-stitch, tent stitch, half-cross stitch, oblique Slav stitch, stem stitch, petit point." See *Bloomsbury Needlepoint: From the Tapestries at Charleston Farmhouse, with Charts of Designs by Duncan Grant, Vanessa Bell & Roger Fry* (London: Ebury Press, 1992), 114–15.

48 *Daily Express*, 18 March 1913, 5, quoted in Collins, *The Omega Workshops*, 42.

49 *Pall Mall Gazette*, 27 March 1913, n.p., quoted in Collins, *The Omega Workshops*, 42.

50 M. M. B., "Post-Impressionist Furniture," *Daily News and Leader*, 7 August 1913, 10, quoted in Richard Cork, *Art Beyond the Gallery in Early 20th Century Britain* (New Haven and London: Yale University Press, 1985), 138.

51 Undated and unsigned letter in C. R. Ashbee Papers, King's College Library, Cambridge, quoted in Isabelle Anscombe, *Omega and After: Bloomsbury and the Decorative Arts* (London: Thames & Hudson, 1981), 31, italics in the original.

52 Roger E. Fry, "The Exhibition of Illuminated Manuscripts at the Burlington Fine Arts Club," *The Burlington Magazine* 13, no. 63 (June 1908): 128–29, 128.

53 "The Ottoman and the Whatnot," *Athenaeum* no. 4652, 27 June 1919, 529–30, reprinted in *Vision and Design* (London: Pelican Books, 1937 [1920]), 40–46, 43.

54 For this see Christopher Reed, *Bloomsbury Rooms*, 241–42; and idem, "Bloomsbury as Queer Subculture," in *The Cambridge Companion to the Bloomsbury Group*, ed. Victoria Rosner, 71–89 (Cambridge: Cambridge University Press, 2014).

55 Richard Shone suggests that Grant and Bell "went into business as decorators in 1922" and suggests "[a]ccounts books were kept, estimates given, advertisements placed in periodicals and theatre programmes," see Richard Shone, "'. . . Decorations domestic ecclesiastical theatrical . . .,'" in *Duncan Grant & Vanessa Bell: Design and Decoration 1910–1960*, 2–6 (London: SPINK, 23 October–22 November 1991), 2. In the 1920s they sold designs through a shop called "Fearnley" on Davies Street in Mayfair and by the late 1930s they were approached to provide designs for Dunbar Hay Ltd.

56 Spalding, *Duncan Grant*, 323.

57 Lee, *Virginia Woolf*, 542.

58 Diary entry, 13 February 1932, in *The Diary of Virginia Woolf*, vol. 4, *1931–1935*, ed. Anne Olivier Bell and Andrew McNeillie (London: The Hogarth Press, 1982), 77.

59 See *The Embroiderers' Guild* (London: Walker's Galleries, 118 New Bond Street W., 1 November to 14 November 1923), cat. nos. 74, 83, 90, 94, 104, 124–28, 130. Ethel Grant also showed work (after a design by Vanessa Bell) at the 1927 Embroiderers'

Guild exhibition, see *The Embroiderers' Guild* (London: Walker's Galleries, 118 New Bond Street W., 26 January to 9 February 1927), cat. no. 142.

60 Clive Bell, "October Shows in London," *Vogue*, early November 1925, 70.

61 *The Arts and Crafts Exhibition Society, Catalogue of the Fifteenth Exhibition, at The Royal Academy, Burlington House,* © *1931* (London: ACES, 1931), see 28, "No. 24. Wyndham Tryon. Spanish Landscape. Woolwork on canvas. Executed and exhibited by Mary Hogarth"; 76, "No. 352. Duncan Grant. Appliqué Church banner. Executed by Mary Hogarth and Mary Symonds"; and 94, "No. 429. Roger Fry. Prie-dieu chair in cross-stitch wool. Executed by Miss Elwes."

62 *Catalogue, Exhibition of Modern British Embroidery, Victoria and Albert Museum, 1st to 30th July, 1932* (London: British Institute of Industrial Art, 1932). See nos. 25, 90, 91, 104, 117, 259, and 262.

63 *Catalogue of the Exhibition of English Needlework (Past and Present) in Aid of the Artists' General Benevolent Institution* (London: 15 Portman Square, W.1. By kind permission of The Lord & Lady Maud Carnegie, 19th February – 12th March 1934), see cat. nos. 240, 243, 244, 246, 250, 251, 253, 254, 258, 264, 265, 266, 273, 275, 310, 320–22, 324, 325, 330–34, 336, 337, 339, and 340.

64 There is a Pathé News film of the exhibition that shows Duncan Grant in the process of drawing a design for an embroidery; see Pathé News, *Needlework De Luxe*, 15 March 1934 [Film ID 1626. 13], https://www.britishpathe.com/video/needlework-de-luxe/query/VIII (accessed 30 June 2014).

65 *Catalogue of an Exhibition of 20th Century Needlework* (London: Ernest Brown & Phillips, [1935]).

66 Barbara Caine, "Bloomsbury Masculinity and Its Victorian Antecedents," *The Journal of Men's Studies* 15, no. 3 (Fall 2007): 271–81, 272.

67 Simon Watney, *The Art of Duncan Grant* (London: John Murray, 1990), 24; Alexandra Harris, "The Antimacassar Restored: Victorian Taste in the Early Twentieth Century," in *Strange Sisters: Literature and Aesthetics in the Nineteenth Century*, ed. Francesca Orestano and Francesca Frigerio, 255–72 (Oxford and Bern: Peter Lang, 2009), 264.

68 Reed, *Bloomsbury Rooms*, 298 [note 51], and see 236–37.

Chapter 5 *Whig's Defeat*: Stitching Settler Culture, Politics, and Identity

Acknowledgments

The revisions of this chapter and the editing of this volume were possible with the generosity of the Centre for Canadian Studies at Mount Allison University, Sackville, NB, where I was W.P. Bell Postdoctoral Fellow, and the collegial support of my colleagues in and out of Hart Hall.

1   Aimee E. Newell, "'Tattered to Pieces': Amy Fiske's Sampler and the Changing Roles of Women in Antebellum New England," in *Women and the Material Culture of Needlework & Textiles*, ed. Maureen Daly Goggin and Beth Fowkes Tobin, 51–68 (Farnham, UK: Ashgate, 2009), 57.

2   Ruth McKendry, *Quilts and Other Bed Coverings in the Canadian Tradition* (Toronto: Key Porter Books, 1979).

3   Barbara Brackman, *Civil War Women*, 69–78 (Lafayette, CA: C&T Publishing, 2000), 74.

4   Heritage Quilt Collection, Agnes Etherington Art Centre (Kingston: Agnes Etherington Art Centre, 2011).

5   Edwin Binney and Gail Binney-Winslow, *Homage to Amanda* (Washington, D. C.: Smithsonian Institution, 1984), 43.

6   Amelia Peck, *American Quilts and Coverlets in the Metropolitan Museum of Art*, 110–11 (New York: MQ Publications, 2007), 110.

7   Stana Nenadic and Sally Tuckett, *Colouring the Nation: The Turkey Red Printed Cotton Industry in Scotland, c.1840–1940*, 23–42 (Edinburgh: The National Museums of Scotland Publishing, 2013), 25; Stana Nenadic, "Colouring the Nation: A New Study of the Turkey Red Pattern Books in the National Museums of Scotland," *Textile History* 40, no. 2 (2012): 140–51.

8   Harry L. Watson, *Andrew Jackson vs. Henry Clay: Democracy and Development in Antebellum America* (Boston: Bedford/St. Martin's, 1998). The rooster replaced the sanctioned donkey emblem in 1828, after Democrat Andrew Jackson was ridiculed and called a jackass by the supporters of John Quincy Adams during an intense presidential campaign.

9   Glyndon G. Van Deusen, *The Life of Henry Clay* (Boston: Little, Brown, 1937).

10 Carl Schurz, *Henry Clay, 1777–1852*, i–xvii (Boston: Houghton Mifflin, 1915), vii.

11 *1861 Canada Census, Huntingdon County*, Library and Archives Canada. In 1861, Don Campbell was absent from the Huntingdon County census report likely because he went elsewhere in the winter to earn additional income while not tending the farm. This is indeed probable, since between the 1840s and 1860s, thousands of settlers left Quebec, some permanently, to work in the mills in the United States as economic conditions worsened in the Canadian province. It was regular practice for farmers to sell their farm implements and husbandry to pay for passage to the United States, essentially walking away from property acquired through land grants. For more on Quebec's migrant workers, see Beatrice Craig, *Backwoods Consumers and Homespun Capitalists: The Rise of a Market Culture in Eastern Canada* (Toronto: University of Toronto Press, 2009).

12 Thomas Dublin, *Women at Work: The Transformation of Work and Community in Lowell, Massachusetts, 1826–1860* (New York: Columbia University Press, 1979).

13 *1851 Canada Census, Glengarry County*, Library and Archives Canada.

14 By 1860, manufactured cloth was widely available in most rural towns in close proximity to shipping routes. At the nearby town of Dundee, Quebec, where Campbell likely purchased the textiles for her coverlet, local merchants would have imported their cloth from either the United States and Britain, or from local manufacturers in Montreal. For imported cloth to arrive in Dundee, it was shipped through the main port of Montreal approximately forty kilometers to the north east and could be easily accessed by the St. Lawrence and Salmon Rivers. Although Dundee was within close proximity, no more than twenty kilometers, to sixty-seven cotton mills just over the border in New York State, textiles would have still made their way through Montreal after travelling north on Lake Champlain (New York State) and west on the Richelieu River (Quebec) before they were distributed to numerous local merchants. The networks of exchange for textiles remained reliant on water transportation, and although Huntingdon County was located forty kilometers overland on corduroy roads from Montreal, it was accessible by water and merchants were able to offer a suitable variety of textiles for local residents.

15 Dublin, *Women at Work*, 14–22, 21. In the years leading up to the Civil War, many cotton producers relocated manufactories to the southern states in efforts to be closer to cotton supplies and reduce the costs of production. With these relocations, the impending conflict over abolitionism, and the subsequent Civil War, cotton prices continued to fluctuate, profoundly influencing the market. During the Civil War years (1861–65), cotton prices rose significantly due to the decrease in supply and the increase in demand for cloth.

16 Roxanne McElroy, *That Perfect Stitch: The Secrets of Fine Hand Quilting* (Chicago: The Quilt Digest Press, 1998). In contrast, utilitarian quilts that were made for warmth and in haste before the onset of winter usually were limited to four to five stitches per inch.

17 Lucy Johnson, *Nineteenth-century Fashion in Detail*, 168–84 (London: Victoria & Albert Museum, 2005), 180.

18 Beverly Gordon, *Textiles, the Whole Story: Uses Meaning, Significance*, 202–45 (New York: Thames and Hudson, 2011), 232.

19 Lucy Orrinsmith, *The Drawing-Room: Its Decorations and Furniture*, 1–9 (London: Macmillan, 1878), 2.

20 Personal communication, 15 January 2016.

21 Lucille Campey, *The Scottish Pioneers of Upper Canada, 1784–1855: Glengarry and Beyond* (Toronto: Natural Heritage Books, 2005), 76. As one of the earliest settlers to Eldon Township, McPherson was part of the group of Highlanders that arrived in the region starting in 1820, eventually claimed land, and contributed to the establishment of the local community.

22 Campey, *The Scottish Pioneers of Upper Canada*, 76.

23 Watson Kirkconnell, *Victoria County Centennial History* (Lindsay, ON: Watchman-Warder Press, 1921), n.p.; "Victoria Supplement" (Ontario Map Ref #10), *Illustrated*

Atlas of the Dominion of Canada (Toronto: H. Belden, 1881). The township map indicates that Andrew McPherson settled on Concession V, Lot 6 and his brothers settled on Concession IV, Lot 4.

24 Kirkconnell, *Victoria County,* n.p.

25 Colin Kidd, *Subverting Scotland's Past: Scottish Whig Historians and the Creation of an Anglo-British Identity, 1689–c. 1830,* 70–96 (Cambridge: Cambridge University Press, 1993), 78; Duncan George Forbes, *Culloden Papers: Comprising an Extensive and Interesting Correspondence from the Year 1625 to 1748* (London: T. Cadell and W. Davies, 1815).

26 Finlay McKichan, "Lord Seaforth and Highland Estate Management in the First Phase of Clearance, 1783–1815," *The Scottish Historical Review* 86, no. 1 (2007): 53.

27 Adrienne Hood and David-Thierry Ruddel, "Artifacts and Documents in the History of Quebec Textiles," in *Living in a Material World: Canadian and American Approaches to Material Culture,* ed. Gerald Pocius, 49–63 (St. John's, NL: Institute of Social and Economic Research, 1991), 53.

28 T. M. Devine, *Clanship to Crofters' War: The Social Transformation of the Scottish Highlands,* 24–42 (Manchester: Manchester University Press, 2013), 27.

29 Gerald Craig, *Upper Canada: The Formative Years, 1784–1841* (Toronto: McLelland and Stewart, 1993 [1963]); J. M. S. Careless, *The Union of the Canadas: The Growth of Canadian Institutions, 1841–1857* (Toronto: McLelland and Stewart, 1977 [1967]).

30 Claire Hoy, *Canadians in the Civil War,* 62–76 (Toronto: McArthur, 2004), 68.

31 *Kirkpatrick and Kirkpatrick Fonds,* Accession # 2269.28, Queen's University Archives, Queen's University, Kingston, ON.

32 Lucille H. Campey, *Les Écossais: The Pioneer Scots of Lower Canada, 1763–1855* (Toronto: Natural Heritage Books, 2006).

33 Frederick J. Seaver, "History of Fort Covington, New York," in *Historical Sketches of Franklin County and its Several Towns* (Albany, NY: J.B. Lyon, 1918), n.p. The American military installation of Fort Covington was established during the War of 1812. The presence of its military personnel would have contributed to the economic conditions of Dundee.

34 Craig, *Upper Canada: The Formative Years,* 244–45.

35 Robert A. Dodgshon, *From Chiefs to Landlords: Social and Economic Change in the Western Highlands and Islands, c. 1493–1820,* 179–94 (Edinburgh: Edinburgh University Press, 1988), 187.

36 Devine, *Clanship to Crofters' War,* 30.

37 Peter D. G. Thomas, *George III: King and Politician, 1760–1770,* 24–42 (Manchester: University of Manchester Press, 2002), 36.

38 Thomas Babington Macaulay, *History of England,* 54–69 (London: Heron Books, 1967), 67.

39 S. Johnson, *A Journey to the Western Islands of Scotland* (Oxford: Oxford University Press, 1924), n.p.

40 Personal communication, January 2016; Lucille H. Campey, *After the Hector: The Scottish Pioneers of Nova Scotia and Cape Breton, 1773–1852*, 234–77 (Toronto: Natural Heritage Books, 2004), 254; Lucille Campey, *The Scottish Pioneers of Upper Canada, 1784–1855*.

41 T. M. Devine and Willie Orr, *The Great Highland Famine: Hunger, Emigration, and the Scottish Highlands in the Nineteenth Century*, 12–24 (Edinburgh: John Donald, 1988), 18.

42 Personal communication, January 2016.

43 Alan G. Macpherson, "An Old Highland Genealogy and the Evolution of a Scottish Clan," Clan McPherson, http://clan-macpherson.org/museum/documents/alang01. pdf (accessed 25 February 2016).

44 Personal communication, January 2016.

Chapter 6 "From Prison to Citizenship," 1910: The Making and Display of a Suffragist Banner

Acknowledgments

I thank Beverley Cook, Museum of London, for her invaluable assistance, Liz Arthur for her perceptive advice and generosity, and Queen's University for funding the research for this project.

1 Despite the hope for the Conciliation bill in June 1910, by the end of the summer it became obvious that it had been shelved. On 18 November 1910 (subsequently called "Black Friday"), "a deputation of 500 women set out for the House of Commons." The treatment they received on this occasion was "unexpected and quite exceptionally brutal." Twenty-nine women (of the 139 who alleged violence) "complained of violence with indecency"; frequently the police twisted, pinched or twisted the women's breasts "in the most public way so as to inflict the utmost humiliation." Lisa Tickner, *The Spectacle of Women: Imagery of the Suffrage Campaign 1907–14* (Chicago: Chicago University Press, 1988), 120–21.

2 For a discussion of suffrage and the GSA, see Liz Arthur, "The Artistic, Social and Suffrage Networks of the Glasgow School of Art's Women Artists and Designers," in *Suffrage and Visual Culture: Art, Politics and Enterprise*, ed. Miranda Garrett and Zoë Thomas, 43–63 (London: Bloomsbury, 2018).

3 The banner is held by the Museum of London. See https://collections. museumoflondon.org.uk/online/object/91239.html for a description and information about the object.

4   According to *Votes for Women*, the weekly newspaper published by the WSPU, the
     colors green, white, violet stood for "give women votes." "The Scottish Exhibition,"
     Votes for Women, 6 May 1910, 521. In the literature, violet is used interchangeably
     with purple, with purple used most frequently.

5   Raphael Samuel, *Theatres of Memory: Past and Present in Contemporary Culture*
     (London: Verso, 2012 [1994]), 25.

6   Heather Pristash, Inez Schaechterle, and Sue Carter Wood, "The Needle as the Pen:
     Intentionality, Needlework, and the Production of Alternate Discourses of Power,"
     in *Women and the Material Culture of Needlework & Textiles, 1750–1950*, ed.
     Maureen Daly Goggin and Beth Fowkes Tobin, 13–29 (Farnham, UK: Ashgate,
     2009), 16.

7   Ibid.

8   Diane Atkinson, *The Suffragettes in Pictures* (London: Museum of London, 2015
     [1996]), 61.

9   Ibid.

10   Clive Edwards, "Women's Home-crafted Objects as Collections of Culture and
     Comfort, 1750–1900," in *Material Cultures, 1740–1920: The Meanings and Pleasures
     of Collecting*, ed. John Potvin and Alla Myzelev, 37–52 (Farnham, UK: Ashgate,
     2009), 39–40.

11   Lynne Walker, "Locating the Global/Rethinking the Local: Suffrage Politics,
     Architecture and Space," *Women's Studies Quarterly* 34, no. 1/2 (2006): 174–96, 193.

12   Not all the activists were British. Of those who signed the banner, Kitty Marion
     [Katherina Maria Schafer], was born in Germany. Alice Paul, from Philadelphia, and
     Lucy Burns, from Brooklyn, later returned to the United States to become activists
     there. See, for example, Christine Woodworth, "The Company She Kept: The Radical
     Activism of Actress Kitty Marion from Piccadilly Circus to Times Square," *Theatre
     History Studies* 32, no. 1 (2012): 80–92; J. D. Zahniser and Amelia R. Fry, *Alice Paul:
     Claiming Power* (Oxford: Oxford University Press, 2014); May Walton, *A Woman's
     Crusade: Alice Paul and the Battle for the Ballot* (New York: Palgrave Macmillan, 2010).

13   "The Scottish Exhibition," *Votes for Women*, 6 May 1910, 521.

14   "Suffragists Revolt in Prison," *Belfast News-Letter*, 15 July 1909, 5.

15   Ibid.

16   "Miss Wallace Dunlop Released," *Votes for Women*, 15 July 1909, 934.

17   Marion Wallace Dunlop was sentenced on 2 July 1909 and began her hunger strike
     on 5 July. "Miss Wallace Dunlop Released," 934. By the time Macbeth exhibited the
     banner at least 110 women had been on hunger strike: "the year's record is that on
     110 occasions the hunger strike has been carried out," and "in thirty-six cases
     forcible feeding has been inflicted." "Prison Record," *Votes for Women*, 18 March
     1910, 382. Although not all the women whose names appear on the banner were
     forcibly fed, all were hunger strikers.

18 Fiona MacFarlane and Elizabeth Arthur, *Glasgow School of Art Embroidery* (Glasgow: Glasgow Museums and Art Galleries, 1980), 17–18.

19 Arthur, 51. For discussions of the formation of the association, see Elspeth King, *The Scottish Women's Suffrage Movement* (Glasgow: People's Palace Museum, 1978); and Leah Leneman, *The Scottish Suffragettes* (Edinburgh: National Museums of Scotland, 2000).

20 Liz Arthur, "Jessie Newbery," in *The Biographical Dictionary of Scottish Women*, ed. E. Ewan, S. Innes, and S. Reynolds (Edinburgh: Edinburgh University Press, 2006), 282. See also, King, 19.

21 Janet Rae, *Warm Covers: A Scottish Textile Story* (Bristol: Sansom & Company, 2016), 77.

22 MacFarlane and Arthur, 17–18. *The Scotsman* referred to her as an "embroiderer of much talent." "Art Publications," *The Scotsman,* 6 November 1902, 3.

23 Francis Newbery, "An Appreciation of the Work of Ann Macbeth," *The Studio* 27 (1902): 41.

24 Macbeth was awarded a silver medal at the exhibition. "Scottish Successes at Turin Exhibition of Decorative Art," *The Scotsman*, 5 December 1902, 8. The panel resides in the collection of Glasgow Museums and is regularly on display.

25 Jessie Newbery was the "first departmental Head of Embroidery" at the GSA; Macbeth succeeded her. Rae, 72.

26 "Savants at Glasgow," *St James's Gazette*, 11 September 1901, 6. The banner, which remains in the collection of the association, is held by the Textile Department, Victoria & Albert Museum, London (LOAN:BRITISH ASSOC.1-2004).

27 Janice Helland, *Professional Women Painters in Nineteenth-Century Scotland: Commitment, Friendship, Pleasure* (Aldershot, UK: Ashgate, 2000), 95–97.

28 Letters written by Macbeth in May 1912 suggest Macbeth was forcibly fed: "I am still very much less vigorous than I anticipated after a fortnight's solitary imprisonment with forcible feedings—& I sleep very badly—but the doctor thinks this will improve when I get away." Ann Macbeth to John Groundwater, 11 May 1912, Glasgow School of Art Archives, quoted in Helland, 97.

29 "The Scottish Exhibition," *Votes for Women*, 8 April 1910, 442.

30 "Women's Suffrage Bazaar in Glasgow," *Glasgow Herald*, 29 April 1910, 5.

31 "Hunger Strikers Success," *Manchester Courier*, 22 July 1909, 10; "The Hunger Strike in Holloway: Twelve Prisoners Released after Terrible Experiences," *Votes for Women*, 23 July 1909, 571: Gladys Roberts, Florence Cooke, Elsie Mackenzie, Mrs. [G] Holtwhite Simmons, Sarah Carwin, Ada Wright, Lilian Dove-Willcox, Theresa Garnett, Mary Allen, Eugenia Bouvier, Irene Sprong, Kathleen Brown.

32 "The 'Hunger Strike': All the W.S.P.U. Prisoners Liberated," *Votes for Women*, 13 August 1909, 1061; *Sheffield Independent*, 2 August 1909, 5. Of those released, the following signed the banner: Alice Paul, Annie Bell, Lucy Burns, Emily Davison,

Mabel Capper, Isabel Kelley, Dorothy Shallard, Kathleen Jarvis. Signatures from Greta Cameron and Margaret West are missing.

33 Elizabeth Cumming, *Hand, Heart and Soul: The Arts and Crafts Movement in Scotland* (Edinburgh: Birlinn, 2006), 36 and 38.

34 The style, often referred to as the "Glasgow Style," is most commonly associated with architect Charles Rennie Mackintosh, his designer wife Margaret Macdonald (both studied at the GSA), and Jessie Newbery.

35 Tickner, x.

36 The first exhibition, the Grand Suffrage Bazaar and Exhibition, was held in London at Prince's Skating Rink in May 1909. See, for example, "At the Women's Exhibition, Knightsbridge: First Impressions," *Votes for Women*, 14 May 1909, 657–58. Like the Scottish exhibition that followed, its purpose was to raise funds for, and awareness of, the WSPU.

37 "The Scottish Exhibition, Glasgow," *Votes for Women*, 15 April 1910, 450.

38 "Women's Suffrage Bazaar in Glasgow," *Glasgow Herald*, 29 April 1910, 5.

39 Ibid.

40 "The Scottish Exhibition," *Votes for Women*, 29 April 1910, 494–95.

41 Ibid.

42 A "Miss Savage" assumed the role of another prisoner; her name does not appear on the banner.

43 "Women's Suffrage Bazaar in Glasgow," *Glasgow Herald*, 29 April 1910, 5.

44 "Suffragettes and the Prime Minister," *Scotsman*, 28 December 1909, 3. Leslie Hall was "sent home with a nurse" upon her release; a third woman arrested at the same time, Mabel Capper, also signed the banner. "Suffragette Released," *Manchester Courier*, 26 January 1910, 3.

45 "The Frog March," *Votes for Women*, 7 January 1910, 225. Martin had been arrested on 21 December 1909. See also, Sylvia Pankhurst, *The Suffragette: The History of the Women's Militant Suffrage Movement* (New York: Sturgis & Walton, 1911), 480–82.

46 Ibid.

47 Pristash, Schaechterle, and Wood, 19.

48 See, for example, "The Campaign in the Metropolis," *Votes for Women*, 1 April 1910, 429; and "The Great March, Saturday, May 28," *Votes for Women*, 6 May 1910, 513. King Edward VII died 6 May 1910; as a result, the date of the "Great March" was changed to 18 June 1910, "out of respect to the memory of our Sovereign King Edward VII." "The Great March, Saturday, June 18," *Votes for Women*, 27 May 1910, 560.

49 The banner was presented to the WSPU and carried in a demonstration in Edinburgh in 1909. See Arthur, "The Artistic, Social and Suffrage Networks of the Glasgow School of Art's Women Artists and Designers," 51.

50 "The Scottish Exhibition," *Votes for Women*, 6 May 1910, 521.

51 "Great Women's Suffrage Demonstration," *The Scotsman*, 20 June 1910, 9.

52 Tickner, 112.

53 Beverley Cook, Curator at the Museum of London, maintains that the size would have required three poles. In conversation with the author, November 2016.

54 Rae, 78.

55 Maureen Daly Goggin, "Fabricating Identity: Janie Terrero's 1912 Embroidered English Suffrage Signature Handkerchief," in *Women & Things, 1750–1950: Gendered Material Strategies*, ed. Maureen Daly Goggin and Beth Fowkes Tobin, 17–42 (Farnham, UK: Ashgate: 2009), 27.

56 Rozsika Parker, *The Subversive Stitch: Embroidery and the Making of the Feminine* (London: The Women's Press, 1984), 200.

57 Goggin, 27.

58 Goggin, 28. See also, Eileen Wheeler, "The Political Stitch: Voicing Resistance in a Suffrage Textile," *Textile Society of America Symposium Proceedings* (2012), Paper 758, http://digitalcommons.unl.edu/tsaconf/758 (accessed 10 February 2017). Wheeler's discussion focuses upon the Terrero handkerchief.

59 Vera Wentworth, Edith Hudson, and Hilda Burkitt. Information about Scottish activist Edith Hudson can be found at http://www.edinburghmuseums.org.uk/pdfs/ws-biog.aspx (accessed 30 July 2017).

60 Joy Kay, "'No time for recreations till the Vote is Won?' Suffrage Activists and Leisure in Edwardian Britain," *Women's History Review* 16, no. 4 (2007): 536.

61 Ibid.

62 "A Piece of Iron Thrown at Mr Churchill," *Scotsman*, 9 December 1909, 9. Her address was given as Hitcham Road, Leyton, Essex.

63 "Suffragette Raid: Over a Hundred Defendents at Bow Street," *East Anglian Daily Times*, 1 July 1909, 10. "106 women and eight men arrested as a result of the attempt of the suffragists to force an entry to the House of Commons."

64 "Suffrage Disturbances," *The Times*, 30 June 1909, 12. Maud Joachim, "a university woman," was the "niece of the famous violinist" [Joseph Joachim, 1831–1907], "The End of Truce," *Votes for Women*, 25 November 1910, 120–22, 122.

65 Edith Hudson, 8 Melville Place, Edinburgh and Elsie Roe Brown, of Leicester, "residing in Archibald Place, Edinburgh." "Suffragette Tactics," *Manchester Courier*, 7 December 1909, 8; "The Leith Suffragist Disturbance," *Scotsman*, 7 December 1909, 7. See also, http://www.edinburghmuseums.org.uk/pdfs/ws-biog.aspx for information about Hudson, an Edinburgh hospital nurse.

66 *The Scotsman* quoted a WSPU member speaking on behalf of Hudson and Roe-Brown: should they be forcibly fed, then in this "Scotland was as bad as England, and worse than Russia." "The Leith Suffragist Disturbance," *The Scotsman*, 7 December 1909, 7.

67 "Some Press Comments," *Dundee Courier*, 13 December 1909, 4.

68 "Ninety-one Hours Without Food," *Votes for Women*, 16 July 1909, 934.

69 Ibid.

70 Leneman, 44–47.

71 "Suffragettes Regain Liberty," *Dundee Courier*, 25 October 1909, 5. See also http:// www.edinburghmuseums.org.uk/pdfs/ws-biog.aspx.

72 *Dundee Courier*, 25 October 1909, 5.

73 Elizabeth Crawford, *The Women's Suffrage Movement: A Reference Guide 1866–1928* (London and New York: Routledge, 2001), 544–46, provides a biographical discussion of Phillips. See also, Mary Phillips, *The Militant Suffrage Campaign in Perspective* (London: Latimer Trend, 1957); and "Woman Suffrage: Release of a Prisoner," *The Times*, 19 September 1908, 2, for an account of her release from prison after her first incarceration.

74 Crawford, 759.

75 Crawford, 338.

76 Crawford, 391. According to Crawford, Massy's mother, Lady Knyvett, was also an active member of the WSPU.

77 "Suffragists Return to Bristol," *Western Daily Press*, 6 September 1909, 6.

78 "Suffragists Return to Bristol," 6.

79 "Suffragists Return to Bristol," 6; Crawford, 391. In her lengthy and insightful discussion of Kenney, Elizabeth Crawford included a quotation from Teresa Billington-Greig who commented on the "strong attraction" between Kenney and Emmeline Pethick–Lawrence, "so emotional and so openly paraded that it frightened me." Crawford, 317.

80 Wentworth would later, in 1912, attend St Andrews University in Scotland. Crawford, 705.

81 "The 'Hunger Strike': All the W.S.P.U. Members Liberated," *Votes for Women*, 13 August 1909, 1061.

82 "The 'Hunger Strike,'" 1061. "'Horrible' Holloway," *Sheffield Independent*, 2 August 1909, 5.

83 Davison acknowledged she had engaged in "two previous hunger strikes and her heart had been seriously affected." "How She Withstood the Hosepipe," *Sheffield Evening Telegraph*, 11 January 1910, 2.

84 "The Hosepipe Incident," *Manchester Courier*, 20 January 1910, 10.

85 Ibid.

86 Jane Purvis, "Remembering Emily Wilding Davison (1872–1923)," *Women's History Review* 22, no. 3 (2013): 353–62, 353.

87 Purvis, 353.

88 Purvis, 359.

89 "Forcible Feeding of Suffragettes," *Cheltenham Chronicle*, 29 January 1910, 5. See also "Forcible Feeding Horrors," *Manchester Courier*, 25 January 1910, 3.

90 Michelle Myall, "'Only be ye strong and very courageous': The Militant Suffragism of Lady Constance Lytton," *Women's History Review* 7, no. 1 (1998): 60–84, 63.

91 Dorothy Pethick, along with Winifred Jones, was forcibly fed from her third day of imprisonment at Newcastle-on-Tyne in October 1909. Both were rushed to a nursing home upon release. "Feeding by Force: Suffragists' Allegations," *Manchester Courier*, 26 October 1909, 10. Jessie Lawes and Nellie Crocker were arrested in July 1909. "Suffragist Furies," *Western Gazette*, 2 July 1909, 12.

92 Goggin, 28.

Chapter 7 *Our Lady of the Snows*: Settlement, Empire, and "The Children of Canada" in the Needlework of Mary Seton Watts (1848–1938)

Acknowledgments

This chapter emerged from a paper given at the inaugural Mary Watts Study Day, Watts Gallery – Artists' Village, Compton where I received a very warm welcome. My thanks to Dr. Nicholas Tromans (Brice Curator) for the invitation to speak on Mary Watts's "Canadian banner" and to Dr. Desna Greenhow and the staff at the Watts Archive for their support of this research by "the Canadian working on Mary Watts."

The research for this chapter was funded by grants from the *Fonds de recherche du Québec – Société et culture* (FRQSC) and the Social Sciences and Humanities Research Council of Canada (SSHRC).

1 I have chosen to refer to her as Mary Seton Watts (1848–1938) since this was the name she herself used on diaries, commonplace books, and for the biography of her husband: M. S. Watts, *George Frederic Watts: Annals of an Artist's Life* (London: Macmillan, 1912). Her family name before marriage was Fraser-Tytler. M. S. Watts Diary, 29 July 1906, Watts Archive, Compton, Surrey. The ninth Governor General of Canada was Albert Henry George, 4th Earl Grey (1851–1917).

2 Governor General Grey to Lord Mountstephen (President of the Canadian Pacific Railway), 13 March 1906, Governor General Grey papers, National Archives of Canada. For more on the banners' St George theme see, Robert Common, "The Missing Banners of Lord Grey," *Embroidery Canada* (November 1981): 5–7; and "To Adorn our College Halls," *Canadian Life and Resource* (c. 1910): 13. By 2006, Canadian craft historian Jennifer Salahub had identified and traced 12 banners in Canada to Grey's project, though the exact number of banners remains unknown. See "Governor General Grey's 'Little Scheme': Majesty in Canada," in *Majesty in*

Canada: Essays on the Role of Royalty, ed. Colin Coates, 98–101 (Toronto: Dundrun Press, 2006).

3   Lord Grey writing to Mary Seton Watts on 27 April 1907 refers to "your lovely Lily on stage in Montreal" in conversation about the banner (Watts Archive, MSW 16/79). First mentioned in Mary Watts's diary in 1891, Lilian Mackintosh Chapman came to live with the Wattses in 1898 as a teenager. At the time of the banner presentation ceremony Lilian was living in Toronto (on Alcina Avenue by May 1910) having moved to Canada shortly after her marriage on 25 September 1906 (M. S. Watts to Mrs. Hatton, 13 September 1906, Watts Archive).

4   Liz Stanley claims that "in a sense it is *only* biography which can make available to us the detailed processes of historical change." Stanley does not mean a "conventional linear 'jigsaw' model of biography," which puts the subject under a microscope, but instead proposes a kaleidoscopic approach to a life for the "feminist biographer." Liz Stanley, "Biography as Microscope or Kaleidoscope? The Case of 'Power' in Hanna Cullwick's Relationship with Arthur Munby," *Women's Studies International Forum* 10, no. 1 (1987): 21.

5   This microhistory approach is grounded in the work of Linda Mahood and Jill Lepore, who refers to it as "histories of self." See Jill Lepore, "Historians Who Love too Much: Reflections on Microhistory and Biography," *Journal of American History* 88, no. 1 (2001): 126; Linda Mahood, *Feminism and Voluntary Action: Eglantyne Jebb and Save the Children, 1876–1928* (New York: Palgrave MacMillan, 2009).

6   A former curator of the Watts Gallery, Richard Jefferies, suggested in conversation that they might have been worked at the Royal School of Art Needlework. While painting her portrait, G. F. Watts befriended Madeline Wyndham who was part of the influential committee of women who helped to found the School in 1872, under the presidency of Princess Christian. "The Royal School of Art Needlework," *Magazine of Art* (1882): 219–20. See also, M. S. Watts Diary, Saturday, 4 July 1891; 29 July 1906.

7   For more on the Chapel and Guild, see Paterson, "Decoration and Desire in the Watts Chapel, Compton: Narratives of Gender, Class and Colonialism," *Gender & History* 17, no. 3 (2005): 714–36; and Veronica Franklin Gould, *Unsung Heroine of the Art Nouveau* ([Compton:] Watts Gallery, 1998).

8   M. S. Watts Diary, 29 July 1906, Watts Archive: "I am beginning my banner – this new banner to be given by the Queen to the children of Canada, I want to put everything into it, that can possibly be thought out – A full rounded aspiration to give to the children there ..."

9   These policies, often predicated on the notion of *terra nullius* (that no one owned the land prior to European assertion of sovereignty), have had lasting effects which continue to be felt in Canada, and are only just being addressed now. As law professor Joanna Harrington explains, "within Canadian law it has been held that

the *terra nullius* concept has no application vis-à-vis the European assertion of sovereignty over lands now part of Canada. On 26 June 2014, in a unanimous 8:0 decision that marked the first time the highest court has recognized the existence of Aboriginal title on a particular site, the Supreme Court of Canada made clear that: 'The doctrine of *terra nullius* never applied in Canada, as confirmed by the *Royal Proclamation* (1763), R.S.C. 1985, App. II, No. 1." (*Tsilhqot'in Nation v British Columbia*, 2014 SCC 44 at para. 69; for Harrington's article: http://craigforcese. squarespace.com/public-international-law-blog/2014/6/30/canada-was-never-terra-nullius.html).

10 Harry Ricketts, *The Unforgiving Minute: A Life of Rudyard Kipling* (London: Chatto and Windus, 1999).

11 Harold Begbie, *Albert Fourth Earl Grey: A Last Word* (London: Hodder & Stoughton, 1917), 128.

12 Governor General Grey to Lord Mountstephen, 13 March 1906, Governor General Grey papers, National Archives of Canada.

13 Salahub, 98.

14 Victoria & Albert Museum Archives, Register Papers T35-1945, Charles Grey to Mr. Bedford, 20 June 1945, quoted in Salahub, 107.

15 Helen Gilbert and Chris Tifflin, eds., *Burden or Benefit?: Imperial Benevolence and its Legacies* (Bloomington: Indiana University Press, 2008), 6–7.

16 Helen Clark, *Raise the Banners High: The City of Edinburgh's Banner Collection* (Edinburgh: City of Edinburgh Museums and Galleries, 2001). I thank Janice Helland for sharing this source with me.

17 Nobel Prize-winning English author Rudyard Kipling Convocation Address in 1907: https://www.mcgill.ca/reporter/33/16/past/ and McGill archives: http://www. archives.mcgill.ca/public/hist_mcgill/conv/convocation.htm.

18 Shurlee Swain, "Beyond Child Migration: Inquiries, Apologies and the Implications for the Writing of a Transnational Child Welfare History," *History Australia* 13, no. 1 (2016): 141. Swain suggests when reformers in the colonies sought to convince local government officials of their cause, they were often asking their husbands or friends to support their voluntary actions. Mary Seton Watts had personal correspondence with Grey and many visits with him are confirmed in her diary. She also knew Kipling through family friends and her dedication to Jebb links the two women as does her work on the HAIA Council.

19 McGill University Archives: Royal Victoria College RG 42. See also, Muriel V. Roscoe, *The Royal Victoria College, 1899–1962,* ([Montreal]: Mutilith, 1964); Margaret Gillett, *We Walked Very Warily: A History of Women at McGill* (Montréal: Eden Press, 1981). The origin of the Royal Victoria College can be traced back to the Montreal Ladies' Educational Association which had offered its members university-level lectures in various subjects between 1881 and 1884.

20 See Deborah Miller, "'The Big Ladies' Hotel': Gender, Residence, and Middle-Class Montréal: A Contextual Analysis of the Royal Victoria College, 1899–1931" (MArch diss., McGill University, 1998).

21 In a letter to Queen Alexandra, Grey explains how the hall where the banner hung was used by the university for convocation and on "other great occasions." Earl Grey to Queen Alexandra, 2 May 1907, McCord Museum Archives, Montréal.

22 See for example, Mahood, *Feminism and Voluntary Action*; F. Prochaska, *Women and Philanthropy in Nineteenth-Century England* (Oxford: Clarendon Press, 1980); and Maria Luddy, *Women and Philanthropy in Nineteenth-Century Ireland* (Cambridge and New York: Cambridge University Press, 1995).

23 Sarah Richardson, "Women, Philanthropy, and Imperialism in Early Nineteenth-century Britain," in *Burden or Benefit?: Imperial Benevolence and its Legacies*, ed. Helen Gilbert and Chris Tifflin, 90–102 (Bloomington: Indiana University Press, 2008), 91. Women of note for this chapter: Henrietta Barnett (co-founder of Toynbee Hall settlement) and her sister the housing reformer Octavia Hill, HAIA founder Eglantyne (Tye) Jebb and her daughters Eglantyne (Save the Children founder) and Louisa (active in HAIA Council), social welfare reformers Maria Rye and Annie MacPherson who founded children's charities in the UK and initiated migration programs to the colonies for young women and then children from 1869 on.

24 For an excellent historical background to the home arts movement, see Janice Helland, *British and Irish Home Arts and Industries, 1880–1914: Marketing Craft, Making Fashion* (Dublin: Irish Academic Press, 2007).

25 See Standish Meacham, *Toynbee Hall and Social Reform 1880–1914: The Search for Community* (New Haven, CT: Yale University Press, 1987).

26 M. S. Watts, *The Word in the Pattern* (London: W. H. Ward, 1904).

27 Mahood, 34. In *Slumming, Sexual and Social Politics in Victorian London* (Princeton, NJ: Princeton University Press, 2004), Seth Koven cites a survey undertaken in 1893 by Louisa Hubbard and Angela Burdett-Coutts that estimated about 500,000 women were "continuously and semi-professionally employed in philanthropy" (295). Additionally, 20,000 supported themselves as "paid officials" in charitable societies. These figures do not include the 20,000 nurses, 5,000 women in religious orders, and 200,000 members of the Mother's Unions, which did a considerable amount of charity work and over 10,000 women who collected money for missionary societies.

28 Stephen Knott, *Amateur Craft: History and Theory* (London: Bloomsbury, 2015). Knott connects the HAIA classes with the notion of "Self-Help" popularized by the Victorian reformer Samuel Smiles in his 1859 book *Self-Help*. Knott, 16.

29 Lydia Murdoch, "Training 'Street Arabs' into British Citizens: Making Artisans and Members of Empire," in *Imagined Orphans: Poor Families, Child Welfare and Contested Citizenship in London* (New Brunswick, NJ: Rutgers University Press, 2006), 123–30.

30 Murdoch, 123–30.

31 Social reformer Maria Rye sailing with her first party of around 70 girls, all 12 years or younger, to Canada from Liverpool in 1869 marks the emergence of UK child migration schemes as a major form of organized welfare intervention. Gordon Lynch, *Remembering Child Migration: Faith, Nation-Building and the Wounds of Charity* (London: Bloomsbury Academic, 2016), 31.

32 For instance, at the highest levels of philanthropic patronage, Queen Alexandra was a royal patron of the HAIA and Barnardo's, among many other charitable organizations. Mary Seton Watts's banner was given on the Queen's behalf and is sometimes referred to as "the Queen's banner." Queen Alexandra was also pictured sending British child migrants off on a ship to Canada and quoted as admonishing the children to "be good." Earl Grey is listed as a Vice-President of Barnardo's in the 1906–1907 Annual Reports, while prominent home arts advocates including the Duke and Duchess of Sutherland and Lord and Lady Aberdeen are listed as Barnardo's trustees and Chairs in the 1895–1896 Annual Reports (Barnardo's Archive, Plaistow, London).

33 Murdoch, 8.

34 Murdoch, 165–66.

35 Ellen Boucher, *Empire's Children: Child Emigration, Welfare, and the Decline of the British World, 1869–1967* (New York: Cambridge University Press, 2014), 27.

36 Between 1869 and the late 1930s, children were sent to Canada from Great Britain by philanthropic organizations, like Dr. Barnardo's (early emigration parties were sent by social reformers Maria Rye (1869) and Annie MacPherson (1870), who sent children for Barnardo until his organization started to send them from 1882). Under child migration schemes enacted by the United Kingdom, an estimated 100,000 British children were brought to Canada. Some were orphans (approx. 2%), some were poor—many came from families who saw no other option. At least at the beginning of the program, the Canadian government subsidized the cost of transporting children from Britain. The children worked as indentured laborers until they came of age. Some were treated well; others were seen as "little workers"; many were abused. The children were supposed to go to school, but this often depended on the farmer's needs and harvest season, regardless of the contract of indenture with the child. Library and Archives Canada "British Home Children, 1869–1932" records: https://www.bac-lac.gc.ca/eng/discover/immigration/immigration-records/home-children-1869-1930/Pages/home-children.aspx; British Isles Family History Society of Greater Ottawa: http://www.bifhsgo.ca/cpage. php?pt=10, accessed 8 October 2017; and Joy Parr, *Labouring Children: British Immigrant Apprentices to Canada, 1869–1924* (Toronto: University of Toronto Press, 1994), 85.

37 Lynch, 13.

38 "State-Directed Emigration: Its Necessity," *Night and Day* (December 1884): 178.

39 Boucher, 13.

40 Lynch, 87, 124.

41 Lori Oschefski, founder of the British Home Children Advocacy & Research Association (BHCARA), claims that with no mother's allowance or welfare, workhouses and institutions like Barnardo's were often the only options, but as soon as a child was placed in one, the parents forfeited their rights. This was as a result of The Custody of Children Act, 1891 (BHCARA resource site: http://canadianbritishhomechildren.weebly.com, accessed 15 July 2017).

42 Saturday, 31 December 1898, M. S. Watts Diary (Watts Archive). This diary has been transcribed by Desna Greenhow as *The Diary of Mary Watts, 1887–1904: Victorian Progressive and Artistic Visionary* (London: Lund Humphries, 2016).

43 The response to British child migration schemes was mixed in Canada with the negative reports generated or supported by Dr. C. K. Clarke one of Canada's most prominent psychiatrists. He gave public talks about the supposed degeneracy of British child migrants and their propensity for criminal behavior. Roy Parker, *Uprooted: The Shipment of Poor Children to Canada, 1867–1917* (Bristol: The Policy Press, 2010), 151–88.

44 An excerpt from an 1888 interview with Thomas Barnardo offers details of the training and residential set up of the charity—"Homes for the Homeless – A Chat with Dr. Barnardo: A Peep at the Stepney Home," *Evening News*, 25 September 1888: "Admission to the destitute is immediate and without the payment or promise of a money gift, without the influence or intervention of patronage . . . Destitution, homelessness, or, in the case of girls, grave moral peril, constitutes the sole condition of eligibility, and such cases are admissible at once. . . . The industrial training of all young inmates is looked upon as a matter of the very first importance."

45 Koven, 90. See http://www.barnardos.org.uk (accessed 25 July 2018).

46 Boucher, 13.

47 Swain and Hillel, 140. The deliberate separation of children from their parents or extended families advocated by sending organizations like Barnardo's was not a new idea in the Canadian context. British child sending agencies had come under severe scrutiny after the scathing 1875 Doyle Report prepared for the British government. The Canadian government responded to the Doyle Report with its own enquiry which exonerated the child migration schemes even though it had been unable to trace 31% of the children placed by the earliest sending agencies (Report available at: Library and Archives Canada "British Home Children, 1869–1932" records: https://www.bac-lac.gc.ca/eng/discover/immigration/immigration-records/home-children-1869-1930/Pages/home-children.aspx, accessed 20 July 2017).

48 See Elizabeth A. Harvey, "'Layered Networks': Imperial Philanthropy in Birmingham and Sydney, 1860–1914," *Journal of Imperial and Commonwealth History* 41, no. 1 (2013): 123; and Shurlee Swain, *History of Child Protection Legislation* (Sydney: Royal Commission into Institutional Responses to Child Sexual Abuse, 2014).

The 1879 Davin Report about the efficacy of Industrial Residential Schools for First Nations, Inuit, and Métis children, established in Canada as part of the aggressive assimilationist policies of the government, similarly recommended the removal of children from home and family to schools which were far away from the reserve lands on which the children's families lived in order to fulfil its educational mandate of assimilating the children into settler colonial culture. The last federally-run residential school, Gordon Indian Residential School in Saskatchewan, closed in 1996 (See *Where are the Children? Healing the Legacy of the Residential Schools*, http://wherearethechildren.ca/en/timeline/research/, accessed 20 July 2017).

49 A history that also includes, and relied upon, the residential school system in Canada designed to assimilate Indigenous children through education and separation from their families, and the vast settlement of Indigenous land through agriculture and farming.

Chapter 8 "Je me declare Dieu-Mère, Femme Créateur": Johanna Wintsch's Needlework at the Swiss Psychiatric Asylums Burghölzli and Rheinau, 1922–1925

All translations from German are by the author unless otherwise noted.

1 Beatrice (Bice) Curiger was only the third woman to curate the Venice Biennale. She defended her curatorial strategies in an interview against a charge of anachronism: "I don't think art is a very powerful instrument to change the world. But it can make you rethink certain things. It can break convention. [...] We have now reached a good moment to defend art from within." Blake Gopnik, "Bice Curiger directs the Venice Biennale," *Newsweek*, 29 May 2011. http://www.newsweek.com/bice-curiger-directs-venice-biennale-67747?rx=us.

2 Rosalie Schallenfeld, *Der Handarbeitsunterricht in Schulen: Werth, Inhalt, Lehrgang und Methodik desselben*, 6th edn (Frankfurt: Hermann, 1878).

3 Thirteen (plus four preparatory drawings) at the Prinzhorn Collection in Heidelberg, fourteen at the Collection Rheinau in Zurich (Psychiatric University Clinic), and three at the Collection de l'Art Brut in Lausanne.

4 Art therapy as we conceive it today did not exist in the early twentieth century. Progressive psychiatrists of the day (starting with William Tuke's moral treatment at the York Retreat, England in the late eighteenth century) advocated work therapy to

keep patients occupied, physically tire them, and facilitate a temporary reprieve from disruptive mental dialogues and thoughts. See Edward Shorter, *A History of Psychiatry: From the Era of the Asylum to Prozac* (New York: Wiley & Sons, 1997).

5   Virginia Woolf, *A Room of One's Own* (London: The Hogarth Press, 1929).

6   Bettina Brand-Clausen and Viola Michely, eds., *Irre ist Weiblich: Künstlerische Interventionen von Frauen in der Psychiatrie um 1900* (Heidelberg: Verlag das Wunderhorn, 2004), 263.

7   The first female student matriculated at the University of Zurich in 1867. Doris Stump, "Zugelassen und Ausgegrenzt," in *Ebenso neu als kühn: 120 Jahre Frauenstudium an der Universität Zürich,* ed. Verein Feministische Wissenschaft Schweiz 15–28 (Zurich: Efef, 1988).

8   Jean-François Wintsch, *Historique*, Lausanne, 5 September 1922 qtd. in Bettina Brand-Claussen, "Zünde Deine Augen an: Gestickte Liebesarabesken von Johannna Wintsch," in *Irre ist Weiblich*, 103.

9   Ibid.

10 Ibid.

11 "2010 Subversive Sorgfalt: Stickereien von Jeanne Natalie Wintsch," Exhibition Archive, Museum im Lagerhaus, St. Gallen, 31 August–14 November 2010. http://www.museumimlagerhaus.ch/en/ausstellungen/archiv/2010subversive-sorgfalt-stickereien-von-jeanne-natalie-wintsch/.

12 G. Palmai and B. Blackwell, "The Burghölzli Centenary," *Medical History* 10, no. 3 (July 1966): 257–65.

13 Diagnostic and Statistical Manual of Mental Disorders, DSM-IV, Code 295.30.

14 Patients often died of infectious disease rather than their mental illness due to chronic overcrowding and poor sanitary conditions in early twentieth-century asylums. It is unknown if Wintsch had further psychotic episodes after her release in 1925 or whether they were managed/concealed by her family.

15 Sadly, the night dress does not survive. Katrin Luchsinger, "Ambivalenz als Strategie," in *Wissen und Nicht-Wissen in der Klinik,* ed. Martina Wernli (Bielefeld: Transcript, 2012), 118.

16 Bleuler qtd. in Luchsinger, 119.

17 Ibid.

18 For a general discussion of the repressive conditions at large mental asylums for the "incurable" in the early twentieth century see Shorter (note 4).

19 Brand-Claussen, "Zünde Deine Augen an," 102.

20 Kantonales Staatsarchiv Zurich (StAZH), Krankenakte Rheinau: Inv. No. 5559 and Krankenakte Burghölzli: Inv. No. 18509.

21 Ibid.

22 Wintsch qtd. in Bettina Brand-Claussen, "Der Ratz Ris hat die Ratte JNW gefangen: Stickereien von Johanna Natalie Wintsch in der Anstalt Rheinau," in *Rosenstrumpf und*

Dornenknie: Werke aus der Psychiatrischen Pflegeanstalt Rheinau 1867–1930, ed. Katrin Luchsinger, Jacqueline Fahrni, and Iris Blum (Zurich: Chronos Verlag, 2011), 58.

23 Ibid.

24 StAZH, Krankenakte Rheinau, Inv. No. 5559.

25 Ibid. and Krankenakte Rheinau, Inv. No.18509.

26 It might be worth noting that in the early twentieth century, far more women than men were diagnosed with schizophrenia. Up to 50% of all female patients institutionalized in "care" facilities such as Rheinau were admitted with this diagnosis. Interestingly, many of these schizophrenic women were unmarried, which poses the uncomfortable question about the validity of their diagnosis. Might some of these women have been institutionalized simply because they were difficult, unconventional, or broke gender conventions of the time? More work needs to be done in this area but for an initial foray, see Karen Nolte, "'... die Unfähigkeit des Weibes, Affektstürmen zu wiederstehen': Hysterie und Weiblichkeit um 1900," in *Irre ist Weiblich*, 53–61.

27 Rita Felski, *The Gender of Modernity* (Cambridge, MA: Harvard University Press, 1995); and Agatha Schwarz, *Gender and Modernity in Central Europe* (Ottawa: University of Ottawa Press, 2010).

28 A discussion of this topic exceeds the parameters of this essay, but see Iris Blum, "Im täglichen Gange der Anstalt: Das Praxisfeld Arbeit in der Pflegeanstalt Rheinau in den Jahren 1870–1930," in *Rosenstrumpf und Dornenknie*, 23–34.

29 Foucault's work underpins the theoretical foundations of this essay but *History of Madness* (1961) and *Discipline and Punish: The Birth of the Prison* (1975) are most relevant. Michel de Foucault, *History of Madness,* trans. Jonathan Murphy and Jean Khalfa (London: Routledge, 2006); *Discipline and Punish: The Birth of the Prison,* trans. Alan Sheridan (London: Penguin, 1991).

30 The historiography of the cultural turn is complex but is rooted in the "new history" associated with the French journal *Annales* (founded 1929). Its supporters advocated interdisciplinarity ("total history") to understand experiences of ordinary subjects and widen the scope of what counts as a historical document. For a recent history of the Annales School, see Peter Burke, *The French Historical Revolution: The Annales School 1929–2014* (Redwood, CA: Stanford University Press, 2015).

31 Roy Porter, "The Patient's View: Doing Medical History from Below," *Theory and Society* 14 (1985): 175–98. For Porter's impact on medical history see Katharina Ernst, "Patientengeschichte: Die kulturhistorische Wende in der Medizinhistoriographie," in *Eine Wissenschaft emanzipiert sich: Die Medizinhistoriographie von der Aufklärung bis zur Postmoderne,* ed. Ralf Bröer, 97–108 (Freiburg: Centaurus Verlagsgesellschaft, 1999), and Volker Hess and J. Andrew Mendelsohn, "Case and Series: Medical Knowledge and Paper Technology, 1600–1900," *History of Science* 18 (2010): 287–314.

32 Katrin Luchsinger, "Bewahren besonderer Kulturgüter," Research Project, Züricher Hochschule der Künste/Institute for Cultural Studies, 2006–2008 and 2010–2013. https://www.zhdk.ch/forschungsprojekt/428678.

33 I appropriate this term from early feminist literary criticism. See, for example, Annette Kolodny, "Dancing Through the Minefield: Some Observations on the Theory, Practice, and Politics of a Feminist Literary Criticism," *Feminist Studies* 6 (1980): 1–25.

34 Michel de Certeau, *The Practice of Everyday Life* (Berkeley: University of California Press, 1984), xviii.

35 Brand-Claussen, "Zünde Deine Augen an," 96.

36 StAZH, Krankenakte Rheinau, Inv. No. 5559.

37 F. Knirs, K. Behrens, and O. Pfister, *Ungewöhnliche Materialien im künstlerischen Schaffen Schizophrener,* Mappe 12 (Basel: Sandoz, 1967), n.p.

38 StAZH, Krankenakte Rheinau, Inv. No. 5559.

39 I take this term from the wonderful title of a conference session recently organized by this volume's editors: "Stitching the Self: Exploring the Power of the Needle," Universities Art Association of Canada Conference, NSCAD University, Halifax, 5–7 November 2015.

40 Brand-Claussen, "Zünde Deine Augen an," 100.

41 Ibid.

42 Heather Pristash, Inez Schaechterle, and Sue Carter Wood, "The Needle as the Pen: Intentionality, Needlework and the Production of Alternate Discourses of Power," in *Textiles: Critical and Primary Sources*, vol. 4, *Identity*, ed. Catherine Harper (London: Berg, 2012), 294.

43 StAZH, Krankenakte Rheinau, Inv. No. 5559.

44 Pfister gifted all the embroideries given to him by Wintsch to the Prinzhorn Collection.

45 Arjun Appadurai, ed., *The Social Life of Things: Commodities in Cultural Perspective* (Cambridge: Cambridge University Press, 1986).

46 The exhibition formed part of the larger "Jubilee Exhibition" organized on occasion of Emperor Franz Joseph's fiftieth jubilee and featured female patients' handicraft (embroidery, basket weaving, flower arranging, knitting, and sewing) as well as carpentry, carving, drawing and painting and literary endeavors by male patients. "Feuilleton: Jubiläums-Ausstellung 1898 in Wien," *Wiener Zeitung*, 6 May 1898, 6.

47 Examples of these early collections are: August Marie's "Mad Museum" at the Salpêtrière Hospitel in Paris, Cesare Lombroso's "Museum of Criminal Anthropology" at the University of Turin, Walter Morgenthaler's collection at Bern's "Kantonale Irrenanstalt," and London's Bethlem Royal Hospital's collection (renamed "Museum of the Mind" in 2015).

48 Prinzhorn quoted in Bettina Brand-Claussen, "The Collection of Works of Art in the Psychiatric Clinic, Heidelberg—from the Beginnings until 1945," in *Beyond Reason: Art and Psychosis* (London: Hayward Gallery, 1997), 7. For a more detailed discussion of the Prinzhorn Collection's origins, see Inge Jarchov, "Die Prinzhorn Sammlung," in *Bilder, Skulpturen, Texte aus psychiatrischen Anstalten, ca.*

1890–1920, eds. Hans Gercke and Inge Jarchov, 15–27 (Königstein: Anthenäum Verlag, 1980).

49 Prinzhorn cemented this link between "art of the mentally ill" and (modern) art in his 1922 book *Artistry of the Mentally Ill*, in which he argued for a common impulse driving all creative endeavors, namely, the desire to put into form psychic states of being. Hans Prinzhorn, *Bildnerei der Geisteskranken: Ein Beitrag zur Psychologie und Psychopathologie der Gestaltung* (Berlin: Springer Verlag, 1922).

50 These terms bring with them a complex and often contested legacy that cannot be addressed here. But see Lucienne Peiry, *Art Brut: The Origins of Outsider Art,* trans. James Frank (Paris: Flammarion, 2001); Roger Cardinal and John Elsner, eds., *Cultures of Collecting* (London: Reaktion, 1993); Roger Cardinal and John Maizels, *Raw Creation: Outsider Art and Beyond* (London: Phaidon, 1996).

51 Brand-Claussen, "Collection of Works of Art," 12.

52 Unfortunately, Prinzhorn was unable to find a permanent exhibition space for his collection and he left Heidelberg in 1921. Hans Gruhle (1880–1958) continued to build the collection and organized several touring exhibitions in the late 1920s. After the National Socialists came to power in 1933, the Psychiatric Institute and its collection of patient art was taken over by Carl Schneider (1881–1946), an early supporter of the T4 extermination program who availed the Prinzhorn Collection to Nazi propaganda such as the notorious "Degenerate Art" Exhibitions of 1937 (Munich) and 1938 (Berlin), which featured photographs of mental patients as well as patient art. See Olaf Peters, *Degenerate Art: The Attack on Modern Art in Nazi Germany, 1937* (New York: Neue Galerie/Prestel, 2014).

53 Seven embroideries were part of "Art of the Mentally Ill" at the Applied Arts Museum in Basel (1929) and the Musée d'Art et d'Histoire in Geneva (1930). Brand-Claussen, "Zünde Deine Augen an," 93.

54 This essay would not have been possible without the seminal work by Bettina Brand-Claussen, former deputy director of the Prinzhorn Collection, and Katrin Luchsinger, Principal Investigator of the "Bewahren besonderer Kulturgüter" Research Project.

55 Foucault, *Discipline and Punish*.

56 Katrin Luchsinger, *Die Vergessenskurve: Werke aus psychiatrischen Kliniken in der Schweiz um 1900. Eine kulturanalytische Studie* (Zurich: Chronos Verlag, 2016).

Chapter 9 Hybrid Language: The Interstitial Stitches of Anna Torma's Embroideries

1 Anne Koval, *Paper Doll* (Sackville, NB: Owens Art Gallery, 2010), 26.

2 Heather Pristash, Inez Schaechterle, and Sue Carter Wood, "The Needle as the Pen: Intentionality, Needlework, and the Production of Alternative Discourses of Power,"

in *Women and the Material Culture of Needlework and Textiles, 1750–1950*, ed. Maureen Daly Goggin and Beth Fowkes Tobin, 13–29 (London: Routledge, 2009), 27.

3   Anna Torma, "Artist's Statement," *2003–2004 New Brunswick Art Bank Acquisitions* (Fredericton: Culture and Sport Secretariat Province of New Brunswick, 2004), 38.

4   Anna Torma, interview with the author, 1 August 2008.

5   Homi Bhabha, *The Location of Culture* (London: Routledge, 1994), 1–2.

6   Carole Boyce Davies, *Black Women, Writing and Identity: Migrations of the Subject* (London: Routledge, 2012), 84.

7   Elaine Showalter, "Piecing and Writing," in *The Poetics of Gender*, ed. Nancy K. Miller, 222–47 (New York: Columbia University Press, 1986).

8   Lucy Lippard, "Up, Down, and Across: A New Frame for Quilts," in *The Artist and the Quilt*, ed. Charlotte Robinson (New York: Knopf, 1983), 18.

9   Pristash, Schaechterle, and Wood, 13.

10 Pristash, Schaechterle, and Wood, 14.

11 Adrienne Rich, "When We Dead Awaken: Writing as Re-Vision," *College English* 34, no. 1, Women, Writing and Teaching (October 1972): 18–30, 18.

12 Pristash, Schaechterle, and Wood, 27.

13 Rozsika Parker, *The Subversive Stitch: Embroidery and the Making of the Feminine* (London: The Women's Press, 1984), 215.

14 John Grande, *Dialogues in Diversity: Art From Marginal to Mainstream* (Tuscany: Paris Publishing, 2006), 31.

15 Anna Torma, interview with Gareth Bate and Dawne Rudman, Interview 88, World of Threads Festival, http://www.worldofthreadsfestival.com/artist_interviews/088_anna_torma_13.html.

16 Katalin Keserü, *Anna Torma: Embroideries* (Budapest: Vigado Gallery, 2002).

17 Edit András *Gender Check: Femininity and Masculinity in the Art of Eastern Europe* (Vienna: Kunst Stiftung Ludwig, 2009), 335.

18 Anna Torma, "The Beauty in Beasts," *The Walrus*, 12 October 2004, https://thewalrus.ca/2004-06-detail/.

19 Torma, "The Beauty in Beasts."

20 Koval, *Paper Doll*, 26.

21 Susan Sellers, *Language and Sexual Difference: Feminist Writing in France* (London: Palgrave, 1991), 139.

22 Hélène Cixous, *Coming to Writing and Other Essays* (Cambridge, MA: Harvard University Press, 1991), 51.

23 Anne Koval, "Anna Torma: Bagatelles," *Selvedge Magazine* (2012): 91.

24 Cixous, *Coming to Writing*, 51.

25 Kirsty Bell, "Affiliations: Anna Torma's Artistic and Mythological Sites," *Les mythologies singulières: Anna Torma, Claire Labonté, Marigold Santos* (Montreal: Le 1700 La Poste, 2016), 52.

26 Robert Storr, *Intimate Geometries: The Art and Life of Louise Bourgeois* (New York: Monacelli Press, 2016), 526.

27 Jerry Gorovoy and P. T. Asbaghi, *Louise Bourgeois: Blue Days and Pink Days* (Milan: Fondazione Prada, 1997), 218.

28 Ann Hamilton, "*Follow* 2011," Ann Hamilton Studio, http://www. annhamiltonstudio.com/videosound/follow.html.

29 Hélène Cixous, "Castration or Decapitation," trans. Annette Kuhn, *Signs* 7, no. 1 (1981): 41–55.

30 This aspect of Torma's work was discussed at the Universities Art Association of Canada conference (University of Waterloo, 2008) where an early version of this paper was given. The point was made that Torma's work, when shown in a gallery, becomes untouchable and thereby forfeits that tactile quality long affiliated with craft and quilts.

31 Laura Marks, *Touch: Sensuous Theory and Multisensory Media* (Minneapolis: University of Minnesota Press, 2002), 2.

32 Bell, 47.

33 Bell, 47.

34 The garden theme is found in Torma's earlier series *Jardin du Wiltz*. This series serves as a journal or diary of her days in various gardens at different moments of her life. There are recognizable gardens from Wiltz, Luxembourg, where Torma was artist in residence at *COOPERATIONS* in the spring of 2005. Here, she collaborated with other artists gathered in this creative community.

35 Koval, "Anna Torma: Bagatelles," 91.

36 Bell, 59.

37 Although tactility is a common response to Torma's art, in the shift from craft to high art her work is now positioned as untouchable to all but the handlers and purchasers of her work, in contradiction to the original intention of the quilt-based medium, hence, the reliance on haptic visuality.

38 Torma, "The Beauty in Beasts."

39 Naomi Schor, *Reading in Detail: Aesthetics and the Feminine* (London: Routledge, 2006), 4.

40 Schor, 4.

41 It should be noted that Torma exquisitely finishes both sides of her quilt, and often, in the gallery the reverse side is visible to the viewer. This was particularly integral to her hanging of *Bagatelles* where the viewers' pleasure of looking was doubled.

42 Janis Jefferies, "Contemporary Textiles: The Art Fabric," in *Contemporary Textiles: The Fabric of Fine Art*, ed. Nadine Monem (London: Black Dog Publishing, 2008), 46, as quoted in Julia Skelly, "Feminist Textiles and Excess," *Cut Cloth* (Manchester: PO Publishing, 2017), https://docs.wixstatic.com/ugd/9ebe01_fbe70a380af2426fb1c490e6778b5c50.pdf. See Julia Skelly's *Radical Decadence:*

Excess in Contemporary Feminist Textiles and Craft (London: Bloomsbury, 2017) on the subject of excess in textile art.

43 Bridget Elliott and Janice Helland, eds., *Women Artists and the Decorative Arts, 1880–1935: The Gender of Ornament* (Aldershot, UK: Ashgate, 2002), 5.

44 Anne Koval, "Her Fingers Dream a Garden," *Anna Torma: Needleworks* (Halifax, NS: MSVU Art Gallery, 2007), n.p.

45 Petra Halkes, "A Life of Lines," *Anna Torma: Tangled, with Past Tales* (Ottawa: L.A. Pai Gallery, 2015), 14.

46 Torma, "The Beauty in Beasts."

47 Emily Apter, *Feminizing the Fetish: Psychoanalysis and Narrative Obsession in Turn-of-the-Century France* (Ithaca: Cornell University Press, 1991), 5.

48 Mary Kelly, *Imaging Desire* (Cambridge, MA: MIT Press, 1997), 142.

49 Anna Torma, email to the author, 7 October 2017.

50 Carol Mavor, *Becoming: The Photographs of Clementina, Viscountess Hawarden* (Durham, NC: Duke University Press, 1999), 104.

51 Red is a symbolic color for Torma and is used frequently in her work, often as a reference to her Hungarian heritage and, more particularly, to traditional Hungarian embroidery work.

52 Torma has a history of working with artists with disabilities and was artist-in-residence at *COOPERATIONS* (Wiltz, Luxembourg) in 2005.

53 Anna Torma, "Artist Statement," *Bodies in Translation: Age and Creativity* (Halifax, NS: Mount St. Vincent Art Gallery, 2017), http://msvuart.ca/index.php?menid=04/02&mtyp=2&article_id=546.

54 Koval, "Her Fingers Dream a Garden," n.p.

55 As curator, when developing this exhibition, I had Torma's earlier works, such as *Draw me a Rose I* (2006), in mind.

56 *Paper Doll* included the work of contemporary artists Cindy Sherman, Ed Pien, Jeannie Thib, Barb Hunt, Lynn Yamamoto, Cybele Young, and Anna Torma.

57 Koval, *Paper Doll*, 27.

Chapter 10 Suturing My Soul: In Pursuit of the *Broderie de Bayeux*

Acknowledgments

I thank the editors of this volume for inviting me to participate. I thank my first readers, Mary M. Fox and Kate Kane. I acknowledge the resources of the Rossell Hope Robbins Library at the University of Rochester, a non-circulating library of medieval studies, where I conducted my research.

1 R. Howard Bloch, *A Needle in the Right Hand of God: The Norman Conquest of 1066 and the Making and Meaning of the Bayeux Tapestry* (New York: Random House, 2006), 42.

2 Shirley Ann Brown, *The Bayeux Tapestry: A Sourcebook* (Turnhout, Belgium: Brepolis, 2013).

3 Madeline H. Caviness, "Anglo-Saxon Women, Norman Knights, and the 'Third Sex' in the Bayeux Embroidery," in *The Bayeux Tapestry: New Interpretations*, ed. Martin K. Foys, Karen Eileen Overbey, and Dan Terkla, 85–118 (Woodbridge, Suffolk, UK: The Boydell Press, 2009), 86–87.

4 "An embroidery of images and texts." Nicole de Reyniès, "Bayeux Tapestry or Bayeux Embroidery? Questions of Terminology," in *The Bayeux Tapestry: Embroidering the Facts of History*, ed. Pierre Bouet, Brian Levy, and François Neveux, 69–76 (Caen, France: Presses universitaires de Caen, 2004), 70.

5 See Bloch, 6–13 for a brief recounting. David Wilson recounts the story in a text that parallels the unfolding visual narrative; see David M. Wilson, *The Bayeux Tapestry* (London: Thames and Hudson, 1985), 174–96.

6 Richard Brilliant, "The Bayeux Tapestry: A Stripped Narrative for the Eyes and Ears," *Word and Image* 7, no. 2 (1992): 98–126, especially 99–100.

7 Bloch, 17.

8 One early exception was Roger Sherman Loomis, "The Origin and Date of the Bayeux Embroidery," *Art Bulletin* 6, no. 1 (1923): 2–7.

9 David Herlihy, *Opera Muliebria: Women and Work in Medieval Europe* (New York: McGraw Hill, 1990), especially Chapter 4.

10 John Munro, "Medieval Woollens: Textiles, Textile Technology, and Industrial Organisation, *c.* 800–1500," in *The Cambridge History of Western Textiles*, ed. David Jenkins, 1:181–227 (Oxford: Oxford University Press, 2003).

11 See, for example, Cyril Hart, "The Bayeux Tapestry and Schools of Illumination at Canterbury," *Anglo-Norman Studies* 23 (2000): 117–67.

12 Pastan and White offer an overview of previous ideas about its patronage, and critique the later model of patronage; see Elizabeth Carson Pastan and Stephen White, "Problematizing Patronage: Odo of Bayeux and the Bayeux Tapestry," in *The Bayeux Tapestry: New Interpretations*, ed. Martin K. Foys, Karen Eileen Overbey, and Dan Terkla, 1–24 (Woodbridge, Suffolk, UK: The Boydell Press, 2009).

13 Carola Hicks, *The Bayeux Tapestry: The Life Story of a Masterpiece* (London: Vintage, 2007), 29–39.

14 Carola Hicks, "The Patronage of Queen Edith," in *The Bayeux Tapestry: New Approaches*, ed. Michael J. Lewis, Gale R. Owen-Crocker, and Dan Terkla, 5–9 (Oxford: Oxbow, 2011).

15 Ibid, 8–9.

16 K. Sutton, "900 Years Ago: The Norman Conquest, The Bayeux Tapestry Complete in Color," *National Geographic* 130, no. 2 (1966): 206–51.

17 Rachel P. Maines and James J. Glynn, "Numinous Objects," *The Public Historian* 15, no. 1 (1993): 8–25, 10.

18 In 2007, it was added to UNESCO's "Memory of the World" (MOW) Cultural Registry. See *Memory of the World: The Treasures That Record Our History from 1700 BC to the Present Day* (New York: HarperCollins and UNESCO, 2012), 80–82.

19 *La Tapisserie de Bayeux/The Bayeux Tapestry/Wandteppich von Bayeux* (Bayeux, France: Edition de Bayeux, n.d.).

20 James Elkins, "On Some Limits of Materiality in Art History," *31: Das Magazin des Instituts für Theorie* 12 (2008): 25–30; Martha Rosler et al., "Notes from the Field: Materiality," *Art Bulletin* 95, no. 1 (2013): 10–37.

21 Bill Brown, "Thing Theory," *Critical Inquiry* 28 (2001): 1–16; Igor Kopytoff, "The Cultural Biography of Things," in *The Social Life of Things*, ed. Arjun Appadurai, 64–91 (Cambridge: Cambridge University Press, 1986).

22 Bayeux Museum, Press Kit, 2015, downloaded January 14, 2016, http://www. bayeuxmuseum.com/en/press_kit_baeux_tapestry_2015.pdf.

23 Isabelle Bédat and Béatrice Girault-Kurtzeman, "The Technical Study of the Bayeux Embroidery," in *The Bayeux Tapestry: Embroidering the Facts of History*, ed. Pierre Bouet, Brian Levy, and François Neveux, 3–11 (Caen, France: Presses universitaires de Caen, 2004).

24 Janet Berlo, *Quilting Lessons: Notes from the Scrap Bag of a Writer and Quilter* (Lincoln, NE: University of Nebraska Press, 2004), 11.

25 These are explained in line drawings on James's website; Bayeux Broderie, accessed February 1, 2016, http://www.bayeux-broderie.com/stitch-bayeux.htm. Her site links to a five-minute Vimeo video with English voice-over in which she demonstrates these stitches: vimeo.com/103599828.

26 Robert Storr, Paulo Herkenhoff, and Allan Schwartzman, *Louise Bourgeois* (London: Phaidon, 2003), 12.

27 Louise Bourgeois, *Destruction of the Father, Reconstruction of the Father: Writings and Interviews 1923–1997* (Cambridge, MA: MIT Press, 1998), 120–22.

28 Deborah Wye, *Louise Bourgeois* (New York: Museum of Modern Art, 1982).

29 Rainer Crone and Petrus Graf Schaesberg, *Louise Bourgeois: The Secret of the Cells* (Munich: Prestel-Verlag, 1998), 91–98.

30 See, for example, Storr, Herkenhoff, and Schwartzman, *Louise Bourgeois*.

31 Storr, Herkenhoff, and Schwartzman, 16.

32 Bourgeois, 222.

33 Most influential is Gaston Bachelard, *The Poetics of Space* (Boston: Beacon Press, 1994). See also Joyce Medina, *Cezanne and Modernism: The Poetics of Painting* (Albany, NY: SUNY Press, 1995).

34 Bruce Metcalf, "Replacing the Myth of Modernism," *American Craft* 53, no. 1 (1993): 40–47, 46.

35 Joan Simon and Susan C. Faxon, *Sheila Hicks: Fifty Years* (New Haven, CT: Yale University Press, 2010), 73.

36 Betty Ring, *Girlhood Embroidery* (New York: Alfred Knopf, 1993).

37 Paula Bradstreet Richter, "Stories from Her Needle: Colonial Revival Samplers of Mary Saltonstall Parker," in *Textiles in New England, II: Four Centuries of Material Life*, ed. Peter Benes, 212–32 (Boston: Boston University Press, 2001), Figure 8.

38 E. Jane Burns, "Love's Stitches Undone: Women's Work in the *chanson de toile*," in *Courtly Love Undressed: Reading through Clothes in Medieval French Culture*, 88–118 (Philadelphia: University of Pennsylvania Press, 2002).

39 Judith Butler, "Performativity," from exhibition *In Terms of Performance* at the Brooklyn Academy of Music, 6 March to 8 May 2018. On-line version at *In Terms of Performance*, Pew Center for Arts & Heritage, http://intermsofperformance.site/keywords/performativity/judith-butler.

40 Carlo Petrini, *Slow Food Revolution* (New York: Rizzoli, 2006); Carl Honoré, *In Praise of Slowness* (New York: HarperOne, 2004).

41 Claire Wellesley-Smith, *Slow Stitch: Mindful and Contemplative Textile Art* (London: Batsford, 2015).

42 Adrienne Rich, *Of Woman Born: Motherhood as Experience and Institution* (New York: Norton, 1976), 283–84.

43 Stendhal, *Rome, Naples, and Florence* (New York: George Braziller, 1960).

Index

Abstract Design in American Quilts
    (Holstein and van der Hoof)
    8–9
"Acanthus" (William and Jane Morris)
    Plate 2.1
African-Americans 8, 9
Against the Cold in General (Szenes) 144
agency 133–4, 136–7
Albertine Schenk (Wintsch) Plate 8.2
Alfoldy, Sandra 54
amateurism 4–6, 38
András, Edit 144
Appadurai, Arjun 9
Apter, Emily 150
Aragon - RE/ICH (Wintsch) Plate 8.1,
    134–5
Archdale, Helen 106
art
    feminist art 9
    fine arts 2, 5
        Brussels Academy of Fine Arts 25–6
    Glasgow School of Art 100–2
    Leisure Arts 61, 62
    needle arts 23–6
    patient art 137–8. *See also* Wintsch,
        Johanna
art history 2, 4, 8–9
artisanal training 116–17. *See also*
    education in needle arts
artistic dress 42
Ashbee, Charles 75
Atkinson, Diane 97–8
Auther, Elissa 9
autobiographical acts 167–8
Autumn (De Rudder, Hélène and Isidore)
    Plate 1.1

Bagatelles (Torma) Plate 9.2, 147–8
Bagenal, Barbara 69
Baltimore Album quilts 87
Barnaby, Alice 3
Barnardo, Dr. Thomas 118, 120, 208n

Bayeux Embroidery Plate 10.1, 155–63
    materiality 160–3
    matrilineal heritage 158–60
bedcover (May and Jane Morris) Plate 2.2,
    46–7
Belgium 21–32
    De Rudder, Hélène 26–9
    exhibitions 29–31
    women's education in needle arts
        23–6
Bell, Kristy 146, 147, 148
Bell, Vanessa 76, 78
Berlo, Janet Catherine 11
*Betty Cornell's Teen-age Knitting
    Book* 51
"Beyond Bricolage" (Berlo) 11
Bhabha, Homi 141
"Black Friday" demonstration 97, 197n
Bleuler, Paul Eugen 129
Bloomsbury Group 67–79, 188n
    masculinity and embroidery 68, 70,
        74–8
    women and needlework 68–74
Bosché, Henriette 31
Botticelli, Sandro 28
Boucher, Ellen 118
Bourgeois, Louise 146, 165–6
    Cells 169–70
    Cell 1 Plate 10.2, 166
British Child Migration Movement 117,
    118–21, 207n, 208n
Broderie de Bayeux Plate 10.1, 155–63
    materiality 160–3
    matrilineal heritage 158–60
Brown, Cheri 61
Brussels
    Academy of Fine Arts 25–6
    exhibitions 29–31
    professional schools 24–5, 27
Brussels needlepoint (D'Olszowska)
    Plate 1.2
Bryan-Wilson, Julia 2

Burden, Elizabeth *34*, 38, 181n
Burden, Jane. *See* Morris, Jane
Burghhölzli psychiatric asylum 129, 130
Burne-Jones, Edward 35, 37, 38, *43*
Burne-Jones, Georgiana 35, *43*, 45

Campbell, Jessie 83
    Whig's Defeat quilt Plate 5.1, 89–96
        design 83, 85, 86, 88
        as McPherson Wedding Quilt
          89–92
        as political quilt 91–5
        textiles 87–8, 195n
Canada 90–5. *See also* Watts, Mary Seton
Carrington (Hampton) 67, 188n
Cells (Bourgeois) 169–70
    Cell 1 Plate 10.2, 166
Chair cover (Bell and Grant) 77
chanson de toile 168
Checinska, Christine 8
Child Migration Movement 117, 118–21,
        207n, 208n
children 149–50
Cixous, Hélèn 145, 147, 152
Clark, Helen 113–14
Clay, Henry 85
cloth. *See* textiles
clothing 40–4, 150–1
Cointet, Guy de 125
collecting as female fetish 149–52
colours 97–8
Cottage Arts Association 115. *See also*
        Home Arts and Industries
        Association (HAIA)
cotton 88, 195n
Cotton (Lemire) 7–8
Coué, Dr Emile 73, 190–1n
*Craft, Community and the Material
        Culture of Place and Politics,
        19th-20th Century* (Helland,
        Lemire and Buis) 10
crafting 11
Crafting Identities (Alfoldy) 54
creative capital 61
critical knitting. *See* Zimmermann,
        Elizabeth
Cultural Threads (Hemmings) 8
Cumming, Elizabeth 101–2
Curiger, Bice 125, 209n

"Daisy" (William and Jane Morris) 35–6
Davidson, Angus 69
Davison, Emily Wilding 108
de Certeau, Michel 132–3
De Rudder, Hélène 26–9
    Autumn Plate 1.1
    Four Seasons, The 28
De Rudder, Isidore 27
De Taeye, Louis 26
de Villermont, Countesses 23
    design 38
    designers 60–1, 62–3
Devine, Tom 93
dialogical transformation in personal and
        institutional identifications 55–60
Dove-Wilcox, Lilian 107
dress. *See also* clothing
    artistic 42
Du Ménil, Hélène. *See* De Rudder, Hélène
Duncan, Ida Riley 51–2
d'Ursel, Riri 21, *22*

écoles professionelles (professional schools)
    24–5, 27
education in needle arts 23–6. *See also*
        artisanal training; Home Arts
        and Industries Association
        (HAIA)
Edwards, Clive 98
effeminacy 68, 74–8
Elliot, Bridget 149
embodied touch 147–9
embodiment 161, 169
Embroiderers' Guild 77–8
embroidery 7
    and Bloomsbury masculinity 68, 70,
        74–8
    Bourgeois, Louise 146, 165–6
        Cell 1 Plate 10.2, 166
        Cells 169–70
        Broderie de Bayeux Plate 10.1, 155–63
        materiality 160–3
        matrilineal heritage 158–60
    De Rudder, Hélène 26–9
        Autumn Plate 1.1
        Four Seasons, The 28
    Grant, Ethel 72–3
        Chair cover 76
        Firescreen 77

Morris, Jane 33–47
  "Acanthus" Plate 2.1
  artistry and embroidery 37–41
  bedcover Plate 2.2, 46–7
  clothing 41–4
  "Daisy" 35–6
  Legend of Goode Wimmen 36–7
  personal relationships 45–6
  photograph *43*
  Red House 35–7
  upbringing 34–5
Our Lady of the Snows (Mary Seton
    Watts) Plate 7.2, 111–14, 122
poetics of 166–9
Silk Rainforest, The (Hicks) 168
Suffragist banner Plate 6.1, 97–109
  banner signatures *99*, 104–9
  exhibitions 102–4
  memories and meaning 97–9
  production 100–2
Torma, Anna 141–54
  Bagatelles Plate 9.2, 147–8
  collecting as female fetish 149–52
  embodied touch 147–9
  Encyclopedia Domestica 146
  Essential Elements 150–1
  feminism 143–5
  Jardin du Wiltz 215n
  l'écriture feminine 145–7
  Man's Island 150–1
  Monster Spirit Plate 9.1, 150, *151*
  Red Fragments I 151–2
  selfhood 152–4
  Vanitas I 152–3
  Vanitas II 154
Wintsch, Johanna 125–37, 138–9
  Albertine Schenk Plate 8.2
  Aragon - RE/ICH Plate 8.1, 134–5
  early signs of mental illness and
    institutionalisation 128–9
  psychiatric asylums 127, 129–34,
    135–7
Woolf, Virginia 69, 71–2
  Leda and the Swan Plate 4.2
Encyclopedia Domestica (Torma) 146
epideictic rhetoric 10, 11
Essential Elements (Torma) 150–1
exhibitions 29–31, 38–9, 54, 77–8,
    102–4, 153

fabric. *See* textiles
female fetish, collecting as 149–52
feminine writing 145–7
femininity 21, 68, 70, 102
feminism 143–5
feminist art 9
feminist theorists 11
Feminizing the Fetish (Apter) 150
fetish, collecting as female 149–52
fine arts 2, 5
  Brussels Academy of Fine Arts 25–6
Fine Cell Work (FCW) 1
Firescreen (Duncan and Ethel Grant) *77*
Foerster, Julie 31
Foucault, Michael 131
Four Seasons, The (De Rudder) 28
Fry, Roger 73, 74, 75, *77*, 78

Garnett, Angelica 72
  Leda and the Swan Plate 4.2
Gehry, Dr. Karl 127
gender 3–4, 38, 68, 149. *See also*
    femininity; feminism; feminist
    art; women
  and social action 115–16, 206n
Germany 52
Gilbert, Helen 113
girls, education in needle arts 23–6
Glasgow School of Art 100–2
Godfrey, Nellie 105
Godwinson, Edith 157
Goggin, Maureen Daly 2, 10
Grafton Group 75
Grant, Duncan 70, 73, 74, 75, 76, 78
  Firescreen 77
Grant, Ethel 72–3
  Chair cover 76
  Firescreen 77
Guenevere (William Morris and Elizabeth
    Burden) 33, *34*, 37

Hadjiafxendi, Kyriaki 4, 10, 11
Hall, Leslie 103
Hamilton, Ann 146
Harris, Alexandra 79
Helland, Janice 149
Hemmings, Jessica 8
Hicks, Carola 157
Hicks, Sheila 149, 168

Holmqvist, Karl 125
Holstein, Jonathan 8–9
Home Arts and Industries Association
        (HAIA) 115–16
homosexuality 70–1
Hope, Lottie 69
Hours, The (Daldry) 67, 187
Howey, Elsie 107
Hudson, Edith 106
Huneault, Kristina 4
Hungary 143–4
"Hunger Strikers' Banner" 104
Hyland, Chris 61

identity 7, 10, 11–12, 17, 168
intellectual property 60–3

James, Chantal 162
Jardin du Wiltz (Torma) 215n
Jebb, Eglantyne 115, 116
Johnson, Samuel 93–4
Jones, Winifred 203n

Kay, Joy 105
Kelly, Mary 150
Kelmscott Manor bedcover (May and Jane
        Morris) Plate 2.2, 46–7
Kenney, Annie 107
Keserü, Katalin 144
Kipling, Rudyard 111, 113, 114
Knit to Fit (Duncan) 52
Knitter's 59
knitting
    mid-century professional knitting
        and knitting craftmanship
        50–2
    Ravelry 64
    Stephen, Adrian 70
    Strachy, Lytton 68, 70–1
    West, Stephen 64–5
    Woolf, Virginia 69
    Zimmermann, Elizabeth 49–50,
        52–64, 65
        dialogical transformation in
            personal and institutional
            identifications 55–60
        intellectual property 60–3
Knott, Stephen 4–5, 116
Kristeva, Julia 145

l'écriture feminine 145–7
Leda and the Swan (Woolf and Garnett)
        Plate 4.2
Legend of Goode Wimmen (William and
        Jane Morris) 36–7
Leigh, Mary 107
Leisure Arts 61, 62
Lemire, Beverly 7
Ligon, Linda 58
Lippard, Lucy 142
Lynch, Gordon 117, 118, 119
Lytton, Lady Constance 108

Macbeth, Anne 100–2, 103, 199n
Man's Island (Torma) 150–1
manufacture 38
Marks, Laura 147
Martin, Selina 103
masculinity 68, 70, 74–8
Massy, Rosamund 107
material agency 133–4, 136–7
material culture studies 2, 3
material turn 9
materiality 160–3
matrilineal heritage 158–60
Mavor, Carol 151
McGill University 111, 112, 114
McPherson, Andrew 83, 89, *90*, 91
McPherson Wedding Quilt 89–92
mental illness. *See* Wintsch, Johanna
Metcalf, Bruce 167
Milwaukee Sentinel 54
mindful deliberation 168–9
Mitchell, Allyson 149
Monster Spirit (Torma) Plate 9.1, 150, *151*
Morrell, Ottoline 73–4
Morris, Jane 33–47
    "Acanthus" Plate 2.1
    artistry and embroidery 37–41
    bedcover Plate 2.2, 46–7
    clothing 41–4
    "Daisy" 35–6
    illness 45, 185n
    Legend of Goode Wimmen 36–7
    personal relationships 45–6
    photograph *43*
    Red House 35–7
    upbringing 34–5
Morris, Jenny 185n

Morris, May 39, 40, 42, 46
    bedcover Plate 2.2
Morris, William 38, 39
    "Acanthus" Plate 2.1
    "Daisy" 35–6
    death 46
    Guenevere 33, *34*, 37
    Legend of Goode Wimmen 36–7
    photograph *43*
    Red House 35, 44
motherhood 145
Murdoch, Lydia 117
Myall, Michelle 108–9

needle arts, women's education in 23–6
"Needle as Pen, The" (Pritash, Schaechtler
    and Wood) 10
needlework 1–2. *See also* embroidery;
    knitting; quilting; sewing;
    stitching
    as art 2–3, 8–9
    as epideictic rhetoric 10, 11
    gendering 3–4
    professionalisation 4–6
    as rehabilitative therapy 73
    transformative nature of 11–12
Nenadic, Stana 84
Newbery, Francis 100–2
Newbery, Jessie 100–2
Newly Born Woman, The 145
Newsletters (Zimmermann) 55–7. *See also*
    Wool Gatherings
    (Zimmermann)

O'Brien, Violet 105
Odo of Bayeux, Bishop 157
Omega workshops 72–3, 75
Orts, Auguste 25–6
Our Lady of the Snows (Mary Seton Watts)
    Plate 7.2, 111–14, 122

Pall Mall Gazette 75
Parker, Mary Saltonstall 168
Parker, Rozsika 105, 143
patient art 137–8. *See also* Wintsch,
    Johanna
Peck, Amelia 8
performativity 167–8
personal relationships 45–6

Pethick, Dorothy 203n
Pethick Lawrence, Emmeline 101, 103
Pfister, Dr. O. 133, 134, 136
philanthropy 115–16, 206n
    British Child Migration Movement
        117, 118–21, 207n, 208n
Phillips, Mary 106, 107, 175n
poetics of embroidery 166–9
political quilts. *See Baltimore Album* quilts;
        Whig's Defeat quilt
Porter, Roy 132
Post-Partum Document (Kelly) 150
Prinsep, Sara 44
Prinzhorn, Hans 137–8
Pristash, Heather 1–2, 10, 11, 97, 142
professional schools (*écoles professionelles*)
        24–5, 27
professionalism 4–6, 38
Prown, Jules 9
psychiatric asylums 127, 129–34, 135–7
    deaths 210n
    patient art 137–8
Purvis, Jane 108

Queen (periodical) 42
quilting
    Abstract Design in American Quilts
        (Holstein and van der Hoof)
        8–9
    Baltimore Album quilts 87
    selfhood 142
    Whig's Defeat quilt Plate 5.1, 83–96
        design 83–6, 88
        as McPherson Wedding Quilt
            89–92
        as political quilt 85, 91–5
        textiles 87–8, 195n

Ravelry 64
Reading in Detail (Schor) 149
Red Fragments I (Torma) 151–2
Red House 33, 35–7, 38, 44
Reed, Christopher 79
rehabilitative therapy 73
relationships 45–6
Rheinau psychiatric asylum 127, 129–30,
        131–2, 134
rhetoric 10, 11, 97, 142–3
Rich, Adrienne 143, 169

Ringgold, Faith 9
Riviere, Joan 70, 189n
Roe-Brown, Elsie 106
Rose, Gillian 9–10
Rossetti, Dante Gabriel 33, 35, 38, 40–1
Royal Victoria College, McGill University
    111, 112, 114

Salahub, Jennifer 113
Salon triennal des Beaux-Arts 30–1
Schaechtler, Inez 1–2, 10, 11, 97, 142
Schenk, Albertine Plate 8.2, 133
schizophrenia 129, 211n
Schoolhouse Press 57
Schor, Naomi 149
Scotsman, The 104
Seamless Yoke Sweater (Zimmermann) 55,
    56, 61, 63
selfhood 141, 142, 152
sensuality 169
sewing 146
    Virginia Woolf Plate 4.1, 69
Showalter, Elaine 11, 142
Silk Rainforest, The (Hicks) 168
"slow" movements 168–9
social action 115–16
    British Child Migration Movement
        117, 118–21, 207n, 208n
social class 88
social media 64
songs 168
Spectacle of Women, The (Tickner) 7
Square Neck Pretzel Sweater
    (Zimmermann) 61–2
steeking 53, 186n
Stephen, Adrian 70
stitching 8. *See also* embroidery
Strachy, Lytton 67–8, 70–1, 74
Styles, John 11
Subversive Stitch, The (Parker) 143
Suffrage movement 7
    "Black Friday" demonstration 97, 197n
Suffrage Signature Handkerchief 105
Suffragist banner Plate 6.1, 97–109
    banner signatures *99*, 104–9
    exhibitions 102–4
    memories and meaning 97–9
    production 100–2
Swain, Shurlee 114, 205n

Szenes, Zsuzsa 144
Szilvitzky, Margit 144

tactility 167. *See also* touch, embodied
tapestry 155
textile history 4
textile scholarship 6–12
textile trade 8
textiles 2, 17, 87–8, 195n
textuality 11. *See also* writing
Tickner, Lisa 7, 102
Tifflin, Chris 113
Times, The 105–6
Tintoretto, Jacobo 125
Tobin, Beth Fowkes 10
Torma, Anna 141–54
    Bagatelles Plate 9.2, 147–8
    collecting as female fetish 149–52
    embodied touch 147–9
    Encyclopedia Domestica 146
    Essential Elements 150–1
    feminism 143–5
    Jardin du Wiltz 215n
    l'écriture feminine 145–7
    Man's Island 150–1
    Monster Spirit Plate 9.1, 150, *151*
    Red Fragments I 151–2
    selfhood 152–4
    Vanitas I 152–3
    Vanitas II 154
touch, embodied 147–9
trade 8
Tryon, Wyndham 78
Tuckett, Sally 84

Ulrich, Laurel Thatcher 7

van der Hoof, Gail 8–9
Vanitas I (Torma) 152–3
Vanitas II (Torma) 154
Venice Biennale 125
Village Voice 59
Vogue Knitting 59, 60
Vogue Knitting Book 50
voluntary social action 115–16, 206n
    British Child Migration Movement
        117, 118–21, 207n, 208n
Voortman, Clara 31
Votes for Women 98, 101, 102, 103, 107

Walker, Lynne 98
Wallace Dunlop, Marion 98–9, 106, 198n
Watney, Simon 79
Watts, Mary Seton 111–22
    artisanal training 116–17
    Our Lady of the Snows Plate 7.2,
        111–14, 122
    self-portrait Plate 7.1
    social action 115–16, 121
Watts Mortuary Chapel 116
Watts-Dunton, Theodore 41, 45
Webb, Philip 35, 45–6
Wentworth, Vera 107
West, Stephen 64–5
Whig's Defeat quilt Plate 5.1, 83–96
    design 83–6, 88
    as McPherson Wedding Quilt 89–92
    as political quilt 85, 91–5
    textiles 87–8, 195n
Wintsch, Johanna 125–37, 138–9
    Albertine Schenk Plate 8.2
    Aragon - RE/ICH Plate 8.1, 134–5
    early signs of mental illness and
        institutionalisation 128–9
    psychiatric asylums 127, 129–34, 135–7
Wisconsin Designer Craftsman
    organization (WDC) 53–4,
    186n
women 10. *See also* Suffrage movement
    Bloomsbury Group 68–9

    education in needle arts 23–6
    social action 115–16, 206n
Women's Day 50–1, 53
Women's Social and Political Union
    (WSPU) banner Plate 6.1,
    97–109
    banner signatures *99*, 104–9
    exhibitions 102–4
    memories and meaning 97–9
    production 100–2
Wood, Sue Carter 1–2, 10, 97, 142
Wool Gatherings (Zimmermann) 57.
    See also Newsletters
    (Zimmermann)
Woolf, Virginia 67, 69, 155
    needlework 69–70, 71–2
    Leda and the Swan Plate 4.2
    portrait Plate 4.1
Workbasket, The 51
Wright, Ada 107
writing 142, 143
    l'écriture feminine 145–7

Zakresi, Patricia 4, 10, 11
Zimmermann, Elizabeth 49–50, 52–64,
    65
    dialogical transformation in personal
        and institutional identifications
        55–60
    intellectual property 60–3

Plate 1.1 Hélène De Rudder, née Du Ménil and Isidore De Rudder, *Autumn*, 1904. Embroidery, 200 × 260 cm. Brussels, Musée de la Ville de Bruxelles-Maison du Roi, inv. E 1904/2/3. © Brussels, Musée de la Ville de Bruxelles-Maison du Roi.

Plate 1.2 Irène D'Olszowska, Round collar of Brussels needlepoint with a pattern of peacocks and flowers, *c.* 1905. Needlepoint, 125 × 18 cm. Amsterdam, Rijksmuseum, BK-BR-364. © Amsterdam, Rijksmuseum, free of copyright.

Plate 2.1 William Morris (designer), Jane Morris (maker), May Morris (maker [?]), "Acanthus," *c.* 1878. 264 × 205 cm. Amgueddfa Genedlaethol Cymru National Museum of Wales.

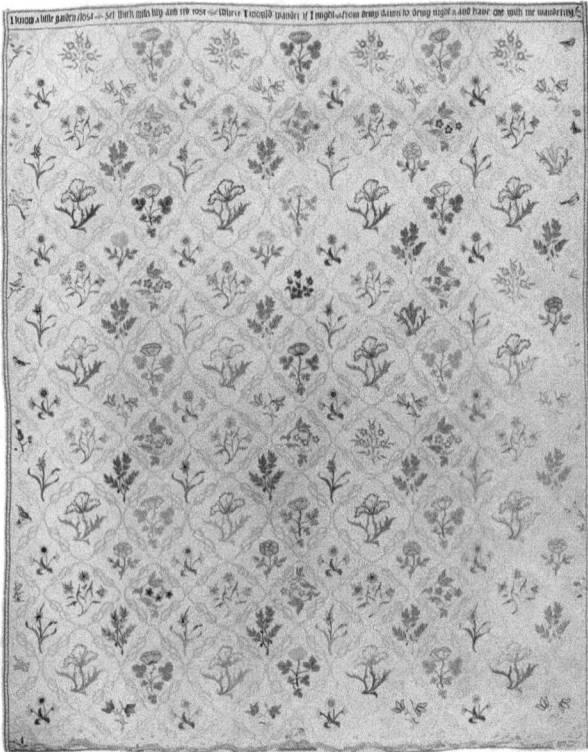

Plate 2.2 May Morris (designer) and Jane Morris (maker), Bedcover (KM233), *c.* 1910. Wool and silk on linen, 261 × 212.5 cm. © Society of Antiquaries of London (Kelmscott Manor)/V&A.

Plate 4.1 Vanessa Bell, *Portrait of Virginia Woolf (née Stephen)*, 1912 [poss. March]. Oil on board, 15¾ × 13⅜″, NPG 5833. © Estate of Vanessa Bell. Courtesy National Portrait Gallery, London.

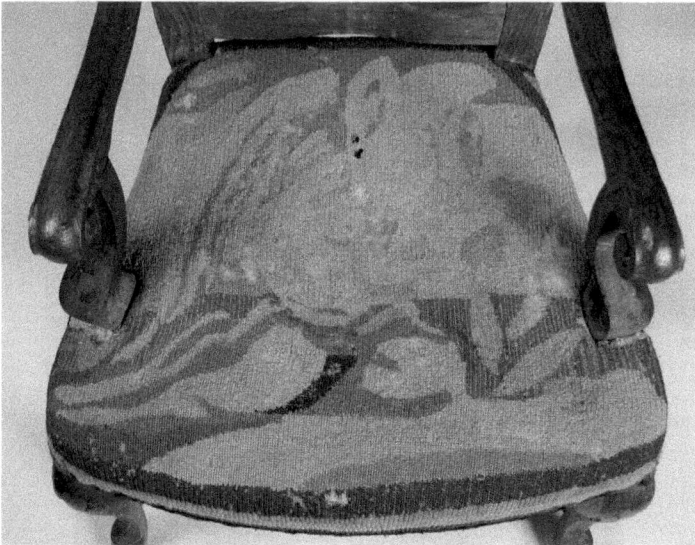

Plate 4.2 Virginia Woolf (embroiderer) and Angelica Garnett (designer), *Leda and the Swan*, chair cover. Monk's House, Rodmell, East Sussex, NT 768172.1. © The National Trust.

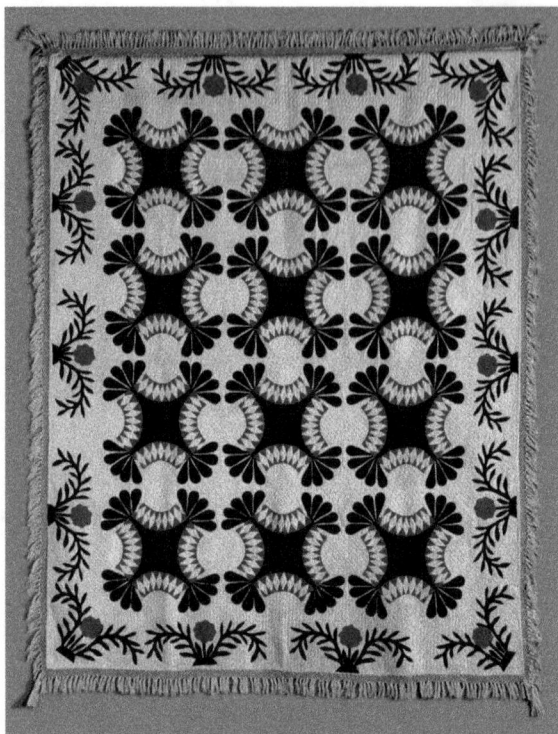

Plate 5.1 Jessie Campbell, *Whig's Defeat, c.* 1860. Hand-sewn, cotton, 222 × 175 cm. Photo courtesy of Agnes Etherington Art Centre, Queen's University, Kingston, ON.

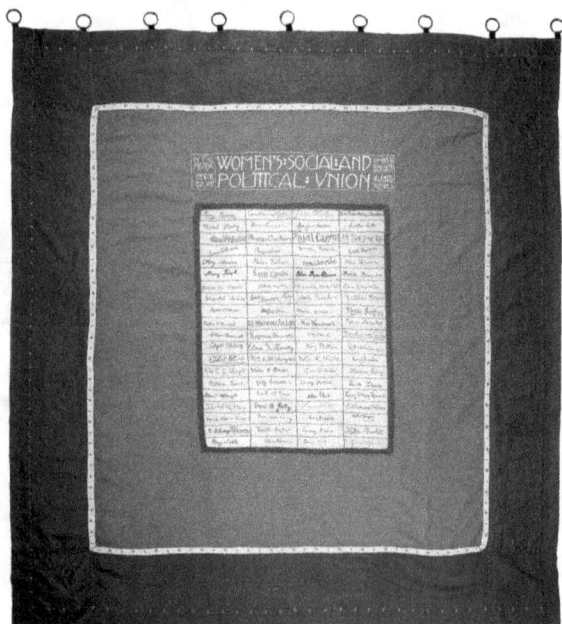

Plate 6.1 Women's Social and Political Union (WSPU), Suffragette Banner, 1910. © Museum of London.

Plate 7.1 Mary Seton Watts (née Mary Seton Fraser Tytler), *Self-Portrait,* watercolor, 1882. © Watts Gallery Trust.

Plate 7.2 Mary Seton Watts, *Our Lady of the Snows*, 1906. Mother of pearl, moonstones, crystal, garnets, aquamarine. Silk and velvet painted and applied on to satin ground, embroidered with gold and silver thread. Collection of McGill University. Presented to the Royal Victoria College, McGill University, Montreal, Canada in 1907. Pictured *in situ* at the Royal Victoria College, 2016. Photograph by author.

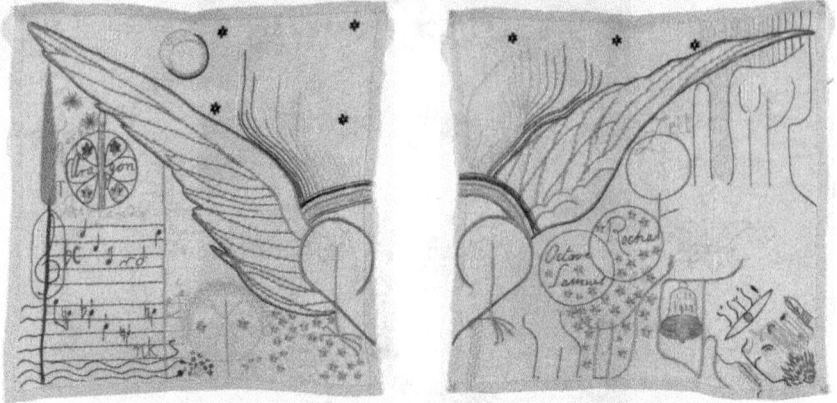

Plate 8.1 Johanna Natalie Wintsch, *Aragon—RE/ICH*, 1924. Silk on linen, 31 × 31 cm. Sammlung Rheinau (StAZH).

Plate 8.2 Johanna Natalie Wintsch, *Albertine Schenk*, 1923. Silk on cotton, 31 × 31 cm. Sammlung Rheinau (StAZH).

Plate 9.1 Anna Torma, detail from *Monster Spirit,* 2008. Silk embroidery on cotton. Photo credit: Anna Torma.

Plate 9.2 Anna Torma, detail from *Bagatelles*, 2011. Silk thread embroidery and watercolor on silk fabric. New Brunswick Museum, Saint John. NB. Photo credit: Istvan Zsako.

Plate 10.1 Installation View of the Bayeux Embroidery. © S. Maurice – Bayeux Museum, Bayeux, France.

Plate 10.2 Louise Bourgeois, *Cell 1*, 1991. Mixed media, 83 × 96 × 108"; 210.8 × 243.8 × 274.3 cm. Photo: Peter Bellamy. © The Easton Foundation/VAGA at Artists Rights Society (ARS), NY.